STAYING IN THE FIGHT

STAYING IN THE FIGHT

How War on Terror Veterans in Congress Are Shaping US Defense Policy

JEFFREY S. LANTIS

UNIVERSITY PRESS OF KENTUCKY

Copyright © 2024 by The University Press of Kentucky

Scholarly publisher for the Commonwealth, serving Bellarmine University, Berea College, Centre College of Kentucky, Eastern Kentucky University, The Filson Historical Society, Georgetown College, Kentucky Historical Society, Kentucky State University, Morehead State University, Murray State University, Northern Kentucky University, Spalding University, Transylvania University, University of Kentucky, University of Louisville, University of Pikeville, and Western Kentucky University. All rights reserved.

Editorial and Sales Offices: The University Press of Kentucky
663 South Limestone Street, Lexington, Kentucky 40508-4008
www.kentuckypress.com

Author builds upon concepts and research originally published in "Military Veterans of the War on Terror: A New Generation of Congressional Foreign-Policy Advocacy," *Journal of Political & Military Sociology* 48, no. 1 (2021). Reprinted with permission of the University of Florida Press.

Cataloging-in-Publication data is available from the Library of Congress.

ISBN 978-1-9859-0039-4 (hardcover : alk. paper)
ISBN 978-1-9859-0040-0 (pbk. : alk. paper)
ISBN 978-1-9859-0041-7 (pdf)
ISBN 978-1-9859-0042-4 (epub)

This book is printed on acid-free paper meeting
the requirements of the American National Standard
for Permanence in Paper for Printed Library Materials.

Manufactured in the United States of America.

Member of the Association of University Presses

Contents

List of Tables   vii
List of Figures   ix
Preface   xi

1. Introduction: War on Terror Military Veterans in Congress   1
2. Military Veterans and Policy Advocacy: Socialization and Representation   20
3. To the Rescue? The Syria Policy Puzzle   35
4. Strained Ties: Saudi Arabia and the War in Yemen   61
5. Veterans and Afghanistan: Ending America's Longest War   86
6. War on Terror Veterans and Public Health   119
7. The Ukraine War and the Fight for Democracy   144
8. Findings and Conclusion   172

Acknowledgments   189
Notes   191
References   199
Index   229
About the Author   233

List of Tables

Table 1.1. Veterans of the WoT Who Served in Congress from 2007 to 2023   6

Table 2.1. Lawmaker Profiles   32

Table 2.2. Case Studies   33

Table 3.1. Sample of Representative Kinzinger's Record of Bill Sponsorship and Cosponsorship   43

Table 3.2. Sample of Representative Gabbard's Record of Bill Sponsorship and Cosponsorship   55

Table 4.1. Sample of Representative Lieu's Record of Bill Sponsorship and Cosponsorship   69

Table 4.2. Sample of Senator Young's Record of Bill Sponsorship and Cosponsorship   81

Table 5.1. Sample of Representative Waltz's Record of Bill Sponsorship and Cosponsorship   94

Table 5.2. Sample of Representative Crow's Record of Bill Sponsorship and Cosponsorship   108

Table 6.1. Sample of Representative Luria's Record of Bill Sponsorship and Cosponsorship   127

Table 6.2. Sample of Representative Stivers's Record of Bill Sponsorship and Cosponsorship   139

Table 7.1. Sample of Representative Gallego's Record of Bill Sponsorship and Cosponsorship   153

Table 7.2. Sample of Representative Meijer's Record of Bill Sponsorship and Cosponsorship   165

Table 8.1. Summary of Findings   178

List of Figures

Figure 1.1. Patterns of Veterans' Representation in Congress: Percent of Members with Previous Military Service   4

Figure 1.2. Experiences of WoT Veterans   13

Figure 2.1. Veteran Lawmaker Policy Advocacy Model   21

Preface

The War on Terror (WoT) generation of military veterans in Congress now represents the largest concentration of veterans with similar experiences in recent conflicts. Sixty-one of the ninety-five veterans in the 118th Congress (2023–25) served in the military in the post-9/11 era, including more than a dozen newly elected members. This group has become a dedicated cohort of lawmakers and defense policy advocates. While the veterans hail from different backgrounds and political persuasions, they frequently acknowledge that their shared bonds help them cooperate across partisan divides. This was certainly the approach adopted by the three West Point graduates from the same graduating class who were elected to Congress in 2022: Representatives John James (R-MI), Pat Ryan (D-NY), and Wesley Hunt (R-TX). These young lawmakers, all combat veterans from the Iraq War, celebrated their similarities, not their political differences, and they told reporters during their orientation on Capitol Hill that the trust and understanding that flowed from their common military experiences would help them transcend partisanship. Cooperation among veteran lawmakers, James stated, would be "essential to move this nation forward" (Carney and Beavers 2022).

This book tells the stories of how WoT military veterans have emerged as an influential new generation of policy activists in Congress that has helped shape critical policy debates. As one of the first in-depth studies of this cohort in Washington, it goes beyond the numbers to provide unique insights into different personalities and their self-professed motivations, policy preferences, and advocacy work. All of the individuals in this study completed active-duty deployments after September 11, 2001, and many were combat veterans from the Iraq or Afghanistan War. After returning home, they continued their public service by running for office to "fight" for select causes in new ways. Their policy interventions and activism on Capitol Hill helped shape policy responses to many different challenges, from the Russian invasion of Ukraine in 2022 and interventions in the civil wars in Syria and Yemen to treatments for illnesses associated with veterans' exposure to toxic "burn pits" during the WoT.

This book also addresses broader questions about the role of veterans in American society. With the long wars in Iraq and Afghanistan now over, what

xi

xii Preface

role will post-9/11 veterans play in public life? Can the common bonds among veterans truly overcome deep ideological and partisan divides? And what types of defense and foreign policy changes should we anticipate with WoT veterans driving political discourse? *Staying in the Fight* offers a timely and policy-relevant account of US responses to international challenges of the twenty-first century and ongoing debates about defense policy.

1

Introduction

War on Terror Military Veterans in Congress

During the chaotic US evacuation of Afghanistan in 2021, a group of members of Congress who were military veterans of the War on Terror (WoT) mobilized quickly to assist citizens, green card holders, and Special Immigrant Visa (SIV) applicants who had aided the American war effort. WoT veterans and their staffs on Capitol Hill created hotlines and coordinated their efforts with government agencies and veterans' groups with contacts on the ground to try to save lives. Along the way, many also became vocal critics of presidential management of the situation. How, they asked, could the Trump and Biden administrations not have a plan for the Taliban's rapid takeover of Afghanistan? Why had the SIV programs dragged on so long, endangering Afghans and their families? Congressman Jimmy Panetta (D-CA), a veteran of the war in Afghanistan, summed up the frustration of many of his peers about the dire situation at the time, calling it "both a professional challenge and a really personal crisis for veterans who served there" (Wire 2021).

The Russian invasion of Ukraine in 2022 similarly activated concerned WoT military veterans in Congress. In the early months of the war, they confronted President Biden's slow response to the crisis and demanded increased military assistance for Ukraine. A bipartisan group of members of Congress that was organized by WoT veterans sent a public letter to the White House demanding shipments of advanced surface-to-air missile systems, the transfer of manned and unmanned aircraft to Ukraine, increased humanitarian aid, and more economic sanctions on Russia. Representative Adam Kinzinger (R-IL), a veteran of the Iraq and Afghanistan Wars and a Lieutenant Colonel in the Air National Guard, said that the United States should enforce of a no-fly zone over Ukraine to give its forces a "fair fight" against Russian invaders. Senator Joni Ernst (R-IA), a combat veteran of the Iraq War, told reporters that

1

watching Ukrainian president Volodymyr Zelenskyy's video address to Congress in March 2022 made her "want to throw on my uniform, you know, and go help." With congressional support, the Biden administration responded by sending more than $100 billion in assistance to Ukraine in the first year of the conflict, including tranches of military aid and increasingly sophisticated weapons systems.

This book is the first of its kind to systematically study the activism of this new generation of veterans in Congress in the defense-policymaking process. These and many other recent examples illustrate the expanding presence and policy influence of veterans of the WoT in Congress today. This study is designed to provide unique insights into the post-9/11 veteran cohort of lawmakers, including their personalities, self-professed motivations, policy preferences, and advocacy work. Though they hail from diverse backgrounds and different parties, this work highlights their many common experiences and concerns: WoT veterans represent the first sizable cohort of veterans with extensive experience fighting foreign wars who chose to do so in the modern all-volunteer force.[1] Indeed, several veterans featured in this study selected combat deployments over other, safer alternatives for their military service. WoT veterans also tended to serve more tours of duty in Iraq and Afghanistan due to force structure demands, with greater likelihood of combat engagements and higher rates of diagnosed post-traumatic stress disorder (PTSD) than previous cohorts of US soldiers (Kelley et al. 2019; Institute of Medicine 2010). As expert Michael Gambone (2021, 1) argues, these shared experiences make veterans in American politics a "distinct subculture" that can be very influential. In addition, once in political office, many of these individuals have remained in the National Guard or Reserves, even as they championed causes related to their own experiences (author's interview, September 16, 2021).

This book explores the impact of these experiences by advancing a multistage model of the engagement of WoT veterans in the policy process. It draws on insights from the expanding literature on policy advocacy (e.g., Tama 2020; Schumacher, Bouris, and Olszewska 2016; Lantis 2019) and debates in civil-military relations about the impact of service experiences on members of Congress (Robinson et al. 2020; Leal and Teigen 2018; Feaver and Kohn 2001). Some of the research questions guiding this project include the following: What are the common characteristics and concerns of the WoT veteran generation in Congress? What does the pattern of growth of WoT veteran representation on Capitol Hill mean for defense policy advocacy? And beyond the quantity of WoT veterans, how do recent military experiences influence the quality and nature of policy debates? What strategies do they pursue to influence executive branch policies, and how do these help to explain puzzling US foreign and defense policy outcomes?

The process model advanced for this study traces the engagement of WoT veterans across different dimensions—from distinctive motivations and traditional and nontraditional strategies for policy influence to measurable outcomes—and it applies the model to ten original case studies of the activism. The study includes a mix of Republican and Democrat veterans of the WoT as well as members from diverse backgrounds. Results speak to popular culture and discourse about veterans' engagement in American politics as well as to debates in the civil-military relations and policy advocacy literature (Lowande, Ritchie, and Lauterbach 2019; Robinson et al. 2020; Lupton 2022; Brooks 2020). The study concludes that WoT veterans can be particularly influential over policy outcomes, unusually creative in their means of influence, and surprisingly collaborative with their fellow veteran legislators.[2]

Generations of Veterans in Congress

The rise of a new generation of lawmakers with military experience reflects a fascinating historical pattern in the United States: Veterans of every major American war have been elected to office in national and state level politics in significant numbers. Distinguished military service records have helped generate popular support for presidential candidates ranging from George Washington to George H. W. Bush (Teigen 2018; Nteta and Tarsi 2016).[3] Similarly, thousands of military veterans have run for Congress and served with distinction throughout the nation's history. These cohorts have often been disproportionately represented on Capitol Hill, and the work of veterans also tends to garner substantial public and media attention (Brooks, Golby, and Urben 2021).

The high-water mark of military veterans' presence in Congress in modern politics was at the end of the Vietnam War era, when more than three-quarters of all lawmakers on Capitol Hill had military experience (DiCicco and Fordham 2018). Veterans from World War II, Vietnam and the Korean War, and those who served during the Cold War all found themselves working together. For example, prominent veterans of the Vietnam War like Bob Kerrey (R-NB), John Heinz (R-PA), Les Aspin (D-WI), and Leon Panetta (D-CA) came from different backgrounds and had very different political beliefs. But when it came to defense policy, they acted in concerted ways predicted by studies of political socialization: nearly all of them sought to limit war operations, promote congressional oversight of the executive branch, and support the care of soldiers and veterans (Bartels and Jackman 2014; Gelpi and Feaver 2002; Zillman 2006). Studies of Vietnam-era veterans have found similarities tied to their experiences, though not all scholars agree on the depth and duration of these connections (DiCicco and Fordham 2018; Sechser 2004).

Patterns of veterans' representation began to change in the early 1970s, though, and the next few decades saw a precipitous decline of their numbers in Congress (see figure 1.1).[4] There were a variety of circumstances behind this change, including retirements, the end of the draft, and the rise of an entire volunteer force (not to mention the increasing complexity and cost for a veteran candidate to mount a successful political campaign). But regardless of the causes, experts have argued that this decline also had significant effects on policy activism. Scholar Danielle Lupton argued that fewer veterans in Congress resulted in "a decreased willingness by the legislature to try to influence the White House on defense and national security issues" and "restrain the president's use of force" (Lupton 2018). Another study lamented, "No one understands the spirit of national service better than an American veteran [and the] perspective of veterans, particularly those who have served in foreign wars, is invaluable when this country's leaders debate putting American forces in harm's way" (Jones 2014). Many worried, for example, that the adventurism of the George W. Bush administration was not tempered as well by the presence of more veterans in government. Only representatives with military experience, they argued, "have the credibility and background necessary to hold the president accountable" (Jones 2014). However, these dynamics began to change again with the arrival of a new generation in Congress.

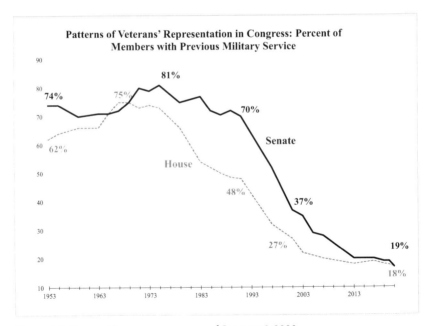

Figure 1.1. Source: Congress.gov, accessed January 6, 2023.

Introduction 5

WoT Veterans in Congress

There are nearly four million veterans of the WoT today in the United States, or about 22 percent of all living veterans.[5] For many voters, WoT veterans who run for Congress seem to embody a spirit of public service and sacrifice. The first veterans of the Iraq and Afghanistan Wars who were elected to Congress were Democrats: in 2006, candidates Joe Sestak (D-PA), Christopher Carney (D-PA), Patrick Murphy (D-PA), and Tim Walz (D-MN) all campaigned on their records of military service, and they upset incumbent Republicans in relatively conservative districts. This marked the beginning of a trend: by the 2020 elections, nearly two hundred veterans had won major party primaries and run for Congress in House and Senate races, including a record number of women. Of that number, fifty-one WoT veterans were sworn into Congress in January 2021, marking the largest new concentration of members with similar service backgrounds in decades.[6]

Beyond the numbers, this book also offers an exploration of the diversity of representation and the quality of the policy debates informed by military experiences. For example, there was also a notable increase in the number of female military veterans of Afghanistan and Iraq. This study highlights the service experiences and political activism of several representatives who were part of the largest female share of any veteran cohort in Congress in US history. Veterans like Senator Tammy Duckworth (D-IL) and Congresswoman Mikie Sherrill (D-NJ) have demonstrated resolve to fight for policies they believe in and challenge executive authority. Duckworth was severely injured while piloting an Army Black Hawk helicopter in Iraq in 2004, and she was elected to Congress in 2012. There, she worked closely with a growing cadre of fellow female veterans to successfully pressure the Defense Department to open all service roles to women, including combat roles.[7] Mikie Sherrill served as a Navy helicopter pilot and battle theater commander during the WoT. She was elected to Congress as a Democrat in 2018, representing the New Jersey Eleventh District, a swing district. Sherrill has been especially active on military and veterans' issues and Afghanistan War oversight, sponsoring the largest number of bills on these subjects of any freshman lawmaker. These examples reflect changing patterns of WoT veterans representation in Congress that are further examined in this study.[8]

Many WoT veterans share experiences in common. As noted, WoT veterans were activated for deployments from National Guard and Reserve units more often than in past wars. The WoT generation also had the highest levels of education of any prior war veteran cohort (Vespa 2020). Building on their training and experience, members of Congress who were deployed to Iraq and Afghanistan served as pilots, military surgeons, intelligence officers, Explosive Ordinance Disposal team members, and in many other positions of responsibility.[9]

6 *Staying in the Fight*

Table 1.1. Veterans of the WoT Who Served in Congress from 2007 to 2023

Name	Political Office	Party	State-District	Time in Congress	Service Branch
Mark Sanford	Representative	R	SC-1	1995–2001/2013–19	Air Force Reserve
Lindsey Graham	Representative then Senator	R	SC-3	1995–present	Air National Guard
Roger Wicker	Representative then Senator	R	MS-1	1995–present	Air Force Reserve
John Shimkus	Representative	R	IL-15/19/20	1997–2021	Army Reserve
Joe Wilson	Representative	R	SC-2	2001–present	Army National Guard
Tim Murphy	Representative	R	PA-18	2003–17	Navy Reserve
Christopher Carney	Representative	D	PA-10	2007–11	Navy Reserve
Joe Sestak	Representative	D	PA-7	2007–11	Navy
Patrick Murphy	Representative	D	PA-8	2007–11	Army
Tim Walz	Representative	D	MN-1	2007–19	Army National Guard
Mike Coffman	Representative	R	CO-6	2009–19	Marine Corps
Tom Rooney	Representative	R	FL-17/16	2009–19	Army
Duncan Hunter	Representative	R	CA-50/52	2009–20	Marine Corps
Brett Guthrie	Representative	R	KY-2	2009–present	Army
Gary Peters	Representative then Senator	D	MI-14/9	2009–present	Navy Reserve
Steve Stivers	Representative	R	OH-15	2011–21	Army National Guard
Steven Palazzo	Representative	R	MS-4	2011–23	Army National Guard
Adam Kinzinger	Representative	R	IL-16/11	2011–23	Air Force
Andy Harris	Representative	R	MD-1	2011–present	Navy Reserve
Steve Womack	Representative	R	AR-3	2011–present	Army National Guard
Todd Young	Representative then Senator	R	IN-9	2011–present	Marine Corps
Jim Bridenstine	Representative	R	OK-1	2013–18	Navy Reserve
Ron DeSantis	Representative	R	FL-6	2013–18	Navy

Introduction 7

Table 1.1. Veterans of the WoT Who Served in Congress from 2007 to 2023 (*Continued*)

Name	Political Office	Party	State-District	Time in Congress	Service Branch
Doug Collins	Representative	R	GA-9	2013–21	Air Force Reserve
Tulsi Gabbard	Representative	D	HI-2	2013–21	Army National Guard
Brad Wenstrup	Representative	R	OH-2	2013–present	Army Reserve
Scott Perry	Representative	R	PA-10/4	2013–present	Army National Guard
Tammy Duckworth	Representative then Senator	D	IL-8	2013–present	Army National Guard
Tom Cotton	Representative then Senator	R	AR-4	2013–present	Army
Ryan Zinke	Representative	R	MT (at large)	2015–17	Navy
Steven Russell	Representative	R	OK-5	2015–19	Army
Martha McSally	Representative then Senator	R	AZ-2	2015–20	Air Force
Ralph Abraham	Representative	R	LA-5	2015–21	Coast Guard Auxiliary
Lee Zeldin	Representative	R	NY-1	2015–23	Army
Dan Sullivan	Senator	R	AK	2015–present	Marine Corps
Joni Ernst	Senator	R	IA	2015–present	Army National Guard
Ruben Gallego	Representative	D	AZ-7	2015–present	Marine Corps
Seth Moulton	Representative	D	MA-6	2015–present	Marine Corps
Ted Lieu	Representative	D	CA-33	2015–present	Air Force Reserve
Trent Kelly	Representative	R	MS-1	2015–present	Army National Guard
Scott Taylor	Representative	R	VA-2	2017–19	Navy
Anthony Brown	Representative	D	MD-4	2017–23	Army Reserve
Brian Mast	Representative	R	FL-18	2017–present	Army

Continued

8   Staying in the Fight

Table 1.1. Veterans of the WoT Who Served in Congress from 2007 to 2023 (*Continued*)

Name	Political Office	Party	State-District	Time in Congress	Service Branch
Don Bacon	Representative	R	NE-2	2017–present	Air Force
Jack Bergman	Representative	R	MI-1	2017–present	Marine Corps Reserve
Jimmy Panetta	Representative	D	CA-20	2017–present	Navy Reserve
Mike Gallagher	Representative	R	WI-8	2017–present	Marine Corps
Roger Marshall	Representative then Senator	R	KS-1	2017–present	Army Reserve
Conor Lamb	Representative	D	PA-17/18	2018–23	Marine Corps
Denver Riggleman	Representative	R	VA-5	2019–21	Air Force
Max Rose	Representative	D	NY-11	2019–21	Army
Steve Watkins	Representative	R	KS-2	2019–21	Army
Elaine Luria	Representative	D	VA-2	2019–23	Navy
Van Taylor	Representative	R	TX-3	2019–23	Marine Corps
Chrissy Houlahan	Representative	D	PA-6	2019–present	Air Force Reserve
Daniel Crenshaw	Representative	R	TX-2	2019–present	Navy
Greg Steube	Representative	R	FL-17	2019–present	Army
Guy Reschenthaler	Representative	R	PA-14	2019–present	Navy
Jared Golden	Representative	D	ME-2	2019–present	Marine Corps
Jason Crow	Representative	D	CO-6	2019–present	Army
Mark Green	Representative	R	TN-7	2019–present	Army
Michael Waltz	Representative	R	FL-6	2019–present	Army
Mikie Sherrill	Representative	D	NJ-11	2019–present	Navy
William Timmons	Representative	R	SC-4	2019–present	Air National Guard
Mark Kelly	Senator	D	AZ	2020–present	Navy

Introduction 9

Table 1.1. Veterans of the WoT Who Served in Congress from 2007 to 2023 (*Continued*)

Name	Political Office	Party	State-District	Time in Congress	Service Branch
Mike Garcia	Representative	R	CA-25/27	2020–present	Navy
Kai Kahele	Representative	D	HI-2	2021–23	Air National Guard
Peter Meijer	Representative	R	MI-3	2021–23	Army Reserve
Andrew Clyde	Representative	R	GA-9	2021–present	Air Force Reserve
August Pfluger	Representative	R	TX-11	2021–present	Air Force
Jake Auchincloss	Representative	D	MA-4	2021–present	Marine Corps
Jake Ellzey	Representative	R	TX-6	2021–present	Navy
Jim Banks	Representative	R	IN-3	2021–present	Navy Reserve
Ronny Jackson	Representative	R	TX-13	2021–present	Navy
Scott Fitzgerald	Representative	R	WI-5	2021–present	Army
Scott Franklin	Representative	R	FL-15	2021–present	Navy
Tony Gonzales	Representative	R	TX-23	2021–present	Navy
Troy Nehls	Representative	R	TX-22	2021–present	Army Reserve
Pat Ryan	Representative	D	NY-19	2022–present	Army
Anna Paulina Luna	Representative	R	FL-13	2023–present	Air Force
Christopher Deluzio	Representative	D	PA-17	2023–present	Navy
Cory Mills	Representative	R	FL-7	2023–present	Army
Derrick Van Orden	Representative	R	WI-3	2023–present	Navy SEAL
Eli Crane	Representative	R	AZ-2	2023–present	Navy SEAL

Continued

10 *Staying in the Fight*

Table 1.1. Veterans of the WoT Who Served in Congress from 2007 to 2023 (*Continued*)

Name	Political Office	Party	State-District	Time in Congress	Service Branch
J. D. Vance	Senator	R	OH	2023–present	Marine Corps
Jeff Jackson	Representative	D	NC-14	2023–present	Army Reserve
Jennifer Kiggans	Representative	R	VA-2	2023–present	Navy
John James	Representative	R	MI-10	2023–present	Army
Max Miller	Representative	R	OH-7	2023–present	Marine Corps Reserve
Morgan Luttrell	Representative	R	TX-8	2023–present	Navy SEAL
Nicholas LaLota	Representative	R	NY-1	2023–present	Navy
Rich McCormick	Representative	R	GA-6	2023–present	Marine Corps/ Navy
Ryan Zinke	Representative	R	MT-1	2023–present	Navy SEAL
Wesley Hunt	Representative	R	TX-38	2023–present	Army
Zach Nunn	Representative	R	IA-3	2023–present	Air Force/Air National Guard

Source: Quorum Federal Database; legislator websites; House Committee on Veterans' Affairs.

When they arrive in Congress, WoT veterans have found opportunities to achieve their policy goals by working closely with advocacy groups. For example, there are a growing number of nonpartisan groups dedicated to the election of more veterans to Congress to pursue shared interests and concerns. The nonpartisan group With Honor was founded in 2017 by veterans of the WoT to promote the election of more WoT veterans to Congress. Its mission is to promote a "less polarized government that works for and is trusted by Americans" in which "elected officials serve with integrity, civility, and courage." This group argued that veterans have many shared experiences that help them to overcome traditional polarization and partisan divides and put country before party. They help fund veterans' campaigns through political action committees but also advocate for policy reform. Other nonpartisan groups like VoteVets and Veterans Campaign also promote veteran involvement in politics. These groups have worked closely with caucuses in Congress such as the For Country Caucus (a bipartisan group of twenty-six veteran representatives and some senators) and claimed policy successes on a wide range of defense and foreign policy issues as well as supporting legislation to promote veterans' health care and benefits (Lowande, Ritchie, and Lauterbach 2019).

Broadly speaking, WoT veterans in Congress also have appeared to be highly committed, focused, and intentional in their work on Capitol Hill. Indeed, this book explores how these many different personalities have drawn on shared experiences for engagement on common causes. For instance, Congressman Michael Waltz (R-FL) is a combat-decorated Green Beret who was deployed to Afghanistan, the Middle East, and North Africa and continued to serve in the National Guard during his political career. He ran for the seat in the Florida Sixth Congressional District in 2018, to succeed retiring Congressman Ron DeSantis (R-FL). Waltz frequently referenced experiences from his tours in combat and working as an adviser in the executive branch in relation to his stances on military affairs as a member of Congress. For example, during the showdown between Russia and the United States over Ukraine, Waltz said that it was critical the Biden administration show strength and resolve toward Putin because he knew "what it is like to face down an adversary" in combat (quoted in Powers 2021). Just weeks before the outbreak of that war, Waltz joined with fellow veteran Democrats, including Congressmen Ruben Gallego (D-AZ) and Seth Moulton (D-MA), to conduct a fact-finding mission to Ukraine, and upon their return, all three veterans intensified their pressure on the White House to provide greater military and humanitarian assistance.

WoT lawmakers have also reported that they feel a sense of camaraderie with fellow veterans in Congress that allows bipartisanship even in an era of extreme polarization. These veterans told me that they immediately recognize their counterparts with shared experiences and have common bonds that bridge partisan and ideological differences. One senior congressional staff member and WoT veteran said that in their experience, cooperation with other veterans was "just easier." "They intuitively get each other," they said, and "speak each other's language" (author's interview, October 15, 2021). Congressman Jason Crow (D-CO), a former Army Ranger, acknowledged that he was "profoundly affected" by his military service and that it "completely changed my outlook and goals for a life of service to the country." Crow said that he was drawn to work with other veterans on Capitol Hill and felt that combat experiences helped create a shared bond. He said that veterans know "we've got to find ways to work together because political sideshows don't get you anywhere" (author's interview, October 26, 2021). Another veteran on Capitol Hill said that military experiences set them apart from civilians and candidly shared that it was sometimes "frustrating to see a lack of creativity on foreign policy and security issues by civilian leaders." "Veterans are used to solving problems immediately,"

12   Staying in the Fight

he said, "but Congress is like a different world" (author's interview, October 15, 2021).

Finally, members of Congress from the WoT generation have also offered strong opinions about US foreign and defense policy that are informed by their experiences. Veterans of Iraq and Afghanistan fought in conflicts that often lacked a battlefront—in wars where their enemies were hidden among the populace and attacks were conducted by insurgents or improvised explosive devices. These types of experiences not only had a profound impact on the mental and physical toll on veterans but also provided them with a unique perspective on the limits of military force. Veterans have often rendered their policy arguments in this context (Sjursen 2017, 12). Mary Kaszynski, director of government relations at the policy advocacy group VoteVets, told me, "Military veterans definitely have distinctive perspectives on issues in Congress. Their direct experiences give them a sense of the real costs of decisions in Washington like putting troops in harm's way and the investment the United States makes in the world" (author's interview, November 16, 2021). In her judgment, "veterans seem to be much more thoughtful about decisions regarding military and security issues. They are more conscious that they and the Congress have a responsibility to support and protect the troops" (author's interview, November 16, 2021; Recchia 2015; Teigen 2015). Another former staff member on Capitol Hill agreed, stating, "Military veterans from Afghanistan and Iraq just know what the military can do. They can help identify the problem and choose a solution; they have contingencies. But veterans also know what the military cannot do or should not do—and that makes a difference" (author's interview, October 12, 2021). Given what they have faced, WoT veterans seem to be especially "persistent and relentless, with a strategic approach to problem-solving." A congressional staff member concluded, "They are engaged because they consistently ask the right questions" (author's interview, November 5, 2021).

Service and Sacrifice

This study also recognizes the heavy price of military service and its impact on public life and policy advocacy processes. Research shows that WoT veterans are about twice as likely to have been deployed in combat zones compared to prior generations of soldiers, and they also suffered injuries at higher rates per capita than in previous conflicts (Watson Institute 2020) (see figure 1.2). More WoT veterans have survived "poly-traumas" (i.e., combinations of severe injuries, such as spinal cord injuries, amputations, burns, blindness, and traumatic brain injuries) than in prior wars (Scott et al. 2006). Prolonged conflicts in Iraq and Afghanistan required more frequent deployments and exposure to the intensity of combat than in any other modern US conflict (Parker et al. 2019; Institute of Medicine 2010).[10]

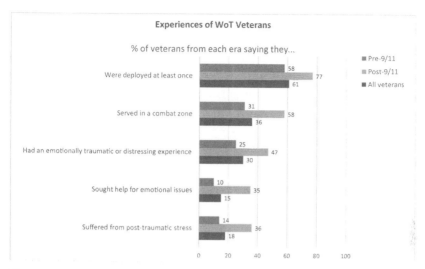

Figure 1.2. Source: Survey of US veterans conducted May 14–June 3, 2019. "The American Veteran Experience and the Post-9/11 Generation."

These experiences, in turn, have impacted the physical and mental health of this generation of veterans. For example, a 2020 report by the US Census found that post-9/11 veterans had the highest chance of having a service-connected disability than any other group of veterans—on average, a 43 percent chance of disability from time serving (Vespa 2020; Glasser 2011). Not only were battlefield injuries a serious risk, but studies have also shown that a high percentage of veterans of the Iraq and Afghanistan Wars were exposed to toxic plumes from "burn pits" used for the disposal of materials at bases in those countries. Studies suggest that these plumes may have contributed to respiratory illnesses and even rare cancers for some veterans (LeBlanc 2011). Surveys also show negative mental health effects of deployments. A 2019 Pew Center study found that 42 percent of post-9/11 veterans said that their experiences have harmed their mental health, compared to just 17 percent of a pre-9/11 cohort of veterans polled. Roughly half of all post-911 veterans say they had emotionally traumatic or distressing experiences while on active duty, and about one-third report that they have sought professional help to address these challenges (Parker et al. 2019). PTSD is the most frequently diagnosed mental disorder among WoT veterans seeking health care from the Veterans Administration (Jakupcak et al. 2009). As one expert told me, "We recognize the effects of military service and a wide definition of trauma from deployments. In many ways, participating in combat itself *is* trauma. It is traumatizing, whether veterans address it directly or not" (author's interview, November 16, 2021).[11]

Do We Need More Veterans in Congress?

This book also grapples with questions about the role of veterans in American politics at a time when many worry that the fabric of US democracy is fraying. President Donald Trump's attempts to politicize the military, coupled with increased partisanship and polarization, seemed to cast civil-military relations in an especially harsh light. In turn, this has prompted new debates about whether the presence of more veterans in high elected office promotes representation and democratic principles or dangerously blurs the lines of the separation between civilian and military control of government (Brooks 2021; Gambone 2021; Rudalevige 2006).

Many American voters support veterans in office and believe they bring significant strengths to the job (Zillman 2006; Teigen 2007, 2018). Studies show that the American electorate associates values with military veterans, including honor, trust, and responsibility (McDermott and Panagopoulos 2015; Teigen 2018). Expert Jessica Blankshain of the Naval War College acknowledges that distinctive experiences for WoT veterans might create different types of attentiveness to select military and foreign policy issues (author's interview, September 30, 2021). According to retired four-star General Wesley Clark (2018), the advantages of military service for members of Congress are unequivocal. He argued in 2018 that the midterm elections would "see a wave of Iraq and Afghanistan war veterans ascend Capitol Hill" and said he believed that was "exactly what our country needs." He added:

> Veterans are running for office in record numbers this year because they believe Washington is broken. What's more, they know the same sense of duty, commitment to results, [and] integrity. . . . Veterans are respectful of institutions. Veterans of my generation returned from Vietnam to help transform the U.S. Army. But young veterans are fed up with political leadership. Politicians sent them into Iraq and Afghanistan without exit plans, leaving them with their fingers in the dike. Now home, they see partisan bickering but no vision for America. They are impatient for change. . . . Voters are starting to see veterans as the antidote to Washington's toxicity, a jump-start for our democracy ironically predicated on the very qualities that distinguish them from most politicians . . . [like putting] country before party.

However, others remain hesitant to endorse stronger representation of the armed forces in civilian government (Nielson and Snider 2009; Brooks 2019). Some believe that lawmakers with past (or even present) military service experience could skew the delicate balance of democratic representation and civilian control of government. Samuel Huntington outlined this argument in his seminal study *The Soldier and the State* (1957)—providing a vision of civilian "objective control of the military," with a clear separation of authority and domains of responsibility into political and military spheres. These boundaries would be defined and respected. Huntington believed "this approach was ideal because it ensured both military deference to civilian authority and the country's military effectiveness in war" (Brooks 2020, 9). This vision imagined a relationship between the two sectors as more transactional than collaborative, a general agreement that a liberal democratic society demanded this type of objective engagement.

Increased representation of former active-duty military veterans, along with guard and reserve officers, in Congress today has led some experts to conclude that the idea of a truly apolitical military leadership is more aspiration than fact (Levinson 2020; Bacevich 2011). Higher rates of guard and reserve duty activation for operations in conflict zones since September 11, 2001, means the United States has effectively adopted an "operational reserve" mode for these forces instead of treating them as a limited, strategic reserve in the past. These units have been called up for deployments at increasingly frequent rates since 2001, and veterans in Congress are not exempt from these actions. For example, former representative Adam Kinzinger (R-IL) is a lieutenant colonel in the Wisconsin Air National Guard whose unit was deployed in 2019 while he was serving in Congress to the US-Mexico border to support security operations ordered by President Trump. Trent Kelly (R-MS), a combat veteran who served multiple tours of duty in Iraq, worked in Congress even while he rose to the rank of major general in the National Guard. Critics raise questions about the propriety of today's situation where veterans may often "have more in common with their active-duty counterparts than with average Americans" (Blankshain 2019; Golby, Feaver, and Dropp 2017).

Critics also charge that military veterans display distinct biases in their approaches to policymaking. One senior military officer interviewed for this book said that while longtime service veterans could provide a "wealth of information" to shape foreign policy, "the problem comes when these individuals don't provide unbiased advice." While a senior military veteran "should provide an assessment of the complex environment, provide recommendations, and try to look at the issue from multiple points of view," they more often do not (author's interview, September 9, 2021). He warned, "For example, a former general officer who does not provide unbiased options or assessments of immigration policies does a disservice to his/her nation . . . if [they] only provide an assessment that supports his/her preferred policy decision, then their experience and background does not help." Their input in the policy process can have the effect of "sidelining, understating, or actively destroying the other potential policy choices" (author's interview, September 9, 2021). These concerns lead

16   Staying in the Fight

many to question whether lawmakers with a hybrid status as Guard members and active politicians may face conflicts of interest.

Finally, experts debate the constitutionality of the modern soldier-statesman model. Some question the propriety of military National Guard and Reserve officers and former military officers also serving in Congress and cite the Incompatibility Clause in Article I, Section 6 of the Constitution that states, "No Person holding any Office under the United States, shall be a Member of either House during his Continuance in Office." They argue that the provision means that members of Congress should not serve in two different posts in the government at the same time, preventing undue influence across the different branches of government. This highlights the tensions associated with whether members of the National Guard or Reserve can also sit in Congress without resigning their commissions. The question reached the US Supreme Court in a 1973 case, *Schlesinger v. Reservists Committee to Stop the War*. An anti–Vietnam War group charged that senators and representatives who held commissions in the National Guard or Reserve forces should be removed as officers in the military (or resign from Congress). While lower courts acknowledged the incompatibility of holding dual offices, the high court sidestepped the substantive details of the question and resolved the case on procedural grounds. What remains is a situation that might challenge Huntington's vision of an apolitical military and one that allows significant policy input from veterans elected to Congress (Recchia 2015).

Military Veterans, January 6, and a Stress-Test for American Democracy

These competing perspectives were put to the test on January 6, 2021, when supporters of President Trump forced a vote in Congress on whether lawmakers should decertify the results of Electoral College vote counts by states in the November 2020 presidential election. According to the US Constitution, the president is elected indirectly through the Electoral College, where votes are allotted to states based on their populations. The winning candidate is required to receive at least 270 out of the 538 electoral votes available (Edwards 2019).[12] This system was formalized in Article II of the Constitution, the Twelfth and Thirteenth Amendments, and the Electoral Count Act of 1887. As the final stage in this process, Congress meets in a joint session to count the electoral votes (essentially recertifying the certificates of ascertainment submitted by the states with their election results). This session is presided over by the vice president of the United States, and these meetings had long been considered standard fare and garnered little media attention (Feerick 2021).

However, when President Trump lost the election in 2020, he and his supporters charged that the presidency had been "stolen" for Joe Biden via rampant electoral fraud. After a series of failed lawsuits, they further determined that the January 6, 2021, certification process in Congress offered a last-stand opportunity to challenge the legitimacy of the election. Trump backers, including members of the Senate and the House, planned to try to challenge the count results of Pennsylvania, Arizona, and possibly other states, with the goal of returning them back to their respective state legislators and electoral officials for reconsideration.[13] They knew that they might have a slim chance to disrupt the proceedings on January 6 through internal (procedural maneuvers) and external (protests and pressure) interventions. Trump used social media to invite protesters to come to Washington, DC, for a rally that day that would feature a keynote address by Trump himself on the Ellipse. Tens of thousands of protesters attended the speech, and thousands marched to the US Capitol building. What followed was an insurrection: At almost the same time that some Republican lawmakers in the Senate made the first of a planned series of objections based on allegations of widespread voter fraud in select states, a mob of protesters outside the Capitol breached police lines and fought with Capitol Police officers to try to gain entry into the building. Hundreds of protesters broke into the Capitol, injuring members of the police, damaging property, and threatening lawmakers with physical harm. At least seven people lost their lives in connection with the January 6 attack, including three law enforcement officers. This tragic break with democratic traditions was labeled by many as an "attempted coup" for Trump to retain power as president in spite of losing the popular vote (Anderson 2022; Raskin 2022).

WoT veterans played important, yet contrasting roles in this story: Some WoT veterans like Representatives Jason Crow (D-CO) and Ruben Gallego (D-AZ) stepped up on January 6 to protect their fellow lawmakers in the face of threats of violence. Their stories are told in further detail later in this book. But other WoT veterans were antagonists in the insurrection. Outside the Capitol building, for example, roughly 10 percent of those charged with violence against the police were military veterans.[14] Of those, the majority of members had served in the military after 9/11, and at least one active-duty Marine officer was also arrested and charged in the attack (Cohen and Rabinowitz 2021). Meanwhile, some WoT veterans were involved in events inside the House chamber: When Congress reconvened on the evening of January 6 to debate certification, 19 of the 139 representatives who voted to sustain objections to the vote counts in Pennsylvania and Arizona were WoT veterans. This represented a sizable 37 percent of the entire cohort (19 out of 51).[15]

These developments raised many interesting questions for further study. The circumstances around the insurrection, coupled with very different roles played by different veterans of the wars in Iraq and Afghanistan, remind us of the fragile and complex nature of the democratic process. They also highlight the complicated relationship between military service and political engagement

18   *Staying in the Fight*

and activism that continues to unfold in American politics. This book will probe different dimensions of these important questions.

Theoretical and Empirical Preview of Book

As noted previously, this book applies foreign policy analysis theories of policy advocacy and entrepreneurship to study the activism of a new generation of military veterans in Congress, and it develops a multidimensional perspective on engagement and entrepreneurship that includes issue framing, personal and political narratives, sponsorship and cosponsorship of legislation, and advocacy coalition formation to achieve measurable objectives (Lynch and Madonna 2017; Bond 2019). This study posits that WoT veteran lawmakers have high levels of motivation and will employ a range of strategies to achieve their defense policy goals. It also recognizes that outcomes of their engagement go beyond formal legislation to include changes in executive branch policies and procedures and engagement on the implementation of initiatives.

This project employs a mixed-method research design to examine propositions on foreign policy advocacy and entrepreneurship. It combines comparative case method (Gerring and Cojocaru 2015; George and Bennett 2005) and descriptive statistics, supported by archival research and original elite interviews. A structured, focused comparison of cases of foreign policy advocacy allows us to examine how veterans in Congress have developed increasingly sophisticated, multilevel strategies to achieve their objectives in US foreign policy. The following cases are developed in the book:

- *Strategic Engagement in the Middle East—Saudi Arabian Relations and the Yemen Civil War*: A bipartisan coalition of WoT veterans, including Representative Ted Lieu (D-CA) and Senator Todd Young (R-IN) challenged executive branch support for Saudi Arabia and its operations in the Yemeni Civil War and placed restrictions on military aid that led to a significant drawdown of US engagement.
- *Ending the Afghanistan War and the Special Immigrant Visa Programs*: Representatives Mike Waltz (R-FL) and Jason Crow (D-CO) were strong supporters of expanding the Special Immigrant Visa (SIV) programs for Afghan interpreters and others to be granted permanent residency in the United States at the end of the war. Waltz and Crow also became personally engaged in trying to manage and respond to Trump and Biden administration decisions regarding the drawdown of US forces in Afghanistan and the chaotic evacuation of refugees from the country in 2021. In 2022, they launched a new campaign to allow former Afghan soldiers to join the US military.
- *The Syria Policy Puzzle*: The story of US engagement in Syria's civil war cannot be fully understood without recognizing the push and pull of key

legislators, including military veterans, against presidential administration policies. Representatives Tulsi Gabbard (D-HI) and Adam Kinzinger (R-IL) were influential voices in Obama and Trump administration decisions regarding Syria, and other veteran lawmakers have engaged in more intense oversight of policies since at least 2014.

- *Veterans Affairs and Health—PTSD and "Burn Pits"*: In the 116th Congress, Representatives Elaine Luria (D-VA) and Steve Stivers (R-OH) helped establish the bipartisan For Country Caucus and cosponsored legislation to bring relief to veterans who may have been exposed to toxic "burn pits" during deployments in Iraq and Afghanistan. They also worked with other veteran lawmakers on Capitol Hill to establish a strong Veterans Affairs response to treatments for PTSD.

- *The Ukraine War and the Fight for Democracy*: The US response to the war in Ukraine in 2022 was greatly influenced by a strong and committed group of WoT veterans in Congress who were dedicated to the cause of defending democracy and giving Ukraine "a fighting chance." While the Biden administration attempted to proceed very cautiously to avoid being drawn directly into the conflict, most WoT veterans in Congress argued that the United States had vital national interests in the struggle against Russia. Lawmakers like Senator Joni Ernst (R-IA) and Congressman Ruben Gallego (D-AZ) helped develop legislation that would dramatically expand US military support. It soon became clear that strong congressional and public pressure, combined with strong advocacy efforts on behalf of Ukraine, seemed to lead in this policy development process rather than follow executive branch preferences.

In summary, these case studies offer valuable insight into WoT veterans' attitudes and behavior in political office—and they have been developed at a time when we are just beginning in earnest to explore these dynamics. This manuscript represents an important contribution to our understanding of this cohort and how experiences in Afghanistan and Iraq have shaped lawmakers' interests and advocacy. Indeed, it offers some of the first scholarship focused on the motivations, behavior, and policy preferences of this distinctive group. This book tells the stories of profoundly interesting ways that WoT veterans maneuver through the minefields of executive-legislative branch tensions and achieve their objectives. From fighting for causes and solving problems like providing health care for burn pit victims to providing safe harbor for Afghan refugees, a new generation of veterans in Congress are making their voices heard. This book illustrates how service and sacrifice often translate into dedication to policy changes and critical and creative strategies to help the US government get there.

2

Military Veterans and Policy Advocacy

Socialization and Representation

When Republicans took control of the US House of Representatives in January 2023, many conservatives demanded that federal spending, including the defense budget, be dramatically curtailed. Kevin McCarthy (R-CA) reportedly cut a deal with a group of lawmakers that they would vote for him to become Speaker of the House if he would implement spending caps and budget cuts. Just days after the start of the 118th session of Congress, though, the House seemed to be in disarray on the question. Leading the opposition to capping defense spending were veterans of the WoT from both sides of the aisle. Representative Tony Gonzalez (R-TX), a career cryptologist in the Navy and a veteran of operations in Iraq and Afghanistan, spoke out against defense spending cuts as "a horrible idea" in the face of threats around the world like Russia's invasion of Ukraine and China's ambitions for Taiwan. He was joined by a bipartisan group of fellow WoT veterans, including Representative Jim Banks (R-IN), a Navy Reservist and Afghanistan veteran, and Representative Jared Golden (D-ME), a Marine combat veteran from Afghanistan. They warned that a large cut to the defense budget would "fly in the face of the tradition of bipartisan defense consensus and supporting freedom and democracy in conjunction with our allies" (quoted in Neukam, January 11, 2023). Within weeks, the House leadership appeared to backpedal on the question of topline budget cuts and instead began to identify line items and programs they might instead try to trim.

Veterans are clearly making themselves heard in today's political process. This chapter details a theory framework for a more systematic study of WoT veterans' policy advocacy in Congress. I posit that the five dimensions of leadership, motivations, preferences, strategies, and voting behavior are all influential

20

in producing changes in defense policy directions or outcomes for the United States. The first of the five dimensions in the process model is the importance of distinctive socialization experiences and motivations of military veterans. The study tells the story of the personalities of a subset of veteran lawmakers and ways that they bring their experiences and personal journeys to bear in the policy process by adding depth and valuable context from exclusive interviews. Second, the process model examines key strategies and processes by which lawmakers gain that influence. This study posits that military veterans in Congress are likely to use advocacy strategies such as issue framing and linking personal and policy narratives. These narratives are not only reflective of their individual experiences; lawmakers quickly recognize ways to effectively link personal and policy narratives for advocacy for select policy positions. Third, WoT veterans may be likely to cosponsor legislation and adopt bipartisanship in their policy advocacy to provide them leverage for congressional oversight and the achievement of comprehensive policy solutions.

Fourth, this study proposes that a new generation of lawmakers has become more active in building policy coalitions that align themselves with the views of interest groups and epistemic communities. This form of insider/outsider advocacy offers junior lawmakers opportunities for influence in a system that is otherwise controlled by party leaders, and it helps to illustrate actor motivations, strategies, and associated policy change over time. And finally, WoT military veterans in Congress may be especially well attuned to adapting to complexity and rapid changes in difficult strategic environments. When they face obstacles in the legislative environment, for example, these activists may demonstrate a level of "mission flexibility" in seeking alternative acceptable outcomes such as oversight or intervention in executive branch policy implementation (see figure 2.1).

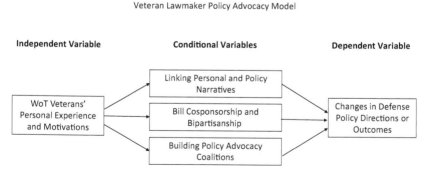

Figure 2.1. Source: Emily Hasecke.

22 *Staying in the Fight*

Each of the sections that follow details how this multidimensional model of veteran activism is grounded in the civil-military relations and policy analysis literature, and they advance several propositions for the study.

Military Service and Distinctive Motivations

Military veteran lawmakers may be especially inclined to become advocates in critical policy decisions as a function of their own personal and professional journeys. The military socialization process provides distinctive experiences that often have lifelong impacts (Elder, Gimbel, and Ivie 1991; Settersten 2006). Indeed, the majority of enlistees in the US military fall between the ages of eighteen and twenty-four, or what socialization theorists refer to as critical formative years. Military training engages socialization processes as components of the physical and mental preparation for the potential rigors of service (Jackson et al. 2012; Shpeer and Howe 2020). This commonly features programs "in which civilian status is broken down and the new identity of military recruit is forged," creating new behavioral norms and expectations (Jackson et al. 2012, 2; Leal and Teigen 2018). As scholar Michael Gambone (2021, 33) argues, "Military service defines the veteran [and] every veteran leaves the service with the stamp of plural military cultures on them. To understand the veteran, it is necessary to understand the military as a culture and an institution."

Previous studies have demonstrated that individual experiences while in the military may also function as heuristics that influence their political attitudes (Fordham 2001; Teigen 2015, 2018).[1] Indeed, Danny Sjursen (2017, 3) asserts that veteran lawmakers often approach issues "from a veteran's as much as a legislator's perspective." How distinctive are military veterans' perspectives on politics? Studies of civil-military relations assert that military experience offers "direct relevance for how leaders evaluate issues," including "the utility of using military force" (Burden 2007; Grossman, Manekin, and Miodownik 2015; Horowitz and Stam 2014; Stadelmann, Portmann, and Eichenberger 2015; Best and Vonnahme 2019). As noted in chapter 1, scholars also argue that common experiences can have "generational effects" on political views of candidates, including military veterans' service (DiCicco and Fordham 2018; Fuhrmann and Horowitz 2015; Bartels and Jackman 2014). Some contend that leaders with certain types of military experience are more likely to initiate militarized disputes or favor more hawkish foreign policy (Stadelmann, Portmann, and Eichenberger 2015). Meanwhile, others maintain that leaders in democratic states who have prior combat experiences are less prone to conflict (Horowitz, Stam, and Ellis 2015; Recchia 2015). Danielle Lupton's (2017) analysis of roll-call data finds that the effects of military service are strongest where the experience is highly salient: in the oversight of war operations.

This study of WoT veterans' socialization experiences also speaks to a much larger debate in the civil-military relations regarding the power of socialization versus self-selection. Most scholars seem to agree that there are distinctive differences in military veterans' attitudes about policy priorities and that they "decide differently on military affairs" (Stadelmann, Portmann, and Eichenberger 2015, 143; Feaver and Kohn 2001; Dempsey 2010; Gambone 2021; Recchia 2015). Research shows that politicians with a military background may estimate the potential costs and benefits of their choices and the types of strategies differently than civilians, for example (Grossman, Manekin, and Miodownik 2015; Hong and Kang 2017; DiCicco and Fordham 2018; Fuhrmann and Horowitz 2015). These arguments are more broadly grounded in socialization theory, which asserts there are strong links between individual experiences and subsequent political activism and engagement (Mannheim [1936] 1955; Sears and Levy 2003; Dudley and Gitelson 2002; Thomas 1971; Leal and Teigen 2018; Wasburn and Covert 2017; Burden 2007; DiCicco and Fordham 2018). However, other studies assert that personal values and ideology have the strongest impact on political behavior and that individuals who "self-select" to join the volunteer military may be driven by their own belief structures (Bachman et al. 2000; Jennings and Markus 1977).

The WoT veterans interviewed for this study expressed a universal opinion on this question: they believe that their experiences in uniform in the post-9/11 era have been profoundly formative. While they are respectful of the views of their civilian counterparts, veterans and experts interviewed for this project describe the unique and valuable perspectives they can bring to the policy process. Former congressman Steve Stivers (R-OH) told me that experience in the military helped him "understand what soldiers go through and how wars can impact them." He added, "Because we are all accumulations of our experiences, I firmly believe that this kind of service gives you unique perspectives" (author's interview, December 6, 2021). Another expert said, "Military veterans . . . know what the military can do. They can help identify the problem and choose a solution; they have contingencies. But veterans also know what the military cannot do or should not do—and that makes a difference" (author's interview, October 12, 2021). One senior congressional staff member told me that veterans' service was very important, arguing, "It's impossible to separate life experiences from work experiences on Capitol Hill" and that military experience is at the core of the identity of many WoT veterans (author's interview, October 14, 2021). Another senior staff member said that veterans clearly had distinct "skillsets" plus a "passion and commitment" to key defense and foreign policy issues that set them apart from some other lawmakers (author's interview, October 13, 2021).

Issue Framing: Linking Personal and Policy Narratives

Distinctive motivations often become the impetus for policy commitments by WoT veterans in Congress, who, in turn, may adopt sophisticated, multilevel

24   Staying in the Fight

advocacy strategies to achieve their foreign policy objectives (Lantis 2019; Green 2019; Curry 2015; Hall and Shepsle 2014). Experiences in the field of combat or military service abroad can help veterans see issues in a specific light. Some may have identified priorities for counterterrorism policy based on first-hand experiences; others have worked with vulnerable refugee populations or foreign nationals aiding the US war effort. Veterans might seek to protect their fellow servicemembers from danger in a war against Russia over Ukraine or to provide care for veterans who have returned from Iraq or Afghanistan suffering physical or emotional wounds of war. To veteran lawmakers, these issues are not ambiguous challenges. They are real problems with names and faces for which they seek solutions. Indeed, many veterans in elected office feel a deep moral imperative and even a personal responsibility to find a resolution.[2]

Accordingly, this study posits that WoT military veterans in Congress may use policy narratives to advocate for preferred foreign policy outcomes in the public arena (Shanahan et al. 2018; Ertas 2015; Nelson 2011; Nelson, Oxley, and Clawson 1997; Entman 1993). Policy narratives can be especially powerful tools for advocacy on salient issues such as war fighting, veterans affairs, or congressional oversight of military operations (Parker and Peters 2015; Sjursen 2017; Cormack 2018; Lupton 2017). In the context of this study, they may help military veterans in Congress draw connections between profound personal and professional experiences and policy needs. Policy narratives supplement studies of policy advocacy and help explain dynamic processes of policy learning, policy change, and coalition formation (Feldman et al. 2004; Akin and Palmer 2000; Yanow 2000). Elizabeth Shanahan et al. (2018, 173) conclude, "Policy debates are necessarily fought on the terrain of narratives, constituted by both formal institutional venues (e.g., floor debates and testimonies in the House or lower chambers) and informal venues (e.g., media, interest group websites, Twitter, YouTube, blogs). Both serve to reflect and shape the contours, elevations, and chasms of the narrative terrain."

Policy narratives are also strategic: linking personal and professional policy narratives often allows lawmakers to broaden the appeal of their preferred positions (Schaffner and Sellers 2010). The use of personal narratives may help establish connections for an audience, which in turn may help generate support for prioritizing issues and affecting change (Gamson 1995; Goffman 1974). Actors "use words, images, and symbols to strategically craft policy narratives to resonate with the public, relevant stakeholders, and governmental decision makers, with the aim of producing a winning coalition" (Shanahan, Jones, and McBeth 2011, 536). For example, in 2019, when WoT veteran lawmakers framed the Trump administration's proposal for direct negotiations with the Taliban at Camp David on the anniversary of September 11 as antithetical and insulting, they were able to effectively steer White House policies away from the plan. And when President Biden announced in 2021 that he intended to order a full withdrawal from Afghanistan, veterans in Congress successfully pressured the administration to expand special visa programs for Afghan citizens who had supported US troops. By helping frame sentiments for or against executive actions, advocates could effectively set the "boundaries to permissive conduct" in foreign affairs (Sobel 2001, x).[3] These foundations help set up the first proposition that will be investigated in this study:

> *Proposition 1: If elected representatives in Congress are veterans of the War on Terror, then they are likely to practice issue framing using personal narratives to advocate for military and defense matters in Congress.*

Bill Cosponsorship and Bipartisanship

Another tool for congressional veteran foreign policy advocates is the development, sponsorship, and cosponsorship of legislation. Members of Congress advance formal legislation to pursue their objectives, and they have a role in appropriations decisions that can help shape policy outcomes (Carter and Scott 2009; Lindsay 1994). Military veterans in Congress traditionally sponsor or cosponsor many bills related to defense policy and veterans affairs, and the WoT generation has continued to reflect this pattern. Indeed, for many junior members of Congress who are WoT veterans, these can constitute large percentages of their legislative portfolio in any given year. This study of bill cosponsorship and cooperation among WoT veterans is noteworthy because it challenges prevailing conceptions of dysfunction (Schultz 2017; Jeong and Quirk 2019; Robinson et al. 2020) and a decline in centrist coalition building in Congress (Thurber and Yoshinaka 2015; Kabaservice 2012).[4] Instead, we explore how WoT veteran advocates may be likely to work in teams and collaborate to achieve defense policy objectives (Kertzer, Brooks, and Brooks 2021).[5] These are instrumental skills, especially for junior lawmakers. As Michael Mintrom (2019, 311–12) argues, "Policy entrepreneurs must be tenacious [and they] must be team players . . . policy entrepreneurs who get along well with others and who are well connected in their local policy contexts are more likely to achieve their policy goals."

Studies have identified a variety of factors that may influence the propensity of lawmakers to cosponsor legislation, including as a way to overcome structural constraints, as a function of personal convictions, and through affinity and shared goals. First, new lawmakers face structural constraints when they arrive at Capitol Hill. Many find that power is consolidated in the modern Congress among establishment party leaders and that newer, younger members of Congress often struggle to make a legislative impact. By default, the vast majority of WoT veterans in Congress today face these disadvantages due to their relative junior status (Hammond 1991; Smith 2007; Fleisher and Bond 1983).

Studies have shown that junior legislators often feel frustrated by a policymaking process dominated by a handful of senior leaders and hierarchical rules and procedures in the 1990s. The centralization of control of the policymaking process by party leaders (especially in the House) and the limited information availability to junior members (Curry 2015) can serve to reduce their potential influence (Hall and Shepsle 2014). Thus, it is perhaps not surprising that representatives in the minority were more likely to choose to leave Congress for the private sector. The 2016, 2020, and 2022 election cycles all saw high numbers of junior retirements.

A second factor driving cosponsorship patterns among veterans may be homophily based on shared experiences (Koger 2003; Garand and Burke 2006; Platt and Sinclair-Chapman 2008; Rocca and Sanchez 2008). Kenneth Lowande, Melinda Ritchie, and Erinn Lauterbach (2019, 1) describe these connections where "shared experiences operate as a critical mechanism for representation" and argue that, in turn, these affiliations and relationships have a demonstrable impact on policy behavior. Homophily can serve as the foundation for coalition building that captures both descriptive and substantive representation (Kessler and Krehbiel 1996; Krehbiel 1995; Koger 2003; Wilson and Young 1997; Best and Vonnahme 2019). Studies have also found similar dynamics occurring among veterans in other institutional settings, from their local communities to group homes (Guerrero and Jason 2020) and community colleges (Harrell 2021).

Third, my research suggests that WoT veterans on Capitol Hill certainly believe that they can cooperate to solve important defense policy problems and seek out bill cosponsorship based on shared perspectives and values. As Representative Mike Waltz (R-FL) observed, "We know each other. We know who has served in Iraq and Afghanistan, and we know that that colors our experiences for how we approach policy issues" (author's interview, October 19, 2021). Congressional staffers with military experience have strong connections too, especially among combat veterans. "We speak each other's language" and "it's very intuitive," said one (author's interview, October 15, 2021). Another staff member and Iraq War veteran agreed. They said that in their experience, "Veterans just seem to have a way of approaching problems that seems different from how other offices on the Hill operate sometimes" (author's interview, August 9, 2021). Newer lawmakers who are WoT veterans may view the political terrain somewhat differently, drawing on their own past experiences of overcoming difficult challenges and obstacles. Some might even see their position as empowered given the narrow majorities in Congress.

In summary, this project posits that military veterans may be likely to seek out and work with their fellow veterans in Congress to develop laws. A preliminary randomized study of data comparing WoT veterans with a randomized sample of nonveterans conducted for this project suggested significantly higher rates for WoT veteran bill cosponsorship than for nonveterans (Lantis 2021), and this is further reflected in higher scores for veterans on the Lugar Center's Bipartisan Index. But does this relationship suggest that WoT military veterans might be more likely than nonveterans to pursue bipartisan solutions to problems? As much as proponents claim that this might be the case (e.g., Barcott and Wood 2017; McCormick 2018; Tyson 2018), the empirical foundations for this assertion are more limited and open to interpretation.[6] For example, according to Robinson et al. (2018), difference in means testing using the *Congressional Record* finds limited evidence that veterans could be more bipartisan than nonveterans. While their research showed that some groups, such as recent Democrat military veterans, might act in more bipartisan ways than nonveterans, data variations made it difficult to draw more statistically significant or robust results.

These arguments provide the foundation for proposition 2:

> *Proposition 2: If elected representatives in Congress are veterans of the WoT, then they are likely to cosponsor legislation with fellow veterans regarding military and defense matters.*

Advocacy Coalitions

Veterans may also seek out and build coalitions to promote issues that they care about, including garnering support from broader coalitions of political action committees, interest groups, and epistemic communities that favor their preferred policy outcomes (Mullen and Ackerman 2018). Junior veteran lawmakers and their staffs may reach out to groups with similar concerns, but they also often find that these groups "come to them" as they begin to rally support for issues (author's interview, October 12, 2021). There are numerous examples of these dynamics at work—from the logical union between veterans of the Iraq and Afghanistan Wars in Congress and groups that champion veterans' health care to concerns about the value of Special Operations troop deployments for counterterrorism operations in the Middle East. Similarly, there is a logic to the idea that coordination of strategies between members of Congress and advocates and interest groups may act as a valuable "force multiplier" in efforts to influence policy outcomes (Lantis 2019), and this strategy further illustrates links between actor motivations, strategies, and issue areas (Sabatier 1986, 1988; Jenkins-Smith 1990).

Experts argue that advocacy coalitions tend to form among "people from various governmental and private organizations who share a set of normative and causal beliefs, and who often act in concert" to achieve policy goals (Jenkins-Smith and Sabatier 1994, 180; Weible, Sabatier, and McQueen 2009). Advocacy coalitions reflect a shared "set of basic values, causal assumptions, and problem

28 Staying in the Fight

perceptions . . . and show a non-trivial degree of coordinated activity over time" (Sabatier 1988, 139). Hank Jenkins-Smith et al. (2014, 192) argue that common stakeholder beliefs and behavior effectively become embedded within informal networks, and these actors "seek allies, coordinate resources, and develop complementary strategies" to achieve mutual objectives.[7]

Both veterans on Capitol Hill and leading lobbyists have come to recognize the synergy they can create through advocacy coalitions. Indeed, congressional staff members work closely with interest groups on major issues—and some acknowledge that interest groups actually help draft key legislation and build a broader advocacy network to achieve desired objectives. Some of the strongest advocacy groups for WoT veterans can be formed on issues that affect large constituencies such as veterans' affairs and public health, though they also engage in advocacy on foreign relations concerns such as military interventions, protection of human rights, and efforts to prevent civilian casualties in distant conflicts. Ultimately, foreign policy advocacy requires a commitment to work both "inside" or "outside" the political system to force change, reflecting insights from studies of social movements and strategic choice (Bergman 2004; Tarrow 1998, 2005; Tilly and Tarrow 2006; Sabatier and Weible 2007; Pierce et al. 2017). Ultimately, veteran lawmakers can become adept at representation, advocacy, constituent services, and policy influence (Lowande, Ritchie, and Lauterbach 2019).

These arguments provide the foundation for the next proposition of this study:

> *Proposition 3: If elected representatives in Congress are veterans of the WoT, then they are likely to build advocacy coalitions with governmental and nongovernmental actors to address military and defense policy concerns.*

Changes in Defense Policy Directions or Outcomes: Beyond the Roll-Call

Military veterans in Congress may be especially well attuned to adapting to complexity and rapid changes in difficult strategic environments. They may demonstrate flexibility when it comes to pursuing certain goals, ranging from blocking troop commitments or responding to concerns of Gold Star families. Veterans in Congress may also seek out more immediate "solutions" to perceived problems through oversight of executive branch policies, consistent with an advocacy and entrepreneurship mode. In contrast to traditional legislative models that focus primarily on bill passage and roll-call voting, this study is designed to capture nuance in the policy process, including incrementalism and efforts at agenda-setting, short of formal legislation (Hersman 2000). The study of the policy advocacy process—and not simply legislation passed by roll-call votes—is itself significant. Indeed, an adaptable policy entrepreneurship model lends itself to analyzing "how actors in the foreign policy space draw attention to problems, advance workable proposals, and link outcomes to symbolic values" (Mintrom and Luetjens 2017, 1,363). The oversight process can also help create informal guardrails and norms that define future policy choices by the executive.

This study adopts a proactive and targeted focus that is partly inspired by Lupton's (2017, 4) assertion that "if military experience should only narrowly matter, scholars must test for the impact of military service where military expertise is highly applicable."[8] Analysis of the initiation of progressive changes focuses most directly on executive policy influence. This helps overcome limitations of studies that demonstrate mixed evidence of connections between veterans' experiences and roll-call voting behavior (Bianco and Markham 2001; Robinson et al. 2018), for example, and it may better capture the contemporary spirit of WoT veteran entrepreneurship on Capitol Hill. WoT veteran lawmakers and their staffs may perceive roadblocks on certain pathways and instead shift or evolve their objectives to reach a reasonable, nearly comparable objective (Lindsay 1992–93).[9]

There appear to be numerous examples of the influence of WoT veterans in contemporary affairs. For example, at a critical moment in August 2013, after Syrian government forces killed hundreds of civilians in a chemical attack, a select group of veterans in Congress banded together to argue that President Obama should *not* conduct a retaliatory strike on Syria because the attack did not pose a vital risk to US national security. Representatives Tulsi Gabbard (D-HI), a freshman lawmaker who had served two tours of duty in Iraq and Kuwait, joined forces with other veterans like Scott Perry (R-PA), a retired aviation battalion commander in Iraq, to form a coalition opposed to intervention. Only Congress could authorize the use of force, they said, and a military strike would likely drag the United States into yet another quagmire conflict in the Middle East. The United States remained on the sidelines of the Syria conflict for years, despite its mounting toll.[10]

WoT veterans on Capitol Hill were also deeply committed to congressional oversight of US military operations in Afghanistan (2001–21), and once again this resulted in both legislation that was introduced, some that passed into law, and a substantial amount of policy advocacy work. For example, when President Trump threatened an immediate withdrawal from that country in 2018, calling the war there "a complete waste," WoT veterans in Congress argued that preventing Afghanistan from becoming a terrorist safe haven required a continued military presence and that it was worth the sacrifice. Representative Mike Waltz joined with fellow veteran Jason Crow (D-CO) to cosponsor a bipartisan oversight bill, the Afghanistan Partnership and Transparency Act, designed to ensure strong congressional monitoring of drawdown operations

30   Staying in the Fight

in the region. Crow (2020), a former Army Ranger said, "I served in Afghanistan and I know firsthand what makes the U.S. military the strongest in the world. . . . The war in Afghanistan must end, but we must do so in a way that ensures lasting peace. The world is watching to see whether America keeps its promises." Months later, after the collapse of Afghanistan, Waltz remained committed to save those in danger in that country, stating, "We are continuing to work with veterans' groups and other nonprofits to try to rescue thousands of stranded Afghans and Americans in Afghanistan. It's a really dire situation." Even though the "State Department just wants this issue to go away," he said, "we're not going to let this go" (Waltz 2021).[11]

Summary: Connectivity, Originality, and Conviction in the Policy Process

This study adopts this multidimensional model of connections between veterans' experiences, motivations, strategies, and objectives. It starts with WoT veterans' unique experiences and motivations that set them apart from other lawmakers. It assumes that veterans in Congress may be especially well attuned to complexity and adaptation to rapid changes in difficult strategic environments. These unique experiences and motivations then have several consequences: (1) WoT veterans are able and inclined to link their personal experiences to create effective policy narratives around foreign policy issues; (2) WoT veterans are inclined toward bill cosponsorship and cooperation on these issues (especially in working with other WoT veterans across party lines); and (3) WoT veterans are inclined toward building broad policy advocacy coalitions with groups outside of Congress. Through these three "conditioning" first-order consequences, we arrive at a broad-based outcome for WoT veterans: they demonstrate distinct flexibility, and even creativity, in how they approach policymaking on foreign policy issues, which appears to give them significant influence. They employ alternative strategies of activism that reflect their conviction and creativity in the policy process. Among these are issue framing, bipartisanship and team building, and the development of advocacy coalitions, designed to try to solve problems and drive the political agenda.

These causal and multistage connections tend to produce a dynamic policymaking process in which the motivated WoT lawmaker channels their energy and concerns into pursuit of objectives using multiple pathways (sometimes simultaneously). Their motivations and convictions become, in turn, the sinews that tie together different aspects of the model. The distinctiveness of veterans' experiences is often necessary as the impetus for pursuit of policy outcomes, and these carry through each stage of the model in shaping desired objectives and finding ways to get there. In addition, this study recognizes that outcomes of their engagement go beyond formal legislation to include changes in executive branch policies and procedures and engagement on the implementation of initiatives. Taken together, these elements help us construct and test a more reflexive model that captures different strategies of influence, undertaken by different types of entrepreneurs, with variation in terms of goals.

Research Design and Methodology

To test this model of advocacy, this study employs a multimethod research design, including interview data, archival work, descriptive statistics, process tracing, and the comparative case method (Gerring and Cojocaru 2015). In-depth case studies allow us to explore how WoT veterans in Congress can develop sophisticated, multilevel strategies to achieve their objectives in foreign policy. Cases trace the motivations and processes of policy development, with a special focus on congressional entrepreneurship and advocacy strategies and outcomes (Ragin 2014; George 1979; George and Bennett 2005). The research methodology is structured: all cases address a standardized set of theoretically relevant questions regarding policy engagement and activism. And it is focused: sections speak to elements of the model in the larger policy process (Kaarbo and Beasley 1999). This approach can be especially useful for theory testing and developing, evaluating "whether evidence shows that the hypothesized causal mechanism linking variables was present and that it functioned as theorized" (Beach and Pederson 2018, 11; Ragin 2013).

Cases selected for this project offer illustrations from a wider universe of possible instances of attempted congressional foreign policy advocacy by veterans of the WoT who were members of Congress elected to serve in 2010 or later. While this study explores the distinctive personalities and commitments of a select group of veterans, I believe the stories may be generally representative of wider populations of WoT veterans. They reflect policy advocacy by lawmakers from different partisan affiliations and ideologies, and with diversity of representation of gender, race, and ethnicity. This group includes five Republican lawmakers and five Democrats, including two female WoT veterans. Furthermore, this group includes members with different experiences in terms of service branches, areas of deployment, state of origin, and personal backgrounds (see table 2.1).

This study also captures the quality of policy debates led by WoT veterans on a range of issues. Indeed, once in office, these lawmakers addressed different issue areas or instances of policy innovation, and advocacy for substantive policy changes during the Obama and Trump administrations (2009–21) as well as the early Biden presidency (2021–22). Cases examine a range of foreign and defense-related issues that either directly or indirectly impact soldiers or veterans and that, in turn, often shape policy advocacy. As a result, the cases help describe significant phenomena in their depth and complexity as well as

Table 2.1. Lawmaker Profiles[a]

Name	Party	State-District	Service in Congress	Lugar Bipartisan Index Score	Bipartisan Ranking in Congress	Service Experience
Representative Steve Stivers	R	OH-15	2011–21	1.601	21	Army National Guard
Representative Adam Kinzinger	R	IL-16/11	2011–23	1.357	36	Air Force
Senator Todd Young	R	IN-9/IN	2011–present	0.58	37	Marine Corps
Representative Tulsi Gabbard	D	HI-2	2013–21	0.807	80	Army National Guard
Representative Ruben Gallego	D	AZ-7	2015–present	0.311	155	Marine Corps
Representative Ted Lieu	D	CA-33	2015–present	0.089	207	Air Force Reserve
Representative Elaine Luria	D	VA-2	2019–23	1.416	32	Navy
Representative Jason Crow	D	CO-6	2019–present	1.012	63	Army
Representative Mike Waltz	R	FL-6	2019–present	0.745	86	Army
Representative Peter Meijer	R	MI-3	2021–23	0.555	44	Army Reserve

[a] Bipartisan scores and ranking data drawn from the Lugar Center's Bipartisan Index coverage of the 116th Congress (2019), with the exception of Peter Meijer (117th Congress). For more perspective, see www.thelugarcenter.org/ourwork-Bipartisan-Index.html.

Source: Quorum Federal Database; legislator websites; House Committee on Veterans' Affairs.

Military Veterans and Policy Advocacy   33

Table 2.2. Case Studies

	Saudi Relations & Yemen Civil War	Special Immigrant Visa Program & Afghanistan War	Veterans Affairs & Public Health	Syria Policy & Intervention Debates	Responses to War in Ukraine
Democrats	Representative Ted Lieu (CA)	Representative Jason Crow (CO)	Representative Elaine Luria (VA)	Representative Tulsi Gabbard (HI)	Representative Ruben Gallego (AZ)
Republicans	Senator Todd Young (IN)	Representative Michael Waltz (FL)	Representative Steve Stivers (OH)	Representative Adam Kinzinger (IL)	Representative Peter Meijer (MI)

suggest lessons for broader generalization (see table 2.2).[12] Cases also represent different periods and balances of power and party control in Congress. And finally, while I do acknowledge that cases reflect instances where members were engaged on the issue at hand—where they appeared to *care* about the particular subject—my research finds that their actual levels of engagement, positions taken, and strategies adopted varied significantly. Furthermore, their behaviors appear to be generally representative of the level of WoT veteran commitment to questions about defense policy, executive-legislative relations, and interests of the wider population of veterans of Afghanistan and Iraq serving in Congress.[13]

To develop these case studies, this project draws on information from primary and secondary sources, including the *Congressional Record*, data on legislative initiatives from the Quorum Federal dataset, previous scholarly work, and media reports. This study also features exclusive information derived from dozens of elite interviews. I used a snowball sampling interview technique that involved outreach to multiple lawmakers and their staffs with prior military experience. More than forty interviews were conducted with officials and experts in Washington, DC, in one of three formats: in-person; online using videoconferencing technology; and by phone. These interviews helped provide a representative sample of interview subjects in order to provide balanced evidence for process tracing in case studies (Theriault 2008). While there are always potential limitations of representativeness and sample bias (Bleich and Pekkanen 2013), the snowball technique allowed me to gather information from a range of different players with different perspectives and to overcome problems like representativeness of sample and potential bias (Lynch 2013). These perspectives reveal how new forms of congressional policy advocacy are having a profound impact on the scope and nature of US foreign and defense policy outcomes.

34   Staying in the Fight

Finally, I should note that this research takes a deep dive into rich case studies to explore how WoT veterans have become policy activists and employed creative strategies to effect policy change. But it is not designed as a comprehensive empirical study of all WoT veterans and voting patterns in Congress. Prior work, along with ongoing research programs from scholars such as Robinson et al. (2018) and Lupton (2017, 2022) offer excellent summaries of these issues, and my own work has been informed by these foundations. While broader studies of voting patterns and efforts to curtail executive authority are needed in the discipline, this study takes an alternative path: I argue that we can learn a great deal about members of Congress from all walks of life, including lawmakers who sometimes do not make the headlines, through rich, qualitative studies of their interests and strategies. Their compelling stories that unfold in the chapters to come illustrate the opportunities and constraints of today's lawmakers and the rise of a new generation of veterans in Congress.

3

To the Rescue?

The Syria Policy Puzzle

United States foreign policy responses to the civil war in Syria have varied over the past decade, and critics have described different government decisions in the conflict as counterproductive, "puzzling" (Carpenter 2013), or even "failed" (Feltman and Balian 2021). Policy outcomes have also dramatically contradicted the stated intentions of US presidents in some cases. For example, President Barack Obama pledged that the United States would adopt a more principled approach to global leadership and protect human rights. Yet, when chemical weapons attacks in Syria killed thousands of civilians, White House policies toward the crisis remained restrained and muted (Krieg 2016; Geis and Schlag 2017). In contrast, President Donald Trump loudly proclaimed his intentions to withdraw the United States from major conflict zones, including removing US Special Forces troops from Syria. But the president's immediate wishes ran up against strong resistance from a growing number of WoT military veterans in Congress and advocacy groups. Trump's calls for retrenchment in Syria went mostly unheeded for two years (author's interview, October 6, 2021), signaling a surprising disconnect between executive branch intentions and actual US foreign policy responses.

This chapter examines the puzzle of US policies toward Syria through the lens of congressional foreign policy advocacy. It focuses on the understudied, yet significant role that WoT veterans have played on these issues in Congress. Representatives Tulsi Gabbard (D-HI) and Adam Kinzinger (R-IL) were WoT veterans who joined with their fellow veteran lawmakers to try to change executive branch policies through activism and oversight. Gabbard was one of the first female combat veterans of the WoT ever elected to Congress, and she advised Presidents Obama and Trump that the United States should remain disengaged from the Syria conflict for strategic reasons. Gabbard was also an

35

36   Staying in the Fight

early public champion of allowing Syrian president Bashir al-Assad to remain in office to help end the war (Lantis 2021).[1] By comparison, Congressman Kinzinger used policy advocacy and bipartisan bill cosponsorship to promote a very different message: that a limited commitment of troops to Syria was in the national security interests of the United States and would fill a critical vacuum of power. As the war dragged on, Kinzinger became a bold antagonist to many of President Trump's statements and policies.[2]

Gabbard and Kinzinger challenged the establishment by using unorthodox strategies to achieve their foreign policy objectives, including conducting personal diplomacy and forming advocacy coalitions with diverse members of Congress and civil society groups. They also advanced bipartisan legislation that garnered support from a range of different lawmakers. Notably, both were successful in helping move the policy needle: The Obama administration quietly dropped its requirement for the removal of Assad, for example, and US troop deployments to Syria continued well beyond the deadlines preferred by President Trump. At this writing, Syria's president Assad has regained control of most of his country and is working to restore his country's engagement in multilateral diplomacy and the global economy.

The Challenge: US Responses to the Syrian Civil War

The war in Syria began in March 2011 when hostilities broke out between the Assad regime and the Syrian military against rebel groups and Islamists. While US officials grew increasingly concerned about the conflict, many were divided over the question of whether they had a true responsibility to become involved. President Barack Obama did demand early in the conflict in 2011 that Assad step down "for the sake of the Syrian people" after harsh attacks on civilian protesters, and he withdrew US diplomats from the country (Schulhofer-Wohl 2021). The United States and its allies also froze Syrian assets and barred commercial transactions with the regime. Nevertheless, the conflict continued and became a drawn-out, full-scale civil war between the Assad regime and rebels. In the first five years of the conflict alone, the Syrian Civil War caused 500,000 deaths and displaced millions of people (Boghani 2016).

This chapter examines the influence of congressional military veterans on US foreign policy responses in a series of challenges or "decision points." One of the first major episodes that illustrated the tensions between the executive and legislative branches on Syria policy occurred when the Syrian military ignored President Obama's threats of a "red line" against the use of chemical weapons. In August 2013, the Assad regime unleashed a Sarin nerve gas attack against rebel-held areas in the Damascus suburbs that killed more than 1,400 civilians. However, instead of a massive response by the United States, President Obama hesitated to act without an authorization for the use of force from Congress and set off an intense debate in Washington about what to do. During the ensuing struggle, fourteen of the sixteen WoT veterans serving in Congress in 2013 argued that greater involvement in Syria was *not* in the national security interests of the United States.

Other challenges presented by the Syrian conflict included the rise of the Islamic State as well as what to do about interventions by outside powers like Iran and Russia. The Islamic State (or ISIS), a radical jihadist terror group, moved into lawless areas of Syria and declared the establishment of a "caliphate" under Sharia law (Remnick 2014; Sinha 2015). The group also began kidnapping and killing Western hostages (Al-Salhy and Arango 2014). Power dynamics shifted again when Russia intensified its military assistance to the Assad regime during the civil war. Syria also drew support from Iran, which had common interests in challenging Sunni regimes allied with the United States in the Middle East like Saudi Arabia. Finally, President Donald Trump repeatedly questioned the strategic value of any intervention in Syria and called for the immediate US withdrawal from conflicts in the Middle East.[3] Trump also announced what the Obama administration had tacitly accepted: the United States was no longer focused on the ouster of Assad to end the conflict in Syria (author's interview, October 12, 2021).

Congressman Adam Kinzinger (R-IL) and the Case for Strategic Troop Deployments in Syria

Representative Adam Kinzinger (R-IL) was among the first veterans of the Iraq and Afghanistan Wars to be elected to Congress in the Republican Party. He came to office in 2011 with strong views on foreign and defense policy, and he quickly began to establish a reputation as a strategic thinker and effective communicator. Kinzinger was very interested in Syria policy given his experience with military service in the Middle East, and the crisis unfolded during his watch as a member of the powerful House Foreign Affairs Committee. Early on, Kinzinger favored strategic interventions in Syria against the Islamic State as well as operations to counterbalance Iranian and Russian involvement in the conflict (author's interview, October 13, 2021). To Kinzinger, missions that used a combination of Special Forces and airpower represented a worthy investment to forestall a much wider regional conflict. Through congressional oversight and frequent appearances on cable news shows, Kinzinger also seemed quite willing to "speak truth to power" on foreign and defense policy matters.

Kinzinger's support for these operations set him up for a clash with incoming president Donald Trump. Trump campaigned for the presidency in 2015 and 2016 as a foreign policy isolationist. His "America First" platform included withdrawing troops from distant conflicts and focusing instead on domestic

38 *Staying in the Fight*

priorities. Trump articulated strong arguments against US involvement in Syria as a private citizen, candidate, and president. In 2018, he doubled down on challenges, stating, "We're knocking the hell out of ISIS. We'll be coming out of Syria, like, very soon. Let the other people take care of it now" (quoted in Browne and Starr 2018). In December 2018, the president finally took definitive action: He announced that the Islamic State was "100% defeated" and that the United States would quickly withdraw all its forces from Syria (quoted in Ryan and Dawsey 2018). Yet Kinzinger and many of his fellow WoT veterans in Congress knew that the threat of radical jihadist terrorism persisted in Syria and beyond. The stage was set for significant clashes between supporters of continued Syria intervention, and these would soon be amplified through social media and cable news coverage.

Distinctive Motivations

Kinzinger entered office with strong commitments to foreign and defense policy. In some ways, this policy advocacy seemed quite consistent with a lifetime of taking up important causes: He was politically active from a young age, and he was elected to a county board seat while he was still a sophomore at Illinois State University. In the aftermath of 9/11, Kinzinger took up another cause: he joined the Air Force and was commissioned as a second lieutenant in November 2003. Kinzinger was a pilot on refueling and reconnaissance aircraft, and he was deployed in both Operation Iraqi Freedom and Operation Enduring Freedom in Afghanistan (author's interview, October 13, 2021). As he tells it, it was during his time on active duty that he determined to run for political office. He said, "I remember thinking if I'm willing to fight and die for my country on the outside, I've got to be willing to fight for it on the inside. So that's when I really . . . cross[ed] that mental Rubicon of saying, you know what, yeah, I think this is something I can do" (quoted in Miller 2010).

Kinzinger returned home from his deployments abroad, announced his candidacy for Congress representing the Illinois Eleventh District, hired a campaign manager, and began making regular trips to Washington, DC, to talk with power brokers and sitting lawmakers. He was clearly determined to try to win the Eleventh District, despite running against a Republican incumbent who had won the district by a substantial margin two years earlier. Kinzinger's personal story, his networking and meetings with other influential officials, and his commitment to serve won over many supporters, though (Miller 2010). He also remained in the Air National Guard and rose to the rank of major.

Kinzinger was elected to Congress at the age of thirty-two, and he was appointed to a choice seat on the House Foreign Affairs Committee. Kinzinger had come to know the Middle East well during his deployments, and he believed that the credibility of US commitments to the Middle East and support for allies should shape engagement (Parlapiano et al. 2017). When President Obama authorized Special Forces operations in the country to fight the Islamic State and counterbalance Russian and Iranian interests in the region, Kinzinger publicly applauded the actions. He argued that a strategic forward deployment of Special Forces in the region could help counterbalance Iranian and Russian interests.

Kinzinger continued to praise strategic interventions in Syria early in the Donald Trump administration. In April 2017, for example, Kinzinger had one of his first opportunities to send a message to the White House about his motivations and concerns. The Syrian military launched a chemical weapons attack against a rebel-held town that killed more than eighty people, including dozens of children. Trump authorized a limited cruise missile strike on the base from which the attack originated. Kinzinger and other lawmakers responded with strong praise for the action taken, stating: "Tonight, the United States stood up for humanity, and sent a clear message to the barbaric Syrian regime, and the entire world. America will not sit idly by, and allow a dictator to butcher his country's men, women, and children. I applaud the President for his swift action against Bashar al-Assad and the Syrian military" (quoted in "Durbin, Kinzinger Support" 2017).

However, by 2018, it became clear to Kinzinger that praise would not be enough to keep Trump committed to Syria. The president had grown increasingly restless and concerned about risks to US lives and national security interests with involvement in the conflict. This news helped mobilize Kinzinger and his colleagues for even more active congressional foreign policy advocacy to stymie the president's plans and slow withdrawal from what they viewed as a smart, strategic troop deployment (author's interview, September 29, 2021). In the end, the product of these actions and variable mission objectives appear to demonstrate the effect of moderate, steady hands on the foreign policy tiller that prevented sudden or dramatic changes that President Trump seemed to prefer.

Issue Framing through Personal Narratives

Kinzinger employed a range of traditional and nontraditional strategies to try to sway Trump administration policies. First, he publicly linked his personal experience to how he believed that critical values like loyalty and responsibility should play out in US foreign policy. The congressman's praise for Trump's response to chemical weapons attacks in 2017 and 2018 reflected this commitment to US engagement. In addition to favoring Special Forces operations,

Kinzinger was also sensitive to the question of US troop support for Kurdish fighters who served a critical role in the conflict in eastern Syria. The Kurds had demonstrated resolve to fight the Assad regime as well as to stand on the frontlines of the war against the Islamic State. Kinzinger said that he recognized in the Kurds the type of commitment that he saw in US forces during the wars in Iraq and Afghanistan, and he was determined to support them as key allies (Hiltermann 2017). As one staff member said, Kinzinger is "deeply committed to loyalty and a sense of duty through service" (author's interview, October 6, 2021). The congressman believed that maintaining troops in the country to assist Kurdish fighters in the struggle against the Islamic State and supporting air operations was a very small investment that yielded substantial gains. The president's plan to hastily withdraw from the region was thus antithetical to the policy narrative Kinzinger supported.

Concerns about loyalty and responsibility came through in many public statements that Kinzinger made in support of the Kurds and continued US engagement in the conflict. In an interview in 2018, for example, he said:

> We don't have a choice about whether we fight terrorism. We're going to fight terrorism. The question is where do we fight them. Do we fight them there, or do we fight them on the streets of America? And I fear that the latter is going to happen if we leave too early. . . . [Withdrawing from Syria] is a gift to Turkey. I think it's a gift to Moscow. I think it's a gift to Iran and certainly a gift to Assad and the rat's nest of ISIS. And, you know, Turkey has been wanting to prosecute the fight against the Kurds. And I think for whatever reason, there was a conversation between the president and President Erdogan. And I think that bodes very badly for the Kurds. ("Republican Congressman and Veteran Shares His Thoughts" 2018)

Kinzinger was also surprisingly open about his strategy to link personal and political narratives. In 2017, he said, "The American people weren't ready for a third intervention in the Middle East [in Syria], but that's because it wasn't sold to them." He added, "We are willing to do very tough things, we are willing to do very difficult things, but we have to have it explained to us why that's important" (quoted in Mattiace 2017).

Kinzinger also framed US engagement in Syria as a strategic imperative. He argued that the United States needed to develop a clear strategy for dealing with the civil war because the threats of regional instability were becoming dire. Kinzinger was also increasingly concerned about the rise of Iranian power and Shiite militant group infiltration of Syria (author's interview, October 13, 2021). As a member of the Foreign Affairs Committee, Kinzinger was privy to a range of information that would have outlined the problem: Iran and Syria were allies, and Iran needed a friendly regime in power in Damascus that would allow Iran to continue to supply its proxy terrorist group Hezbollah in Lebanon. Iran and Syria also had shared interests in destabilizing Israel. When the war threatened to topple Assad, Iranian leaders stepped in to provide support by recruiting and arming Shia militia forces to fight on behalf of the regime. In addition, Iran sent thousands of military advisers to Syria from its own Islamic Revolutionary Guard Corps elite Quds Force as well as units from Iran's regular army. They even mobilized thousands of Hezbollah fighters from Lebanon to fight alongside Syrian military units. To counter these moves, Kinzinger believed that US engagement in the region, perhaps with just a few thousand Special Forces, along with airpower, could effectively help balance the region. When challenged on whether he supported an "endless war" with the deployments, Kinzinger shot back that he was actually in favor of "preventing an endless war" in the Middle East through this measured intervention (quoted in Sonmez 2019). Ultimately, the congressman said, "I am suggesting we take a stand for what is right, what is just, and what is in the best interest of the United States and freedom loving people around the world. We need a long-term strategy in Syria that leads to a solution of peace and an end to the ongoing deadly conflict" (quoted in Wolfgang 2018).

Bill Cosponsorship and Bipartisanship

Kinzinger pursued several different forms of bipartisanship, including caucus groups, committee work, and bipartisan bill cosponsorship. First, the congressman was a founding member of the bipartisan Friends of a Free, Stable and Democratic Syria Caucus in the House. Within two years, membership had grown to more than fifty lawmakers. This caucus provided a vehicle in Congress for members to share information on the conflict in Syria, to meet with experts and key personnel for further education on this crisis, and to work to advance national and international efforts to bring justice and accountability to Syria (Kinzinger and Boyle 2017). The group was expressly bipartisan, drawing Republicans and Democrats together, including many military veteran lawmakers like Representatives Don Bacon (R-NE), Mike Waltz (R-FL), and Seth Moulton (D-MA) (Denham 2019).

Second, Kinzinger pursued bilateral cooperation through discussions with his counterparts on the House Foreign Affairs Committee and other leaders in government with shared concerns. Kinzinger was a member of the House Committee on Foreign Affairs and subcommittees focused on the Middle East, North Africa, and international terrorism. Bipartisanship was "really in the congressman's DNA," one staff member said, and "his time in the service reinforced the importance of teamwork" (author's interview, October 13, 2021). Through these contacts, Kinzinger quickly became aware that Trump's own advisers were becoming exasperated with the president's erratic approach to the issue. In 2018, when Defense Secretary James Mattis resigned in protest of Trump's plans to withdraw from Syria, Kinzinger reached out again to his counterparts across the aisle to mobilize to change policies. He found common ground, for example, with Representative Cheri Bustos (D-IL) and Minority Leader Chuck Schumer (D-IL), who believed that the White House was making rash decisions that were not strategic and deliberate in nature.

Third, Congressman Kinzinger became active in sponsoring and cosponsoring legislation on Syria over time, even as he explored alternative strategies for policy influence. He and his staff were proactive in advancing legislation: In his decade of service between January 2011 and January 2021, Kinzinger served as the primary sponsor of nearly 100 bills, and he cosponsored another 1,200. Of those, approximately 340 bills were focused on international affairs, armed forces, and national security, demonstrating Kinzinger's overriding commitment to these critical issues (see table 3.1) ("Kinzinger" 2021).

One of the hallmarks of Kinzinger's international affairs legislation was a strategic view of the relationships between key actors and the balance of power in the Middle East. For example, in 2012 he cosponsored the bipartisan H.R. 1905, the Iran Threat Reduction and Syria Human Rights Act of 2012, which was designed to tighten commercial transactions and trade with Iran and Syria. While much of the legislation addressed Iran, the section regarding Syria required the imposition of sanctions against any person involved in providing goods to Iran and Syria that might be used to commit serious human rights abuses against its people. This bill was broadly supported, and it passed through both houses of Congress and was signed into law in 2012. A year later, Kinzinger cosponsored H.R. 893, the Iran, North Korea, and Syria Nonproliferation Accountability Act of 2013, with Democrat Brad Sherman (D-CA) as well as fellow veterans Jim Bridenstine (R-OK) and Ted Poe (R-TX). This bill addressed concerns about the proliferation of dangerous weapons to adversaries or conflict zones. And even though the introduction of the bill seemed to foreshadow the Assad regime's use of chemical weapons in August 2013, it did not gain significant traction to move out of committee (author's interview, September 28, 2021).

By 2018, the Syria conflict had truly metastasized: Kinzinger became a cosponsor of the bipartisan bill H.R. 390, the Iraq and Syria Genocide Relief and Accountability Act of 2018. This bill was cosponsored by a wide assortment of lawmakers, including some of the most conservative Republicans, several military veterans, and eight Democrats. It called for information gathering and support of entities that are investigating crimes against humanity and war crimes in Iraq and Syria, and it was passed and signed into law that year. H.J. Resolution 77 in 2018 represented a similar effort to help frame the conflict in Syria and promote a more strategic approach to relations with Turkey and the

Table 3.1. Sample of Representative Kinzinger's Record of Bill Sponsorship and Cosponsorship

Label	Title	Introduced	Status
H.R. 5142	To award posthumously a Congressional Gold Medal, in commemoration to the servicemembers who perished in Afghanistan on August 26, 2021	August 31, 2021	Passed Original Chamber
H.R. 1228	Libya Stabilization Act	February 23, 2021	Passed Original Chamber
H.R. 5272	Taliban Recognition Prevention Act	September 17, 2021	Introduced or Prefiled
H.R. 5071	To direct the Secretary of Defense to submit daily reports on the evacuation of Afghanistan	August 23, 2021	Introduced or Prefiled
H.R. 4914	Havana Syndrome Attacks Response Act	August 3, 2021	Introduced or Prefiled
H.R. 3985	Averting Loss of Life and Injury by Expediting SIVs Act of 2021	June 17, 2021	Passed Original Chamber
H.R. 4471	Improving Veterans Access to Congressional Services Act of 2021	July 16, 2021	Introduced or Prefiled
H.R. 3513	Afghan Allies Protection Act of 2021	May 25, 2021	Introduced or Prefiled
H.Res. 317	Condemning the genocide against Uyghurs and other minority groups by the People's Republic of China	April 14, 2021	Introduced or Prefiled
H.R. 1699	Iran Sanctions Relief Review Act of 2021	March 9, 2021	Introduced or Prefiled
H.R. 1014	Veterans National Traumatic Brain Injury Treatment Act	February 11, 2021	Introduced or Prefiled
H.R. 475	Health Care Fairness for Military Families Act of 2021	January 25, 2021	Introduced or Prefiled
H.R. 7952	Veteran Benefits Enhancement and Expansion Act of 2020	August 7, 2020	Introduced or Prefiled
H.R. 7155	National Commission on Modernizing Military Installation Designations Act	June 11, 2020	Introduced or Prefiled
H.Res. 906	Calling on the President to invoke the Defense Production Act to respond to COVID-19	March 23, 2020	Introduced or Prefiled
H.R. 6208	Protecting American Space Assets Act	March 11, 2020	Introduced or Prefiled

Continued

44 Staying in the Fight

Table 3.1. Sample of Representative Kinzinger's Record of Bill Sponsorship and Cosponsorship (*Continued*)

Label	Title	Introduced	Status
H.R. 4305	PAWS for Veterans Therapy Act	September 12, 2019	Passed Original Chamber
H.R. 550	No War Against Iran Act	January 15, 2019	Passed Second Chamber
H.R. 5338	Global Hope Act of 2019	December 6, 2019	Passed Original Chamber
H.R. 5605	United States–Israel PTSD Collaborative Research Act	January 14, 2020	Introduced or Prefiled
H.R. 4873	Syrian Partner Protection Act	October 28, 2019	Introduced or Prefiled
H.R. 4370	TBI and PTSD Treatment Act	September 18, 2019	Introduced or Prefiled
H.R. 3565	Veterans Health Savings Account Act	June 27, 2019	Introduced or Prefiled
H.R. 31	Caesar Syria Civilian Protection Act of 2019	January 3, 2019	Passed Original Chamber
H.R. 2796	Afghan Allies Protection Act of 2019	May 16, 2019	Introduced or Prefiled
H.R. 2481	Gold Star Family Tax Relief Act	May 2, 2019	Introduced or Prefiled
H.R. 1706	No Assistance for Assad Act	March 13, 2019	Introduced or Prefiled
H.R. 299	Blue Water Navy Vietnam Veterans Act of 2018	January 5, 2017	Passed Original Chamber
H.R. 5694	Afghan Allies Protection Amendments Act of 2018	May 7, 2018	Introduced or Prefiled
H.R. 3548	Border Security for America Act of 2017	July 28, 2017	Out of Committee
H.R. 4238	Iranian Proxies Terrorist Sanctions Act of 2017	November 3, 2017	Introduced or Prefiled
H.R. 1698	Iran Ballistic Missiles and International Sanctions Enforcement Act	March 23, 2017	Passed Original Chamber
H.R. 4869	Comprehensive Strategy to Destroy ISIL Act of 2016	March 23, 2016	Introduced or Prefiled
H.R. 4257	IRGC Sanctions Act	December 15, 2015	Introduced or Prefiled
H.R. 3858	Veteran-Centered Access to Coordinated Health Care Act of 2014	January 13, 2014	Introduced or Prefiled

Table 3.1. Sample of Representative Kinzinger's Record of Bill Sponsorship and Cosponsorship (*Continued*)

Label	Title	Introduced	Status
H.R. 1130	Iron Dome Support Act	March 13, 2013	Introduced or Prefiled
H.R. 893	Iran, North Korea, and Syria Nonproliferation Accountability Act of 2013	February 28, 2013	Introduced or Prefiled
H.R. 1775	Stolen Valor Act of 2012	May 5, 2011	Passed Original Chamber
H.R. 5712	Veterans Jobs Act of 2012	May 10, 2012	Introduced or Prefiled
H.R. 4133	United States–Israel Enhanced Security Cooperation Act	March 5, 2012	Passed Original Chamber

Source: Quorum Federal Database 2021. Search terms: *Armed Forces and National Security*; *Foreign Trade and International Finance*; and *International Affairs*.

fate of the Kurds. The resolution was expressly bipartisan and it outlined several strong demands, including calls for Turkey to end military operations in northeast Syria and a pledge of greater support for the Kurds. Kinzinger also cosponsored the bipartisan H.R. 1706, or the No Assistance for Assad Act, which barred any assistance to the Syrian government for stabilization or reconstruction activities. It also required the Department of State to report to Congress on the delivery of humanitarian aid to Syria.

Finally, in an interesting twist, Kinzinger also found common ground with fellow veteran and Democrat representative Tulsi Gabbard in cosponsoring H.J. Resolution 33 in 2015. This called for a restrictive authorization of the use of military force for President Obama to carry out strikes on the Islamic State in Syria. Their shared goal was restricting the latitude of presidents who had heretofore interpreted AUMFs from early in the WoT rather liberally. Presidents Bush and Obama had made clear that they believed they had the authority to use any types of US forces needed, including ground troops, for operations in foreign conflict zones. This resolution countered that the use of ground troops should be sharply circumscribed, and it set a very high bar for congressional reporting requirements (Weed 2017). It would authorize the use of force against defined targets in the Islamic State and "associated persons or forces," and it was designed to repeal past authorizations. Other Republicans who championed these limits included Senators Lindsey Graham (R-SC), Jeff Flake (R-AZ), and Tim Kaine (D-VA). They authored a series of draft AUMF resolutions that

46 *Staying in the Fight*

were opposed by the White House and did not ultimately receive support from majorities in Congress.

Advocacy Coalitions

It became clear by 2018 that part of the struggle over Syria policy was an advocacy game. President Trump issued a series of announcements expressing frustration with the costs of US commitments, and actors inside and outside the government tried to advocate for continued moderation and pragmatism in operations like the Special Forces commitment to Syria. For example, in early 2018, Trump complained that the United States had gotten "nothing out of $7 trillion [spent] in the Middle East over the last 17 years" (quoted in Gearan and Morello 2018), and he followed that with a series of tweets in which he asked, "Does the USA want to be the Policeman of the Middle East, getting NOTHING but spending precious lives and trillions of dollars protecting others who, in almost all cases, do not appreciate what we are doing? Do we want to be there forever? Time for others to finally fight" (Haaretz 2018). In response, Kinzinger and his colleagues practiced congressional foreign policy advocacy that helped stymie the president's plans and slow withdrawal from this strategic commitment.

Kinzinger and his colleagues in the Syria Caucus found that their views aligned well with key actors inside and outside the government that supported engagement in Syria. Moderates in Congress, along with high-ranking officials of the early Trump administration, including National Security Adviser McMaster, Defense Secretary Mattis, and Secretary of State Tillerson, all backed strategic engagement in Syria and tried to counter drawdown demands by the president (author's interview, October 13, 2021). The caucus was joined by leaders of the Republican Party, including Senators Graham and McCain (R-AZ), Chairman of Senate Foreign Relations Bob Corker (R-TN), and House Speaker Ryan (R-WI), all of whom were sympathetic to the idea that selective military operations might help stem the humanitarian crisis and counterterrorism. These lawmakers found like-minded supporters among experts from think tanks with diverse ideological orientations, including the Center for Strategic and International Studies, the Atlantic Council, and the Heritage Foundation, who sponsored forums in favor of engagement and stabilization.

This advocacy coalition struggle came to a head in late 2018, when Trump followed a drumbeat of public statements with an order for a Syria pullout coupled with a series of tweets and videos. Kinzinger and others were stunned by the seemingly abrupt action by Trump, and he activated a coalition of top advisers, civil society actors, and members of Congress who began pushing back almost immediately against the order. A Trump loyalist, Senator Lindsey Graham, said that he felt "blindsided" by the decision and he was "pretty annoyed."

He decried it as "dangerous" and "a disaster in the making." Kinzinger attacked the decision as a challenge to strong and consistent foreign policy advice. Specifically, he charged that it was "obvious" that Trump was ignoring his advisers and urged the president to keep politics out of decision-making. The congressman added, "Fighting terrorism is not a choice that the United States makes, it's a choice that's made for us. The question of the choice we make is where do we fight them?" He continued, "Do we fight them in Syria, do we fight them in Iraq or do we ultimately fight them here at home or in the streets of Europe?" (quoted in Gstalter 2018).

Some members of the coalition that favored continued involvement also took bold steps: Defense Secretary James Mattis, who strongly objected to the president's shift in policy, abruptly resigned after a fiery meeting with Trump. So, too, did Brett McGurk, special envoy for the global coalition to defeat the Islamic State (Lazaroff 2018). Conservative think tanks including the Heritage Foundation lashed out against this threat to long-term US security interests in Syria and the Middle East, while others warned that abandoning the Kurds in the fight would be dangerous (Hiltermann 2018). Pentagon officials also began to quietly slow-walk the order, saying that they needed more time to achieve a successful withdrawal. Later, they leaked to the press that at least two hundred to four hundred soldiers would remain in Syria for stabilization operations. In January 2019, National Security Adviser John Bolton issued a new set of preconditions for US withdrawal from Syria and reassured key allies in the region that US troops intended to stay until the Islamic State was eradicated and regional governments could come to some agreement on the fate of the Kurds. The number of forces expected to remain also grew over time to a rumored one thousand soldiers (Nissenbaum and Youssef 2019). US troops would remain in the country, and in proximity to Iranian-backed forces, even as they faced the potential resurgence of the Islamic State in Syria. The outcome of this case suggests that despite the president's call there was not a fundamental change in US foreign policy (author's interview, September 29, 2021).

Outcome

Congressman Kinzinger and his colleagues seemed to be successful in the campaign to maintain strategic engagement in Syria for years. Early calls for withdrawal by President Trump successfully countered by a network of actors committed to strategic operations and planning. One former senior national security official acknowledged that they chose to resist the president's demands by slow-walking any response. He said, "The president thinks out loud. Do you treat it like an order? Or do you treat it as part of a longer conversation? We treated it as part of a longer conversation." The official added, "By allowing Trump to talk without acting, we prevented a lot of bad things from happening"

48   *Staying in the Fight*

(quoted in Filkins 2019). The stance of the proengagement coalition was also reinforced by circumstances, including the continued military attacks using chemical weapons and the looming influence of Iranian-backed forces in the region, which actors were able to leverage in support of their position.

Finally, there are several fascinating postscripts to this story: In October 2019, President Trump unilaterally announced that US troops would withdraw from northeastern Syria. This redeployment of several hundred soldiers would leave Kurdish allies in the region unprotected and provide a tacit green light to Turkey to attack them. The surprise news was met with shock and outrage in Washington. Insiders reported that leaders in the Department of Defense and staff members in the National Security Council were "completely stunned" by the decision (Laporta, 2019). Congressman Kinzinger quickly joined a large chorus of challengers of the president's decision. He and his Democrat colleagues condemned the action as a betrayal of US interests in the region. Critically, they were joined by critics like Senate Majority Leader Mitch McConnell (R-KY) and Senator Graham, who called the move "a stain on America's honor" (quoted in Widener 2019). Senators Mitt Romney (R-UT) and Chris Murphy (D-CT) put out a joint statement that read: "The president's decision to abandon our Kurdish allies in Northern Syria . . . is a betrayal that will have grave humanitarian and national security consequences." They promised to vote for a resolution demanding an immediate foreign policy change of course. In the end, Pentagon officials maintained the presence of roughly one thousand US troops to assist the Kurds.[4]

Kinzinger also became an outspoken critic of President Trump's efforts to overturn the results of the 2020 presidential elections, which culminated in the insurrection on January 6, 2021, that included the attack on the US Capitol. In the wake of this crisis, Kinzinger and his colleague Liz Cheney (R-WY) spoke out against the insurrection and joined the Select Committee in Congress to investigate it. Kinzinger said that the insurrection and Trump's "big lie" that he had won the popular election were "dangerous to democracy." He also announced that he would not run for reelection in 2022, concluding that Trump's challenges to democracy represented the kind of thing he was "willing to put my career, and frankly, my life on the line for when I was in the military" (quoted in Pfingsten 2021). The January 6 committee began its work in July 2021, and following investigations of the organization and execution of the attack on the Capitol it produced a final report in December 2022.

Representative Tulsi Gabbard (D-HI): Traditional and Unorthodox Strategies of Policy Advocacy

Tulsi Gabbard was one of the first female combat veterans of the WoT elected to Congress, and she served as a Democrat representative of Hawaii from 2013 to 2021.[5] Gabbard believed that the civil war in Syria was a tragedy, but that the US government's fateful decision to take the side of insurgents against Syria's government actually worsened the situation. Western intervention did not help end the conflict, she argued, but rather prolonged it and fueled greater instability and terrorism in the region. The prudent way to manage this crisis, she asserted, was to take a long-term perspective and balance power in the region by accepting the restoration of control by Assad (Rogin 2019). Short of that, the country and its people would face a longer war; jihadist terror groups would gain footholds in the region, and many more people would suffer and die (Harris 2019).

This case study is the story of a military veteran who was once considered a rising star of the Democratic Party in Congress, but whose unorthodox positions and ideological inconsistencies ultimately led her to align with conservative and even libertarian views. Representative Gabbard said at the time that her antiwar position on Syria was directly informed by her military service experiences, but critics on the left seemed to reject this connection and charge instead that she was parroting pro-Assad and even pro-Russian policies (Windrem and Popkin 2019). Over time, Democrats identified other problems with Gabbard's record, including past negative remarks toward the LGBTQ community and her decision to meet with president-elect Donald Trump in November 2016 to talk about Syria. Gabbard was seen as ideologically "unpredictable," raising questions about whether she could be counted on to support party initiatives (author's interview, September 16, 2021). After a failed presidential bid in 2019–20, Gabbard concluded that she had no place in the Democratic Party and announced that she would leave Congress.

But Gabbard's policy advocacy was not done: She returned to the National Guard and then returned to the public spotlight about a year later as a regular contributor on Fox News who espoused conservative pro-Trump positions. In 2022, Gabbard declared herself no longer a Democrat, calling that party an "elitist cabal," and she regularly criticized Biden administration policies. Gabbard strongly opposed US involvement in the Ukraine War, for example, and challenged government programs for diversity, equity, and inclusion (Rossomando 2023).[6] Reports in 2023 suggested that she was considering a run for a Senate seat in Hawaii and would be open to serving as a vice presidential candidate on a future Republican ticket.

Distinctive Motivations

Gabbard was born in American Samoa in 1981 and grew up in a multicultural household (Basu 2015). Gabbard's upbringing clearly influenced her later decisions to engage in public service and her style of policy advocacy. Her father, Mike Gabbard, was elected to the Honolulu City Council and later won a seat

50 *Staying in the Fight*

in the state senate as a Republican.[7] Tulsi Gabbard was home-schooled along with her siblings for most of her education, and she attended Hawaii Pacific University and majored in International Business (Phillips 2015). In 2002, at the age of only twenty-one, Gabbard became the youngest person ever elected to the Hawaii State House of Representatives, and she seemed to quickly make her mark in the legislature (author's interview, September 16, 2021).

Gabbard's military service helped to define her personal experiences and her political profile. She decided to enlist in the Army after the September 11, 2001, terrorist attacks, saying that she wanted to "go after" those responsible. Gabbard joined the National Guard in April 2003, and she was deployed as a field medical specialist for two tours of active duty in Iraq and Kuwait with the Hawaii Army National Guard Twenty-Ninth Infantry Brigade Combat Team. During her 2005 deployment at a base in the Sunni Triangle in Iraq, she earned a Combat Medical Badge when her unit came under fire (Mendoza 2013). These were formative events. When she returned home from Iraq, Gabbard took a position as a legislative aide for Senator Daniel Akaka (D-HI) in Washington. She continued her involvement with the guard and was commissioned as a second lieutenant to serve as a military police platoon leader in the Twenty-Ninth Brigade. In 2008, Gabbard again voluntarily deployed with her unit to the Middle East and worked in training facilities with Kuwaiti National Guard troops.

After returning home from her second deployment, Gabbard won election to the Honolulu City Council, and in 2012, she ran for a seat in the US House of Representatives as a Democrat representing Hawaii's Second Congressional District (the same district in which her father had campaigned almost a decade earlier). She defeated the former mayor of Honolulu in an upset victory in the Democratic primary and went on to win the 2012 election easily.[8] Gabbard's election victory was notable for several reasons. Gabbard was quickly recognized as a rising star in the Democratic Party in Washington, and she brought a great deal of energy and enthusiasm to public service. Establishment leaders saw her, as the first American Samoan and first Hindu American elected to Congress and the youngest female member of Congress at the time, as a symbol of the future of the party. House Minority Leader Nancy Pelosi immediately appointed her to coveted seats on the House Armed Services and Foreign Affairs committees, and she was named vice-chair of the Democratic National Committee. MSNBC host Rachel Maddow quipped that it seemed at the time Gabbard was "on the fast track to being very famous" (author's interview, September 16, 2021).

However, even as Gabbard's star rose in the Democratic Party, her ideological stances, policy positions, and advocacy work did not always mesh with those of the party establishment. For example, Gabbard resisted major gun control initiatives, and she opposed the Obama administration's Trans-Pacific

Partnership trade deal with Asia.[9] Drawing on her own experiences and frustrations with the Iraq War and what she saw as the failed concept of regime-changing military interventions, Gabbard publicly challenged the foreign policies of her own president and party leadership. "Too often we have found, throughout our country's history, we have people in positions of power who make offhanded comments about sending a few thousand troops here, fifty thousand there, a hundred thousand there, intervening militarily here, or starting a war there—without seeming to understand or appreciate the cost of war," she argued. "If our troops are sent to fight a war, it must be the last option. Not the first" (quoted in Sanneh 2017). In early 2016, she cited these views as one of the reasons that led her to resign from the Democratic National Committee leadership post, stating her decision was rooted in "my strong belief that we must end the interventionist, regime change policies that have cost us so much." She went on, "This is not just another 'issue.' This is THE issue, and it's deeply personal to me" (Reuters 2016). Gabbard endorsed and campaigned for Senator Bernie Sanders for the Democratic nomination for the presidency.

Broadly speaking, it appeared that Gabbard's more challenging foreign policy positions were rooted in a foreign policy philosophy of pragmatism, something that had been reinforced during her military service (author's interview, March 20, 2017). She believed that the United States should sometimes make the hard choices to support foreign leaders and regimes, including Syria's president Bashir al-Assad, Egyptian leader Abdel Fattah el-Sisi, and Indian prime minister Narendra Modi in the interest of broader geostrategic stability. These positions set her apart from fellow Progressives and suggested a situational stance that defied easy ideological categorization. The media seized on these contradictions, calling Tulsi Gabbard a "Democrat that Republicans love and the DNC can't control" (Phillips 2015). But these positions also caught the eye of conservatives, and Gabbard received positive coverage on outlets like Breitbart News and the One America News Network. She later went on to become a pundit and temporary host of television programs broadcast on Fox News and those networks.

Issue Framing through Personal Narratives

As the Syria conflict intensified over time, Gabbard continued to try to push back on the idea of liberal interventionism on Capitol Hill. She knew that there was public pressure for action and that intervention was favored by many in Obama's inner circle, but she instead sought to keep the focus on jihadist terrorism as the real threat. This call for pragmatism ultimately placed Gabbard outside of the mainstream position of establishment Democrats. But she was not alone: Chairman of the Joint Chiefs of Staff Martin Dempsey publicly expressed similar caution on Syria policy at the time, stating, "We have learned from the

52 Staying in the Fight

past 10 years that it is not enough to simply alter the balance of military power without careful consideration of what is necessary to preserve a functioning state. We must anticipate and be prepared for the unintended consequences of our action" (quoted in Ackerman 2013). As one knowledgeable congressional staff member said of the debates, Gabbard "was deeply committed to the issue" and "knew that some flag officers in the Pentagon also supported her position" (author's interview, March 20, 2017).

The Assad regime's use of chemical weapons in August 2013 and the subsequent debate in the US government over how to respond represented the first of many instances where Gabbard's strident position publicly contradicted the establishment. The president and many members of Congress believed that Syria should be punished militarily for crossing the "red line," but Obama decided that he would request an authorization for the use of military force from Congress (author's interview, March 20, 2017). Gabbard participated in critical House Foreign Affairs Committee hearings on Syria in August and September 2013, and she attended classified briefings with administration officials before deciding to speak out against intervention. Drawing directly on her personal and professional military experiences, she issued a public statement on her position, stating:

> I am sickened and outraged by the carnage and loss of lives caused by the use of chemical weapons in Syria. It is with gravity that I have carefully considered all the facts, arguments and evidence and soberly weighed concerns regarding our national security and moral responsibility. As a result, I have come to the conclusion that a U.S. military strike against Syria would be a serious mistake. I will therefore vote against a resolution that authorizes the use of military force in Syria. I will also strongly urge my colleagues to do the same. . . . As a soldier, I understand that before taking any military action, our nation must have a clear tactical objective, a realistic strategy, the necessary resources to execute that strategy—including the support of the American people—and an exit plan. The proposed military action against Syria fails to meet any of these criteria. . . . We should learn from history; we cannot afford to be the world's policeman. The United States should not insert itself in the midst of a civil war that is rooted in sectarian hatred and animosity between various warring religious groups. (Quoted in Catalina 2013)

This statement against the White House position garnered substantial attention in the media and Washington politics, especially because Gabbard was a military combat veteran and a freshman member of Congress. She was also one of the very few Democrat members willing to speak out publicly on the matter, and this was interpreted at the time as a signal of resistance to intervention from the progressive wing of the party (author's interview, October 12, 2021).[10]

Even as the Obama administration pulled back from the idea of a retaliatory strike in September 2013, the US government was quietly gearing up for clandestine operations in Syria. Gabbard knew from her post on the Foreign Affairs Committee that the Obama administration had begun shipping light weapons and munitions to Syrian rebel groups fighting the Assad regime during the summer (Londono and Miller 2013). She became increasingly vocal in her challenges to US intervention, and she employed her own personal narrative: Gabbard said that she opposed US military operations in Syria because she had seen firsthand the costs of war. She stated, "For too long, our leaders have failed us, taking us from one regime change war to the next, leading us into a new cold war and arms race, costing us trillions of our hard-earned taxpayer dollars and countless lives. This insanity must end." She escalated her challenges during the 2015 and 2016 presidential campaigns, and she charged that Hillary Clinton's "humanitarian interventionist" stance was hawkish and would draw the United States into broader military involvement in the Middle East (author's interview, September 16, 2021; Johnson 2016).

Bill Cosponsorship and Bipartisanship

Tulsi Gabbard's critical questions about the nature and need for US intervention in Syria resonated with a diverse group of lawmakers on the political left and right. Gabbard found support from progressives as well as ready allies among Republicans who shared her views on challenging President Obama's foreign policy agenda. Again, there was a certain pragmatism in her approach, including on the question of removal of Assad, that resonated with some conservatives. Gabbard and her staff saw these connections as opportunities to help advance legislation with like-minded colleagues (author's interview, September 16, 2021).[11] Meanwhile, the congresswoman frequently cited her commitment to bipartisanship by linking it back to her "tremendous" life-changing experiences in the military (Lahut 2020).

One of the more interesting arguments that Gabbard offered for US restraint and bipartisanship toward the Syria question was to draw parallels to Iraq and Afghanistan: The congresswoman said that she had studied Syria carefully and that based on her conversations with members of the Syrian opposition, religious leaders, and humanitarian workers in the region, the United States should not try to "pick sides" in the civil war. The real threat was radical jihadist terrorism, not the Assad regime, she argued. Vested parties had offered a "powerful and consistent" message: "There is no difference between 'moderate' rebels and al-Qaeda (al-Nusra) or ISIS—they are all the same" (quoted in Howard 2017). The humanitarian crisis would continue so long as great powers

54   *Staying in the Fight*

intervened in the proxy war. And if the Assad regime were toppled, extremist groups like al-Nusra and al-Qaeda would rush into the vacuum.

Gabbard adopted an active legislative agenda focused on pragmatic objectives. During her first term in office (113th Congress, 2013–15), for example, she sponsored or cosponsored a wide range of bills, 242 in total, including a number on veterans affairs. In her second term in office (114th Congress, 2016–17), Gabbard sponsored or cosponsored 294 bills ("Representative" 2017). More than 200 of those bills were related to the armed forces, international affairs, veterans' affairs, and national security. Gabbard also sponsored or cosponsored twenty-nine bills that were targeted at counterterrorism and the Syrian conflict, either directly or indirectly (see table 3.2).

Gabbard found support for some of her bills from across the political spectrum. For example, she reached out to Tea Party members in the Senate, including Rand Paul (R-KY) and Ted Cruz (R-TX), to try to advance companion legislation against Syria intervention. Meanwhile, Gabbard joined with antiwar Democrats who opposed the use of force in Syria and again defied the efforts of the party leadership and president to convince them to reverse their position. During her second term in office (2015–17), Gabbard became much more active legislatively in trying to challenge the Obama administration's programs to arm Syrian rebels. The congresswoman found allies in conservative House Tea Party members like Justin Amash (R-MI), Thomas Massie (R-KY), and others, and she adopted a targeted, bipartisan approach to limit the use of US government funds that might possibly reach al-Qaeda, the Islamic State, and other groups that challenged the Syrian regime. In 2015, she joined with Representative Austin Scott (R-GA) to introduce H.R. 258, a bipartisan cosponsored bill designed to end covert assistance to anti-Assad rebels in Syria (author's interview, October 6, 2021). Gabbard offered a strong case for pragmatism in US foreign policy, issuing press statements that outlined "ten commonsense reasons why the US policy in Syria is wrong." She warned that the US position was short-sighted and that the overthrow of the Assad regime would only create a vacuum of power in the region. Islamic extremist groups and perhaps Iranian influence would flow into the country, she warned (Howard 2017).

By 2015 and 2016, it appeared that this bipartisan legislative pressure against focusing on Assad might be working: The United States began offering its endorsement of Russian government efforts to negotiate peace in Syria. Secretary of State John Kerry stopped referencing the demand for the ouster of Assad and instead argued that it was in everyone's interests to seek a wider peace. That could involve a power-sharing deal brokered by the Russians and involving representatives of all sides (Tisdall 2015). These developments coincided with an increased focus by the Obama administration on its war against the Islamic State and areas of its declared "caliphate" in Syria. The success of the

Table 3.2. Sample of Representative Gabbard's Record of Bill Sponsorship and Cosponsorship

Label	Title	Introduced	Status
H.Res. 1195	Condemning Turkey's attacks on United States forces and allies and Turkey's continued support for terrorist organizations	October 16, 2020	Introduced or Prefiled
H.Res. 1165	Condemning Azerbaijan's military operation in Nagorno-Karabakh and denouncing Turkish interference in the conflict	October 1, 2020	Introduced or Prefiled
H.R. 8261	Presumptive Benefits for War Fighters Exposed to Burn Pits and Other Toxins Act of 2020	September 15, 2020	Introduced or Prefiled
H.Con.Res. 83	Directing the President pursuant to section 5(c) of the War Powers Resolution to terminate the use of Armed Forces in or against Iran	January 8, 2020	Passed Original Chamber
H.R. 1865	Further Consolidated Appropriations Act 2020	March 25, 2019	Enacted
H.Res. 771	Censuring the President of the United States.	December 18, 2019	Introduced or Prefiled
H.Con.Res. 77	Directing the President pursuant to section 5(c) of the War Powers Resolution to remove Armed Forces from Syria	November 21, 2019	Introduced or Prefiled
H.R. 1595	Secure and Fair Enforcement Banking Act of 2019	March 7, 2019	Passed Original Chamber
H.R. 2200	Frederick Douglass Trafficking Victims Prevention and Protection Reauthorization Act of 2018	April 27, 2017	Enacted
H.Res. 1156	Expressing concern about the threat posed to democracy and the democratic process by theocratic groups operating in Bangladesh	November 20, 2018	Introduced or Prefiled
H.Res. 1069	Requiring the President to seek congressional authorization prior to any engagement of the United States Armed Forces	September 13, 2018	Introduced or Prefiled

Continued

56 Staying in the Fight

Table 3.2. Sample of Representative Gabbard's Record of Bill Sponsorship and Cosponsorship (*Continued*)

Label	Title	Introduced	Status
H.R. 1698	Iran Ballistic Missiles and International Sanctions Enforcement Act	March 23, 2017	Passed Original Chamber
H.Res. 355	Condemning in the strongest terms the terrorist attacks in the United Kingdom in 2017	May 24, 2017	Enacted
H.Res. 239	Supporting ongoing efforts by the government to respond to drought and food insecurity in the Horn of Africa	April 3, 2017	Introduced or Prefiled
H.Res. 220	Expressing the sense of the House of Representatives regarding past genocides, and for other purposes	March 22, 2017	Introduced or Prefiled
H.Res. 729	Expressing support for the expeditious consideration and finalization of new, robust, and long-term military assistance to Israel	May 13, 2016	Enacted
H.Con.Res. 75	Expressing the sense of Congress that the atrocities perpetrated by ISIL include war crimes and genocide	September 9, 2015	Passed Original Chamber
H.R. 907	United States–Jordan Defense Cooperation Act of 2015	February 12, 2015	Enacted
H.R. 4534	POSTURE Act	February 11, 2016	Introduced or Prefiled
H.Res. 600	Reaffirming United States can use all available options, including military force, to prevent Iran from acquiring a nuclear weapon	February 3, 2016	Introduced or Prefiled
H.Res. 524	Condemning in the strongest terms the terrorist attacks in Paris, France, on November 13, 2015	November 16, 2015	Enacted
H.Res. 396	Calling on the government of Bangladesh to protect the human rights of all its citizens and prevent extremist groups	July 29, 2015	Introduced or Prefiled
H.R. 1654	To authorize the defense and training to the Kurdistan Regional Government, and for other purposes	March 26, 2015	Introduced or Prefiled

Table 3.2. Sample of Representative Gabbard's Record of Bill Sponsorship and Cosponsorship (*Continued*)

Label	Title	Introduced	Status
H.R. 1568	Protecting Religious Minorities Persecuted by ISIS Act of 2015	March 24, 2015	Introduced or Prefiled
H.Con.Res. 107	A concurrent resolution denouncing the use of civilians as human shields by Hamas and other terrorist organizations	July 16, 2014	Enacted
H.R. 4411	Hezbollah International Financing Prevention Act of 2014	April 7, 2014	Passed Original Chamber
H.R. 850	Nuclear Iran Prevention Act of 2013	February 27, 2013	Passed Original Chamber

Source: Quorum Federal Database 2021. Search terms: *Armed Forces and National Security; Foreign Trade and International Finance;* and *International Affairs.*

US and allied struggle against the Islamic State appeared to cement a shift in broader strategic objectives in the region.

Advocacy Coalitions

The advocacy model of foreign policy decision-making expects that groups will lobby and frame competing policy narratives to provide a logic for their preferred positions. The events of August and September 2013 appeared to catalyze a coalition of actors inside and outside the government to oppose military intervention. Gabbard joined with Progressives and liberal Democrats, as well as Tea Party conservatives and civil society groups, to oppose the president. They tried to counter the moral imperative argument for intervention using several main arguments. First, they drew strong parallels between the buildup to the Iraq invasion in 2003 and the rhetoric they were hearing about Syrian president Assad. The administration contended there was a "clear and compelling" case that had proven Assad was a "thug and murderer," but the opposition coalition responded that they found such claims eerily familiar to the buildup to the Iraq War in 2003 (Memmott 2013). Liberal representatives like Alan Grayson (D-FL) teamed with GOP colleagues to help whip votes against the president's call for a congressional authorization of the use of force.

Second, Gabbard and other advocates argued that a Syrian intervention portended an endless war, and if any operations were approved at all, this should occur in the form of a restrictive congressional authorization for the use of military force. Gabbard found like-minded allies in this struggle, including

58   Staying in the Fight

fellow WoT veteran Tammy Duckworth (D-IL). Together, they claimed that the costs of a Syria intervention would not outweigh the benefits and that the United States was already overcommitted to two other wars in the Middle East. Meanwhile, Tea Party Republicans in the House like Justin Amash (R-MI) argued, "I don't think the American people are ready to go to war based on circumstantial evidence. The case for going to war is not that strong." On August 28, 2013, nearly seventy members of Congress—including fifty-five Republicans and fifteen Democrats—sent an open letter to the president calling on him to seek authorization for the use of military force.

Gabbard and her staff worked closely with civil society actors, including peace groups to oppose greater intervention in Syria. One of the groups that provided strong support was the nonpartisan Veterans for Peace organization, which worked directly with Gabbard's office to help provide outside support and lobbying in favor of her initiatives, including helping to draft H.R. 608, the Stop Arming Terrorists Act. A spokesperson argued, "As veterans we took an oath to preserve and defend the Constitution of the United States. The threat to the Constitution comes not from Russia, China, or the Islamic State, but from within the walls of Washington D.C. where the Congress and the Executive branch have enmeshed the country in ongoing unnecessary, illegal and unconstitutional wars." In many ways, the organization helped support Gabbard's own talking points regarding Syria. That bipartisan initiative was also supported by groups like the Progressive Democrats of America, the US Peace Council, and Veterans for Peace (author's interview, October 12, 2021).

Gabbard's close working relationship with civil society groups was starkly illustrated in late 2016 when she took a weeklong "fact-finding trip" to Syria that was partially funded by peace groups, including the Cleveland, Ohio–based Arab American Community Center for Economic and Social Services. The congresswoman met directly with Syrian president Bashar al-Assad during her trip, the first time that a high-ranking US official had spoken to the leader in years (author's interview, September 16, 2021). Gabbard also met with Lebanon's newly elected president Michel Aoun, Lebanese prime minister Saad Hariri, the US ambassador to Lebanon, and nonprofit groups and members of the clergy. Of her meeting with the dictator, she said, "Given the opportunity, I felt it was important to take it. I think we should be ready to meet with anyone if there's a chance it can help bring about an end to this war." Gabbard argued that her trip further convinced her that the US should stop aiding any rebels fighting against Assad in the war-torn country. She called the rebel groups "terrorists" and argued, "The U.S. must stop supporting terrorists who are destroying Syria and her people. The U.S. and other countries fueling this war must stop immediately. We must allow the Syrian people to try to recover from this terrible war . . . and focus our attention on defeating al-Qaeda and ISIS" (quoted in Serhan 2017).

While the visit did give Gabbard insights into the geostrategic situation on the ground in Syria, this attempt at personal diplomacy was pilloried in the media and by many on Capitol Hill.[12] House Speaker Nancy Pelosi (D-CA) and other party leaders criticized Gabbard for not reporting the planned trip and challenging US official policies. Representative Adam Kinzinger (R-IL), a fellow Iraq veteran, said that the act was wrong—it effectively "legitimized his dictatorship and in turn, legitimized his genocide against the Syrian people" (Scoville 2017). Critics subsequently charged that Gabbard was integrating Syrian talking points directly into her own advocacy efforts (Heffernan 2017).

Outcome

Representative Gabbard's foreign policy advocacy appears to have contributed to several important developments. Her overall approach was multifaceted, reflecting her experiences in the military and the need for variable missions and objectives. Gabbard sought to dissuade establishment Democrats and Republicans from a military response to a chemical weapons attack in Syria in 2013, joining a majority of WoT veterans who opposed this action. She continued to challenge overt and covert military interventions in Syria. If she could not achieve a complete halt to those operations, she sought to at least direct the uses of force toward terrorist groups including al-Qaeda and the Islamic State through legislative guardrails on assistance policies. Her activism, along with that of others, appeared to help shape the types of nonlethal military aid provided and, ultimately, the capabilities of forces meant to destabilize the Assad regime (Lantis 2021).

At this writing (in the fall of 2023), the Syrian Civil War seems to have reached a stalemate in most regions of the country; human rights groups suggest that hundreds of thousands of Syrians have died or disappeared in the war. However, the US government's position toward the Syria conflict has evolved significantly over time. President Obama's initial calls for the ouster of Assad gave way to quieter diplomacy and sanctions programs by the Trump administration. President Biden and his advisers appear to have adopted a middle ground: Publicly, the United States would maintain its pressure and sanctions on the Assad regime in order to try to isolate it, but they would no longer demand the removal of the president as a requirement to end the war. But privately, administration officials began to explore ways to engage with Syria on critical questions including the fight against the Islamic State and efforts to counterbalance growing Iranian influence in the region (Ryan 2023). In 2023, Assad returned triumphantly to public diplomacy by attending an Arab League summit meeting in Saudi Arabia after an eleven-year suspension.

Gabbard has also had an interesting professional arc: Following her failed bid for the Democratic Party presidential nomination, the four-term representative from Hawaii's Second District announced that she would not run for reelection to Congress in 2020. Gabbard transferred her Army National Guard commission from Hawaii to a reserve unit based in California and completed several tours of duty working as a civil affairs officer. In 2021, newly promoted Lieutenant Colonel Gabbard launched a podcast, became more active on social media, and began to appear regularly on Fox News as a critic of Biden administration policies. Gabbard appeared to relish her role as a "political outsider" and a "maverick," and many observers speculated that she might be planning a future run for higher office (author's interview, October 12, 2021). As the Ukraine War unfolded, Gabbard became a champion of restraint, and critics once again charged that she was parroting the Russian government's talking points by warning the United States not to become more engaged in that conflict (Khaled 2022). But Gabbard remained unapologetic. As one close observer of Gabbard commented, "I don't think it's a surprise that she plays for the long ball," Hart said. "She always takes jobs with an eye for future growth, whether as a presidential candidate or a vice presidential candidate. So, why should this be any different?" (Grube 2020).

4

Strained Ties

Saudi Arabia and the War in Yemen

The United States actively supported Saudi Arabia's military involvement in the civil war in Yemen during the Obama and Trump administrations, even as that conflict endangered the lives of millions of people. The war that began in 2014 as a struggle between rival factions for control of the country quickly expanded, and the UN World Food Programme soon called the situation in Yemen the "world's worst humanitarian crisis." Concerned WoT veterans in Congress did begin to challenge US military assistance policies to Saudi Arabia when evidence emerged that Saudi operations were causing civilian casualties. They argued that the United States was effectively complicit in Saudi violations of human rights: the kingdom was using military aircraft purchased from the United States, piloted by personnel trained by the United States and refueled by US aircraft, to carry out attacks on targets that were informed by US intelligence collection (Malley and Pomper 2021).

This chapter analyzes how veterans of the WoT in Congress on both sides of the political aisle became powerful advocates to change executive branch policies toward Saudi Arabia and its intervention in Yemen. Case studies of the activism of Republican senator Todd Young (R-IN) and Democrat representative Ted Lieu (D-CA) illustrate how outspoken junior members and military veterans joined ranks with fellow lawmakers to influence executive branch policies through committee work, obstruction, oversight, and even social media campaigns. Senator Young used a range of instruments at his disposal, including bipartisan activism and engagement through the Senate Foreign Relations Committee (SFRC) to leverage change US foreign policies. Congressman Lieu employed both direct and indirect challenges to White House policies that included grassroots advocacy and lobbying and a social media campaign. Furthermore, these cases demonstrated the effectiveness of congressional oversight: in

February 2021, President Joe Biden announced that the United States was formally ending its support for Saudi-led military actions, calling the conflict a "humanitarian and strategic catastrophe" (quoted in Knickmeyer 2021).

The Challenge: Relations with Saudi Arabia during the Yemen Civil War

US foreign relations with Saudi Arabia and Yemen have been complicated by a Western dependency on Saudi oil, historical developments, and geopolitics in the Middle East region. The United States is a longtime ally of the Kingdom of Saudi Arabia, which became independent in 1932. As the Saudi royal family consolidated its control over the country, Western oil companies like Gulf Oil, Royal Dutch Shell, and Standard Oil of California established a strong presence there. The discovery of large deposits of oil in Saudi Arabia, along with its geographic location and significance, helped position the country as a critical strategic partner for the West (Gause 2018a). While tensions sometimes flared between Saudi Arabia and the United States over issues like oil production and supply and concerns about Saudi financing of extremist groups, they generally remained strong (Ottaway 2009).

The United States has a number of security concerns and interests in the Middle East that benefit from engagement with Saudi Arabia, including stable relationships with the Sunni majority, steadfast support for Israel's right to self-determination and defense, and efforts to counterbalance against other players in the region like Iran (Miller 2017). These objectives have not always been complementary, of course, but they were elements of a larger effort to promote stability in the region (Gause 2018b). The United States has served as a major supplier of arms and military assistance for Saudi Arabia, and the kingdom has helped facilitate negotiations between the Israelis and Palestinians. Presidents and the Congress have traditionally supported robust arms sales, military-to-military exchanges, and education and training programs. US defense contractors have sold advanced F-15 fighters, reconnaissance aircraft, and missile defense systems to Saudi Arabia (Abramson 2021). Finally, Saudi Arabia has also played a critical, albeit complicated and controversial, role in counterterrorism and the US WoT (Blanchard and Prados 2007; Kostiner 2009; Long 2019; Bin Khaled Al-Saud 2017).[1]

However, the kingdom's direct intervention in the Yemen civil war and the actions of Saudi crown prince Mohammed bin Salman (or MBS) strained relations with the United States. Like the Syria case, the conflict in Yemen has its roots in the Arab Spring revolutions of 2011. Facing a popular uprising and political violence, Yemen's longtime president, Ali Abdullah Saleh, handed over power to a deputy, Abd-Rabbu Mansour Hadi. Unfortunately, this did not prevent a conflict between the government and the Houthis, an armed group based in the north of the country whose members adhere to a branch of Shia Islam. The Houthis had strong backing from Iran, and they took advantage of a fractured political climate to gain territorial control over a wide area in the north of the country. In 2015, they overtook the capital city of Sana'a, and the former government, including President Hadi and key officials, fled to the south (Hill 2017). That March, the kingdom announced it was launching Operation Decisive Storm, a military campaign involving ten countries and using sophisticated military hardware, especially aircraft, designed to push the Houthis back and restore order to the country. As coalition forces conducted airstrikes against Houthi positions, the United Arab Emirates also began an active training and arming program for militias in the south of Yemen (Johnsen 2021). However, operations did not go according to plans, and the civil war and proxy war in Yemen continued. While casualty estimates from the conflict vary, a UN agency reported that an estimated 249,000 people had died by the end of 2021, mostly due to indirect causes like the lack of food, health services, and infrastructure.

Saudi Arabia's presentation of its plan to launch Operation Decisive Storm marked the first of several major decision points for the United States government. The Obama administration faced an immediate question of whether to support Saudi Arabia in this venture. The close diplomatic relationship between the two countries allowed officials from the kingdom to pitch this operation to top officials in the United States as a brief and surgical set of strikes that would address instability in Yemen, and Washington offered its support for its early air operations.[2] Indeed, some officials in the Department of Defense were enthusiastic about support for a regional ally taking the lead in a military operation that could promote regional stability. One senior Pentagon official actually called it at the time: "something we've dreamed of" (Oakford and Salisbury 2016). However, the US government soon faced another decision point in determining whether it would continue to support Saudi Arabia after reports surfaced that Saudi operations had likely killed thousands of innocent Yemenis (Oakford and Salisbury 2016). A centerpiece of the US effort in question was an aerial refueling program using KC-135 tankers to deliver millions of tons of jet fuel to Saudi aircraft involved in the war (author's interview, August 16, 2021). In addition, the Saudi coalition–imposed blockade of Yemeni ports created a chokehold on the goods arriving in that country, including humanitarian assistance needed to fend off mass starvation. Finally, news that MBS had been implicated in ordering the 2018 murder of journalist Jamal Khashoggi forced the question of how much the United States could continue to support Saudi Arabia (Aghamohammadi and Omidi 2018). Opponents of US aid to Saudi Arabia in Congress felt compelled to respond to these challenges and advanced their campaign to stop US support for Saudi Arabia.

64   Staying in the Fight

Representative Ted Lieu (D-CA) and the Campaign to Stop Support for Saudi Arabia in the Yemen War

Air Force veteran Congressman Ted Lieu (D-CA) was determined to challenge the Obama and Trump administrations' foreign policy engagement with Saudi Arabia during the late 2010s. This is the story of a committed veteran lawmaker who overcame adversity in his own life and found his own style of leadership and successful strategies for influence. Congressman Lieu recognized opportunities for leverage and influence over US foreign policy toward Saudi Arabia and the broader balance of power in the Middle East. Lieu employed a number of traditional and nontraditional strategies in an attempt to change executive branch foreign policies. In the end, his advocacy helped contribute to significant shifts in Trump and Biden administration policies toward Saudi Arabia.

Distinctive Motivations

Ted Lieu is a member of Congress from California who has served in the Air Force in both active duty and the Reserves since 1995. Born in Taipei, Taiwan, Lieu immigrated with his family to Cleveland, Ohio, when he was still young. According to Lieu, his family struggled, but ultimately "achieved the American Dream" by saving enough money to open a small retail store that developed into a chain (quoted in Yam 2020). Lieu worked long hours as a youth in the family business and excelled at his studies. He was admitted to Stanford University, where he double-majored in political science and computer science (Congressional Veterans Caucus 2021).

Lieu's military career began when he accepted a Reserve Officer Training Corps scholarship from the Air Force that would include active-duty service after graduation from college. Lieu was committed to both his training and studies, and he demonstrated a great deal of tenacity when faced with a challenge. For instance, when Lieu failed a vision examination and the Air Force prepared to discharge him, he wrote a series of appeals to high-ranking officers to gain a commission and continue to serve. Lieu was allowed to do so and graduated as a commissioned lieutenant in the Air Force (author's interview, November 5, 2021). He then attended Georgetown Law School on scholarship and later began active-duty service at the Los Angeles Air Force Base in El Segundo, California, where he worked in the Judge Advocate General (JAG) Corps. Looking back, Lieu said that he was personally inspired by military and public service: "I believed I could never fully give back what this country had given me as the son of immigrant parents who were able to achieve the American dream" (quoted in Doblansky 2016).

Over the next four years on active duty, Lieu found respect and personal meaning through military service. He said that growing up, there were times when he "did not feel like [he] belonged," and this had motivated him to enlist in the military to both prove his place in America and to serve the country that gave his family opportunity. In the armed forces, Lieu noted that he "felt seen for his missions and rank, rather than just his race" (quoted in Yam 2020), and he saw his military service in the operation as particularly formative and interwoven with his life's journey. Lieu was deployed in several locations in the Asia-Pacific theater and in Iraq. During a posting to Guam in 1996, he participated in Operation Pacific Haven, which airlifted thousands of Kurds out of a mountainous region of northern Iraq and brought them to Guam before Hussein's forces could attack them (author's interview, October 4, 2021). To Lieu, Operation Pacific Haven was an example of how a well-intentioned government could use its resources to save people who were under threat because of their identity (McDonald 2017). He received the Air Force Humanitarian Service Medal for his efforts in the operation, and he later transferred back to a base in Southern California, where he completed the remainder of his active-duty commitment and transferred to the Reserves. At this writing, Lieu serves as a colonel in the Reserves.

Lieu's political career quickly took off following his active-duty service, including clerking for the Ninth Circuit Court of Appeals in Los Angeles and practicing law at a private firm. Lieu was elected to the Torrance City Council and, later, to the California State Assembly. He was selected for leadership posts in the assembly and was seen as a rising star in Democratic state politics. In 2011, he was ranked one of the top twelve "worth watching" lawmakers in the nation by *Governing Magazine*, and he was elected to the state senate in 2014. Among his causes in the state legislature were climate change and antiracist legislation. In 2014, Lieu was elected to the US Congress to represent the Thirty-Third district of California Congress, filling a seat vacated after forty years by Congressman Henry Waxman (D-CA).[3] Lieu's arrival in Washington helped him begin a new stage of his journey. From the outset, Lieu's leadership and humble demeanor stood out among his peers, and he was elected president of the Democratic freshman class by his colleagues (Green 2014b). He displayed what one knowledgeable senior congressional staff member said were the principles that were "drilled into" members of the military like duty, honor, commitment, and persistence (author's interview, November 5, 2021). He was appointed to high-profile committees, including the House Judiciary Committee and the House Foreign Affairs Committee (HFAC) (Allen 2017). Finally, Ted Lieu also gained national media attention during the Trump administration by publicly challenging the president on Twitter, stating, "If I'm not going to be doing things or speaking out, then I should give this job to someone else" (McDonald 2017).

Issue Framing: Linking Personal and Policy Narratives

The period of escalation of US involvement in the war and reports of increasing civilian casualties (2015–17) directly overlapped with Lieu's first term on

Capitol Hill. Lieu was in a special class of legislators when he entered Congress in 2015: he was one of twenty representatives who were officers in the National Guard while simultaneously serving in Congress (author's interview, November 5, 2021). From the start, Lieu recognized his military status as interwoven with his life story and his political career. He and other veterans were called up for military operations while in Congress, and some received promotions and commendations for their actions. During Lieu's own promotion ceremony to the rank of colonel—attended by Democrat minority leader Nancy Pelosi (D-CA) and WoT military veterans Seth Moulton (D-MA) and Ruben Gallego (D-AZ)—Lieu said, "As the son of immigrant parents who were able to achieve the American dream, I joined the Air Force on active duty and decided to continue to serve in the Reserves to give back to America—an exceptional country of boundless opportunity that has given so much to my family. . . . I look forward to continuing to serve our nation as an officer and as a Member of the House of Representatives." He concluded, "In both these solemn duties, I pledge to always honor the Air Force's core values: integrity first, service before self, and excellence in all we do" (quoted in "Congressman Lieu Promoted to Rank of Air Force Colonel" 2016).

Congressman Lieu drew together his military background and expertise with his personal concerns about human rights to determine that US backing of a flawed Saudi military operation in Yemen should be confronted. Notably, Lieu's staff members have acknowledged that he did not enter office with an established agenda on Yemen. Rather, he identified the issue in his first months on Capitol Hill "as one where he believed that he could make a difference" based on a combination of factors: Lieu was interested in Middle East politics and human rights, and he saw the Yemen case as a potential legal and security problem. He and his staff also believed the congressman could make his mark on the issue because "nobody else was really talking about Yemen at that point." When news circulated of a tragic mistaken Saudi bombing of a Yemeni wedding party that fall, staffers said that they asked around on the Hill: "Is anybody else doing anything about this?" And the answer was no (author's interview, November 5, 2021). Lieu and his staff also received encouraging signals from State Department officials that this was indeed a serious concern and that the congressman should pressure the Defense Department for answers (author's interview, November 5, 2021). In September 2015, just weeks into the Saudi coalition air operations, Lieu sent letters to Obama administration officials requesting clarification on protections for civilians and requesting that the United States "cease aiding coalition airstrikes in Yemen until the coalition demonstrates that they will institute proper safeguards to prevent civilian deaths" (Norton 2016b). Lieu also raised "serious questions" about coalition operations and cited a United Nations report that claimed nearly three thousand civilians had been killed in the first few months of Saudi airstrikes. He identified these actions as possible "war crimes" by early 2016 (Norton 2016b).

Lieu's personal and professional experiences led him to frame his opposition narrative to government policy in several ways: First, he challenged the general expansion of executive branch authority regarding the use of force in relation to congressional authority. Lieu's own study of constitutional law informed his criticisms of the Obama administration's quiet decision in March 2015 to provide support for Saudi-led military effort to restore Yemen's deposed regime (Mazzetti and Schmidt 2016). As the number of civilian casualties increased dramatically, Lieu and other members of Congress issued more vocal statements regarding the degree of commitment and the legitimacy of the executive branch's authority to authorize the use of force. The congressman publicly questioned the Obama administration's actions, and within months, he had cosponsored bills that would bar the sale of more American bombs and missiles to Saudi Arabia until the administration provided new guarantees on Saudi behavior (author's interview, September 10, 2021).

Second, he expressed strong opposition to the operation in Yemen—characterizing it as illegitimate and possibly illegal—and he ramped-up his oversight on the issue to pressure the administration to curtail the scope of US and Saudi involvement in the war (LaForgia and Wong 2020). Lieu was especially focused on challenging the continuation of US aerial refueling operations for Saudi jets that carried out attacks in Yemen and Saudi regime human rights violations. According to one congressional staff member, Lieu really saw this through a strategic approach to problem-solving. He described it as "similar to an Air Force checklist for a pilot before you fly a plane: Issues arise and you think through them systematically. A long checklist of strategic and tactical considerations to figure out how to solve problems. You also consistently ask the right questions about the best pathways for moving forward" (author's interview, November 5, 2021). For example, during a committee hearing with the newly appointed chairman of the Joint Chiefs of Staff General Joseph Dunford, for example, he challenged the executive branch's rationale for the war, asking, "What is the U.S. national security interest in supporting the Saudi-led air coalition in Yemen? Why is this coalition dropping bombs on civilians nowhere near military targets? How is the U.S. going to stop that from happening?" (Lieu 2015b). As the conflict wore on, Lieu drew even stronger connections between his military experience and opinions on Yemen. He said, "Having served on active duty in the U.S. Air Force, and as a graduate of Air War College, I understand that in the fog of war no battle plan will be executed perfectly . . . however, the apparent indiscriminate airstrikes on civilian targets in Yemen seem to suggest that either the coalition is grossly negligent in its targeting or is intentionally targeting innocent civilians" (quoted in Norton 2016a).

Third, Lieu sought to make a moral appeal to stop US involvement in the war. Yemen policy helped him find a broader audience and effectively vaulted him to center stage as a public challenger of the legitimacy of support for Saudi

68 *Staying in the Fight*

Arabia during the Trump administration. Lieu appeared more frequently on cable news programs and issued more social media challenges against Trump as an unconstitutional, immoral, and illegitimate president (author's interview, November 5, 2021). He said US support for Saudi Arabia in the crisis in Yemen was both "a moral issue and a criminality issue" and explained the legal liability for aiding and abetting war crimes that many State and Defense Department officials could potentially face if the United States continued to fund and support Saudi-led efforts in Yemen (LaForgia and Wong 2020; author's interview, October 4, 2021).[4]

Bill Cosponsorship and Bipartisanship

Congressman Ted Lieu's approach to legislative challenges and congressional oversight of US military operations in the Middle East was determined but also highly bipartisan. Indeed, most of the major legislative initiatives Lieu advanced regarding Saudi policy and Yemen were cosponsored by colleagues in the Republican Party. Two of the areas where he found strong foundations for a bipartisan approach were in his collaboration with fellow WoT military veterans and through his work on the HFAC. Lieu's office regularly partnered with many fellow veterans, including Mikie Sherrill (D-NJ), Jimmy Panetta (D-CA), and Ruben Gallego (D-AZ) (author's interview, October 4, 2021).

Congressman Lieu's first legislative engagement with Saudi foreign policy was in 2015 when he called for the United States to halt its participation in coalition airstrikes in Yemen. This followed the news of another Saudi attack that resulted in the deaths of civilians and Red Crescent volunteers in Yemen (Lieu 2015a). In the spring of 2016, Lieu and colleagues challenged the Obama administration's announcement of a $1.15 billion sale of military supplies to Saudi Arabia by introducing bipartisan resolution (H.J. Res. 90) that would place limitations on the transfer of munitions. He stated the bill would send a clear message that civilian casualties in Yemen are unacceptable and that the United States would not support their military actions until they ensure that civilians will not be harmed (Lieu 2016). This represented companion legislation to a similar bipartisan initiative in the Senate, S.J. Resolution 32, which was cosponsored by Senators Chris Murphy (D-CT) and Rand Paul (R-KY). However, these bills failed to gain enough support, and US backing of Saudi Arabia continued.

In 2017, Lieu joined with Republicans to challenge what they saw as an executive overstretch, particularly the president's claim that Authorizations for the Use of Military Force from 2001 and 2002 served as legal authority to support Saudi Arabia in Yemen. They also introduced legislation in 2017 that would place conditions on the sale of precision-guided munitions to Saudi

Strained Ties 69

Table 4.1. Sample of Representative Lieu's Record of Bill Sponsorship and Cosponsorship

Label	Title	Introduced	Status
H.R. 5497	BURMA Act of 2021	October 5, 2021	Passed House
H.R. 7429	Russian Digital Asset Sanctions Compliance Act of 2022	April 6, 2022	Introduced in House
H.R. 3967	Honoring our PACT Act of 2021	June 17, 2021	Passed House
H.R. 6930	Asset Seizure for Ukraine Reconstruction Act	March 3, 2022	Introduced in House
H.R. 6846	Corruption, Overthrowing Rule of Law, and Ruining Ukraine: Putin's Trifecta Act	February 25, 2022	Introduced in House
H.R. 6601	Saudi Arabia Legitimate Self Defense Act	February 4, 2022	Introduced in House
H.Res. 895	Strongly condemning ongoing violence and human rights abuses stemming from Cameroon's Anglophone crisis	February 1, 2022	Introduced in House
H.R. 6351	Climate Solutions Act of 2021	December 30, 2021	Introduced in House
H.R. 5142	To award posthumously a Congressional Gold Medal, in commemoration to the service members who perished in Afghanistan on August 26, 2021	August 31, 2021	Became Public Law
H.R. 5314	Protecting Our Democracy Act	September 21, 2021	Passed House
H.R. 1155	Uyghur Forced Labor Prevention Act	February 18, 2021	Passed House
H.Res. 317	Condemning the ongoing genocide and crimes against humanity being committed against Uyghurs and other minorities in China	April 14, 2021	Passed House
H.R. 6089	Stop Iranian Drones Act	November 30, 2021	Introduced in House
H.Res. 767	Expressing the sense of the House that it is the duty of the Department of Defense to reduce environmental impact of all military activities	November 3, 2021	Introduced in House
H.R. 5543	Vet CENTERS for Mental Health Act of 2021	October 8, 2021	Introduced in House

Continued

70 Staying in the Fight

Table 4.1. Sample of Representative Lieu's Record of Bill Sponsorship and Cosponsorship (*Continued*)

Label	Title	Introduced	Status
H.R. 5297	National POW/MIA Memorial and Museum Act	September 20, 2021	Introduced in House
H.R. 1448	PAWS for Veterans Therapy Act	March 1, 2021	Became Public Law
H.Res. 585	Condemning the atrocities and crimes against humanity being perpetrated against religious and ethnic minority women in Xinjiang, China	August 10, 2021	Introduced in House
H.R. 3985	Averting Loss of Life and Injury by Expediting SIVs Act of 2021	June 17, 2021	Passed House
H.R. 3385	HOPE for Afghan SIVs Act of 2021	May 20, 2021	Passed House
H.R. 711	West Los Angeles VA Campus Improvement Act of 2021	February 2, 2021	Became Public Law
H.R. 4104	Vanessa Guillén Military Justice Improvement and Increasing Prevention Act	June 23, 2021	Introduced in House
H.Res. 490	Reaffirming the importance of the United States to promote the safety, health, and well-being of refugees and displaced persons	June 22, 2021	Introduced in House
H.R. 256	To repeal the Authorization for Use of Military Force Against Iraq Resolution of 2002	January 11, 2021	Passed House
H.Res. 445	Condemning all violence and human rights abuses in Ethiopia, and calling on the Government to remove all Eritrean troops	May 28, 2021	Introduced in House
H.R. 3492	Gold Star Families Benefits Protection Act	May 25, 2021	Introduced in House
H.R. 2734	Veteran Families Health Services Act of 2021	April 21, 2021	Introduced in House
H.R. 2506	SAUDI WMD Act	April 14, 2021	Introduced in House
H.R. 2108	War Powers Act Enforcement Act	March 19, 2021	Introduced in House
H.R. 1111	Department of Peacebuilding Act of 2021	February 18, 2021	Introduced in House
H.R. 669	Restricting First Use of Nuclear Weapons Act of 2021	February 1, 2021	Introduced in House

Table 4.1. Sample of Representative Lieu's Record of Bill Sponsorship and Cosponsorship (*Continued*)

Label	Title	Introduced	Status
H.J.Res. 15	Providing for congressional disapproval of the proposed foreign military sale to the Kingdom of Saudi Arabia	January 15, 2021	Introduced in House
H.Res. 32	Impeaching Donald John Trump, President of the United States, for high crimes and misdemeanors	January 11, 2021	Introduced in House
H.R. 748	CARES Act	January 24, 2019	Debate
H.R. 550	No War Against Iran Act	January 15, 2019	Debate
H.Con.Res. 83	Directing the President pursuant to the War Powers Resolution to terminate the use of US Armed Forces to engage in hostilities in or against Iran	January 8, 2020	Passed House
H.R. 2881	Secure 5G and Beyond Act of 2020	May 21, 2019	Passed House
H.R. 5543	No War Against Iran Act	January 7, 2020	Introduced in House
H.Res. 768	Calling on African governments to protect and promote human rights through internet freedom and digital integration	December 17, 2019	Introduced in House
H.R. 299	Blue Water Navy Vietnam Veterans Act of 2019	January 8, 2019	Became Public Law
H.R. 663	Burn Pits Accountability Act	January 17, 2019	Introduced in House
H.R. 6869	Violence Against Women Veterans Act	September 25, 2018	Introduced in House
H.R. 2703	Legal Services for Homeless Veterans Act of 2017	May 25, 2017	Introduced in House
H.R. 2123	Enhancing Veterans' Access to Treatment Act of 2015	April 30, 2015	Introduced in House
H.R. 590	International Human Rights Defense Act of 2015	January 28, 2015	Introduced in House

Source: Quorum Federal Database 2022. Search terms: *Armed Forces and National Security*; *Foreign Trade and International Finance*; and *International Affairs*.

Arabia, including the requirement to avoid civilian casualties. By this time, Lieu had successfully generated a bipartisan legislative approach to promote congressional oversight of the situation. They argued that Saudi Arabia had violated standards for the protection of civil rights and that the United States needed to sharply limit the type of assistance it was providing. Lieu later joined Representative Ted Yoho (R-FL) to introduce legislation through the HFAC to place conditions on all air-to-ground munitions sales to the Kingdom of Saudi Arabia, including reducing civilian casualties, facilitating humanitarian aid, and targeting US-designated terrorist organizations (Naiman 2017).

By late 2017, Lieu and his colleagues modified their approach to challenging Saudi assistance by attaching amendments to the National Defense Authorization Act (NDAA) that stepped up congressional oversight. The House passed Lieu's amendment to the omnibus legislation that would require the Departments of Defense and State to report to Congress on whether Saudi Arabia was abiding by commitments to avoid civilian causalities in Yemen. Lieu believed the bill brought critical accountability to the administration's actions (Lieu 2017). With support in the House and Senate, the 2018 NDAA that included Lieu's provision was signed into law by President Trump (author's interview, November 5, 2021). News of potential Saudi involvement in the killing of journalist Jamal Khashoggi in October 2018 prompted even greater scrutiny of Trump administration policies. In November 2018, the Trump administration quietly announced that it would suspend aerial refueling operations for Saudi jets in the war in Yemen. To critics, this seemed to be a tacit admission of potential problems with those missions but, at the same time, represented a move that might forestall more serious US retrenchment. The White House did not announce the suspension of major weapons sales to the kingdom, nor did they directly condemn MBS and Saudi officials for the killing.

The spring of 2019 brought renewed legislative pressure on the Trump administration. Lieu joined with fellow critics of Trump administration policies to vote to invoke the War Powers Resolution to curtail support for Saudi Arabia. This effort was broadly bipartisan in nature. It was cosponsored by progressives on the left like Representative Ro Khanna (D-CA) along with far-right conservatives, including Representatives Matt Gaetz (R-FL), Mark Meadows (R-NC), and Rand Paul (R-KY). Trump ultimately vetoed the measure in April 2019, arguing, "We cannot end the conflict in Yemen through political documents. Peace in Yemen requires a negotiated settlement" (quoted in Landler and Baker 2019). In 2019, Lieu and his colleagues also pursued a permanent legislative ban on KC-135 refueling support for Saudi attack jets. Lieu joined with Representatives Yoho and Malinowski (D-NJ) to introduce the Yemen Refueling Prohibition Act, which would stop the United States from providing the in-flight refueling of Saudi or Saudi-led coalition aircraft conducting missions in Yemen. Recognizing that the act might not be signed into law by the president, Lieu and his colleagues successfully advanced an amendment to the 2020 NDAA that imposed constraints on overall commitments, established certification requirements for US assistance to Gulf partners operating in Yemen, and blocked aerial refueling operations for two years (author's interview, September 10, 2021). Lieu worked hard to ensure that the amendment would stay in the final legislation, and the final NDAA became law on January 1, 2021. As a result, Lieu and his colleagues could celebrate a victory by using the legislative process to achieve the critical goal of restricting US involvement in the war.

Advocacy Coalitions and Lobbying

Congressman Lieu was one of the first voices in Congress to challenge Obama administration policies on Saudi Arabia and Yemen. Indeed, staff members candidly admitted that at the beginning they felt "like we were alone on this one" (author's interview, November 5, 2021). But Lieu's foreign policy advocacy in this area reflected a deep conviction fueled by a synergy between his legal and military training. Lieu believed that he had an obligation from his experience in the JAG Corps to kind of "teach and represent the law" by calling out "war crimes" in Yemen before any other lawmakers (author's interview, November 5, 2021). He worried about legal and political responsibility on the part of the United States, stating that the government could not legally "outsource war crimes"; rather there is an inherent "liability" (author's interview, November 5, 2021). Lieu and his staff began talking to the press right away about their concerns, and he started to build alliances with fellow lawmakers, such as WoT veterans Democrat Debbie Dingell (D-MI) and Republican Ted Yoho (R-FL), on the matter. On the Senate side, Lieu was soon to find a bipartisan group of like-minded allies in Senators Chris Murphy (D-CT), Rand Paul (R-KY), Todd Young (R-IN), and Jeanne Shaheen (D-NH). Together, these lawmakers drafted letters and promoted congressional oversight through HFAC hearings, letters, and public media appearances challenging Obama and Trump administration decisions.

Congressman Lieu was highly active in engaging with advocacy coalitions to leverage changes in US foreign policy. He worked closely with advocacy groups to build pressure on the Obama and Trump administrations—and he skillfully demonstrated the kind of inside/outside advocacy strategies that newer members of Congress appear to have mastered. Beginning in 2016, Lieu's office coordinated its efforts with a variety of groups, including VoteVets, Win Without War, and Swords Into Ploughshares. Another group that supported legislative appeals was the Center for American Progress. Congressional staff members acknowledged that those groups helped specifically with briefings,

74   Staying in the Fight

letters, amendments to National Defense Authorization Acts, and other legislation targeting US support and arms sales to Saudi Arabia (author's interview, August 16, 2021). Together, they also issued a series of public statements calling on Congress to block sales at least long enough to give lawmakers time to "give these issues the full deliberation that they deserve." At one point, groups like CODEPINK and similar organizations, including RootsAction.org and the Yemen Peace Project, began circulating a petition calling on representatives to sign a letter that Lieu had penned calling out the administration's role in support of Saudi airstrikes that killed civilians. In a coordinated effort, Lieu worked with Amnesty International experts who documented airstrikes by the Saudi Arabia–led coalition to demand a halt to US policies (Prupis 2016).

Later, Lieu and his staff closely coordinated development and passage of the Yemen Refueling Prohibition Act with outside advocacy groups. This bill, cosponsored by Republican and Democrat lawmakers, was designed to stop US planes from providing in-flight refueling of Saudi or Saudi-led coalition aircraft conducting missions in Yemen. Lieu publicly promoted the bill, arguing that the United States had a legal and moral responsibility to ensure that it was not aiding war crimes in Yemen. His staff worked closely with civil society groups to help build a groundswell of popular support for action, including Peace Action and US Labor Against War to promote the bill. His office also courted support from the AFL-CIO, along with nonpartisan human rights groups like the International Rescue Committee and Veterans Against the War (author's interview, October 4, 2021).[5]

Outcome: Changing US Defense Policy

The foreign policy advocacy of Congressman Ted Lieu and his colleagues appeared to gather momentum over time and influence executive branch decisions. This case study shows how Lieu regularly drew connections between his experiences and training in the military and his activism on Yemen policy. He regularly cited legal restrictions on executive action, as well as appealed Saudi policy on moral and humanitarian grounds. It is also notable that while his challenges and criticism of US policy did not wane over time, Lieu did appear to shift his strategy somewhat to achieve greater influence. What started out as bold legislative and public challenges to supplying arms and assistance to Saudi Arabia became more surgical activities designed to effect change from the inside and outside. In addition to legislative activism, like Lieu's amendments to NDAAs, Lieu also found ways to tap into a groundswell of support for closer scrutiny of Trump administration policies.

These challenges created powerful pressure on US operations. Perhaps the most focused of Lieu's efforts employed a mix of different strategies to try to stop the aerial refueling of Saudi jets, which he said he found "completely bizarre" (Stewart and Strobel 2016). He called out the actions that were taken by those refueled airplanes, such as bombing attacks that killed civilians, as especially inhumane. Lieu and his colleagues hailed the Biden administration's decision in February 2021 to end all major US military support for Saudi Arabia as a great humanitarian victory. Taken together, Lieu's commitments and initiatives appear to have had a profound influence on the arc of US foreign and security policies in this period. HFAC thus emerged as a leading group for congressional oversight and scrutiny of US policies toward Saudi Arabia and Yemen. Dozens of lawmakers are also on record opposing US sales of high-technology weapons to Saudi Arabia.

Senator Todd Young (R-IN) and the Unexpected Fight over Saudi/Yemen Policy

The civil war in Yemen and the Saudi-led intervention by an international coalition presented the United States government with a series of critical decisions. As noted, US connections to this conflict began when a Saudi-led international coalition intervened against the Houthis in March 2015, and the war intensified in its scope and severity over time. Not only did violence on the ground and airstrikes produce high casualties and destruction, the Saudi coalition also enforced a blockade of supplies and assistance flowing to the Yemeni people. Millions of civilians were thus caught between violence and deprivation, facing destruction of their homes and basic infrastructure, acute hunger, and displacement. According to a United Nations Panel of Experts on Yemen, the blockade of ports was especially pernicious, as the coalition was "using the threat of starvation as a bargaining tool and an instrument of war" (quoted in Norwegian Refugee Council 2018).

Tensions between the president and Congress over the question intensified in the first years of the Trump administration. President Trump argued that the United States should provide steadfast support for Saudi Arabia and work to counter the spread of terrorism and Iranian influence in the region. However, WoT veterans in Congress on both sides of the aisle became increasingly concerned about the implications of the war for US interests in the Middle East. Republican senator Todd Young from Indiana was a Marine veteran who supported the Trump administration on many issues, but he also played a pivotal role in challenging policies toward Saudi Arabia and Yemen. His willingness to confront Trump officials and demonstrate "diligence and sustained attention" on the matter through congressional oversight and activism helped make a significant difference in policy outcomes (Shesgreen 2018).

Distinctive Motivations

Todd Young was born in Pennsylvania in 1972, and his family moved to Indiana when he was still a child. Young was a promising athlete in high school, and

76 *Staying in the Fight*

he earned an appointment to the US Naval Academy in Annapolis, where he competed as a varsity soccer player. Young graduated in 1995 and was commissioned as a junior officer in the US Marine Corps. He served as an intelligence officer with a squadron based at the Cherry Point Marine Corps Air Station in North Carolina and was deployed near the border between the United States and Mexico. Young later became a recruitment director in the Chicago area. As a member of the reserve, he went on to earn several graduate degrees, including a master's in business administration (MBA) from the University of Chicago and a law degree from the University of Indiana. Young received an honorable discharge at the rank of captain in 2005, and he began to build political connections by working in the office of Senator Richard Lugar (R-IN) and in the conservative Heritage Foundation (author's interview, October 15, 2022).

After graduation from law school, Young joined his family's firm in southern Indiana. In 2010, he ran for his first political office representing the Ninth House District in Congress. Young campaigned on a conservative platform and touted his military experience and public service commitment. He said that he would be an important voice in Washington for veterans' affairs issues, along with energy policy and fiscal policy. He pledged to fight for conservative causes, including gun rights and pro-life policies, and against President Obama's health care programs (Indiana 9th District Congressional Debate 2010). Buoyed along by a larger Tea Party conservative movement, Young beat a well-known Democrat incumbent in the race and joined a cohort of new lawmakers who set out to change the way Washington conducted business.

Once in office, Young carried through on many of his conservative campaign commitments, earning a solid "A" rating from the National Rifle Association and supporting initiatives for smaller government. Notably, though, he also began to distinguish himself as part of a new generation of WoT veterans committed to working across the aisle to achieve their goals on select issues. Citing the influence of his mentor, Senator Lugar, Young characterized his bipartisan work in the House of Representatives as "unapologetically pragmatic" (author's interview, August 16, 2021). One of his colleagues described Young as "laser-focused on policy" and said that he was "willing to take risks. He doesn't spend a lot of time worrying about the political ramifications of wading in" (quoted in Desiderio 2021). Young himself said in an interview that foreign policy "should be a nonpartisan exercise" (Desiderio 2021; Cahn 2015). Furthermore, his seat on the House Armed Services Committee allowed him to become directly engaged on military and security issues.

In 2016, Young ran for an open Senate seat in Indiana, where he once again reminded constituents during his campaign that he was a former Marine who knew how to get things done. According to one biography, "Young is no bleeding-heart peacenik, nor is he a libertarian-leaning isolationist. He's a methodical, clean-cut defense hawk who trained as a rifle platoon commander in the Navy after graduating from the U.S. Naval Academy" (Shesgreen 2018). During the campaign, he said, "More than anything else, this election is about who Hoosiers can trust. It's about character. Either [voters] place their trust in a Marine who lives here in Indiana . . . or they place their trust in a career politician [Evan Bayh] who's cashed out and has an unseemly post-Senate career he doesn't want to talk about" (quoted in Groppe 2016). In the end, Young won the election by ten points with support primarily from rural voters, and he moved over to the Russell Senate Office building in January 2017 to advance his policy agenda. Young's actions in the House coupled with his victory in a tough Senate race also illustrate another important characteristic of the lawmaker that played out through his military service and early career in Washington: a willingness to take calculated political risks.

Issue Framing: Linking Personal and Policy Narratives

Senator Young's assessments of US support for Saudi intervention in the Yemeni civil war appear to have been greatly shaped by his personal and policy narratives. Similar to Ted Lieu, two of Young's concerns were for strong congressional oversight of executive branch authority and ending the connection between US policies and human rights violations in Yemen. And, like Lieu, Young did not take office knowing that he would become a congressional foreign policy advocate for Yemen. Rather, he was drawn to this issue based on concerns that it was a unique policy area that he believed "no one was paying attention to" in the Senate, and he saw an opportunity to "make a difference" (author's interview, October 15, 2021). One congressional staffer said that Young was attuned to security and defense policy problems like Yemen as a direct result of his military training and strategic thinking (author's interview, October 16, 2021).

Young earned a coveted seat on the SFRC when he took office in 2017, and he regularly used this position to call out Saudi responsibilities for the human rights catastrophe in Yemen. He often said that he had gained an interest in international politics and greater empathy through his military service. In one interview, for example, Young said that in the Marines, he interacted with "different types of people from different places, from different socioeconomic backgrounds, races and ethnicities and different life experiences." He added, "That's one way and perhaps the best way to cultivate empathy, is by exposing oneself to people who are different from you, and working through differences, and identifying commonalities and then working on projects together" (quoted in Bock 2021). Young also described how his work in military training and intelligence for counternarcotics missions and counterterrorism raised his awareness of the power of public service. As a result, the senator said, "I think I'm more sensitized to the gravity of decisions associated with committing our men and

78 *Staying in the Fight*

women to military engagements and the importance of trying to avoid them at all costs" (Bock 2021).

Young became especially concerned that US support for Saudi airstrikes and the Saudi-led blockade of international assistance to the people of Yemen were causing mass starvation. When his appeals to the Trump administration failed to yield desired results, Young personalized the issue and became somewhat of a political gadfly for the White House. Young argued publicly that the Yemen war "offends the sensibilities of all Americans—that there are countries in this day and age that are using food as a weapon of war" (quoted in Shesgreen 2018). He called the Saudi coalition action to block ports a "starvation blockade" and warned in 2018 that he might be willing to join with Democrats to cut off all funding for the US military intervention in Yemen. His rationale for these actions was once again based on his experiences. Drawing on his own counterterrorism military training and role in the SFRC, he warned that because the Islamic terrorist organization Al-Qaeda in the Arabian Peninsula (AQAP) was headquartered in Yemen, "starving people—denying them basic humanitarian assistance—leads to radicalization. We don't want to create more terrorists" (quoted in Jordan 2019).

Young's personalization of the campaign against US-Saudi policies began to coalesce around an issue that, to him, truly typified injustice: in 2015, Saudi airstrikes had destroyed several large cranes at the Yemeni port of Hudaydah, a strategic access point for offloading relief supplies for the population. Under heavy pressure, members of Congress rallied US government funding of new dock cranes that could be constructed on site for humanitarian relief operations. But in the summer of 2017, the Saudi government refused permission for the cranes to be delivered to Yemen and constructed (Roblin 2018). The senator seized on the issue and began to privately lobby the Saudi regime and the Trump administration to shift their policies. But when these efforts hit a dead end, Young turned a public spotlight on the issue by calling an SFRC hearing where he called out the governments. He described the acute problems with hunger and malnutrition and the need for international aid, and he said, "I want to ensure that the Saudis get all the public credit—or shame—they deserve" for impeding the cranes (author's interview, August 16, 2021).

Young also recognized that as a senator he had even greater leverage through procedural actions. In 2017, the senator placed a hold on the confirmation of a nominee for a key legal adviser position at the State Department, Jennifer Newstead, until Young was satisfied that the Trump administration would pressure the Saudi regime to lift a blockade on international relief aid, including the cranes for the port of Hudaydah (De Luce and Gramer 2017). Young confessed in an interview at the time that "I decided to use my prerogatives as a senator, all the tools in the toolkit." He also personally lobbied Secretary of State Tillerson and his successor, Mike Pompeo, to examine US and

Saudi policies and try to reduce civilian casualties (Shesgreen 2018). When this action prompted responsiveness from the Trump side, Young said that he was satisfied his strategy had worked: "They showed some flexibility . . . and I gave them their attorney" (quoted in De Luce 2017).

Bill Cosponsorship and Bipartisanship

Todd Young pursued bipartisanship on select foreign policy concerns from the start of his time in Washington, and his SFRC seat meant that he witnessed the inconsistencies and problems with Trump administration policies toward Saudi Arabia and Yemen firsthand. The senator saw, for example, how the White House continued to propose large packages of military assistance worth tens of billions of dollars for Saudi Arabia with seemingly few limits on their expected behavior. Young began to partner with a variety of Democrats in the Senate, including fellow veteran Jack Reed (D-RI), a West Point graduate and former paratrooper in the Eighty-Second Airborne, along with Brian Schatz (D-HI) and Chris Murphy (D-CT). Murphy described Young as "very good at thinking of ways to use legislation and letters as a means to push players inside Washington, outside Washington, into action" (quoted in Desiderio 2021). One congressional staff member said that Young was especially inclined to work with fellow veterans like Reed because "they speak each other's language" and that the partnership was "very intuitive" (author's interview, October 15, 2021).

There were numerous examples of bipartisanship in Young's activism toward Saudi and Yemen policies. In 2018, for instance, Young joined Senator Bob Menendez (D-NJ) in advancing cosponsored bipartisan legislation designed to increase congressional oversight. The Saudi Arabia Accountability and Yemen Act of 2018 demanded that the Saudi regime be held accountable for the Khashoggi killing and urged the Trump administration to help end the war. Young promoted the bill, arguing that the legislation actually provided "the Trump administration leverage it should use to push all parties in Yemen to engage in good faith and urgent negotiations to end the civil war and address the world's worst humanitarian crisis. Our national security interests and our humanitarian principles demand nothing less" (quoted in Swarens 2018). In addition, following a 2018 SFRC hearing, Young supported new versions of legislation that would place conditions on US assistance. Young backed S.J. Res. 54 that was driven by Senator Sanders, but he also supported modified legislation in S.J. Res. 58, which would prohibit the United States from participating in or paying for aerial refueling operations. This language was eventually incorporated into the NDAA for 2019 and passed by both houses of Congress. The Trump administration objected to some of the language in the bill, but ultimately signed the NDAA into law (author's interview, September 21, 2021).

80 Staying in the Fight

Young also partnered with liberal Democrat senator Jeanne Shaheen of New Hampshire. Explaining his rationale at the time, Young said that working with Democratic colleagues was "the only way to get things done in a body where you need 60 votes."[6] Young and Shaheen talked regularly about how to curtail US military assistance, training, and even arms sales to Saudi Arabia. The arms sales dimension of the relationship was of particular interest to the two senators. Congressional majorities had long supported arms sales to Saudi Arabia and allied Gulf states, and this had become very lucrative for US defense contractors (Levine 2019). A proposed major overhaul of the Royal Saudi Air Force arsenal with advanced F-15 fighter jets was an important dimension of relations in the 2010s. But these arms sales could also be linked directly and symbolically with the Saudi offensive in Yemen, and lawmakers seized on the issue as a point of possible leverage in the relationship (author's interview, October 15, 2021).

Bipartisan legislative challenges to the Trump administration continued to gather momentum. Indeed, by early 2020, there appeared to be strong bipartisan consensus that Congress should either invoke the War Powers Resolution (WPR) to bring a halt to US operations in the region or repeal the 2001 or 2002 Authorizations to Use Military Force (which helped launch the WoT and wars in Afghanistan and Iraq). Discussions of invoking the WPR circled around growing fears that President Trump might use Saudi Arabia as a launching point for military strikes against Iran. Young and his colleagues supported a series of initiatives, including draft legislation in the House called the "No War Against Iran Act" (H.R. 550), which would prohibit the use of federal funds for any use of military force against Iran without explicit congressional authority. Once again, it is critical to note that these were broad bipartisan legislative initiatives designed to curtail presidential authority (author's interview, October 14, 2021).

Young also joined senators Tim Kaine (D-VA) and Bernie Sanders (I-VT) in advancing legislation challenging the Trump administration's authorization to use military force in Yemen. One bill cosponsored by Young and Kaine would repeal the 1991 and 2002 authorizations for the use of military force in the Middle East amid escalating tension between the US and Iran (author's interview, September 21, 2021). This challenge by Young was especially noteworthy because few Republicans were criticizing the Trump administration for continuing operations in the Middle East at the time. Young openly acknowledged that his willingness to take risks and question authority, mindful of the costs of war paid by soldiers and civilians, was influential in his decision-making. He also quietly supported the enactment of the WPR to stop US support for Saudi coalition operations in Yemen. This effort began in 2018 when Senator Sanders introduced S.J. Res. 54 in the Senate, to "direct the removal of United States Armed Forces from hostilities in the Republic of Yemen that have not been authorized by Congress (except for those U.S. forces engaged in

Strained Ties 81

Table 4.2. Sample of Senator Young's Record of Bill Sponsorship and Cosponsorship

Label	Title	Introduced	Status
S. 2898	Unemployment Insurance Systems Modernization Act of 2021	September 29, 2021	Introduced or Prefiled
S. 2280	VETS Safe Travel Act	June 24, 2021	Introduced or Prefiled
S. 4765	A bill to amend title 10, United States Code, to eliminate the inclusion of certain personally identifying information from the information furnished to promotion selection boards for commissioned officers of the Armed Forces, and for other purposes	September 30, 2020	Introduced or Prefiled
S. 4244	A bill to amend title 3 of the Social Security Act to provide for improvements to state unemployment systems and to strengthen program integrity	July 21, 2020	Introduced or Prefiled
S.Res. 502	A resolution recognizing the 75th anniversary of the amphibious landing on the Japanese island of Iwo Jima during World War II	February 13, 2020	Enacted
S. 2826	A bill to require a global economic security strategy, and for other purposes	November 7, 2019	Introduced or Prefiled
S. 2528	A bill to require the director of National Intelligence to submit to Congress a report on the purpose, scope, and means of expanded Chinese influence in international organizations, and for other purposes	September 19, 2019	Introduced or Prefiled
S. 1881	Veterans Expedited TSA Screening Safe Travel Act	June 18, 2019	Passed Original Chamber
S. 2114	A bill to provide the legal framework and income tax treatment necessary for the growth of innovative private financing options, and for other purposes	July 15, 2019	Introduced or Prefiled

Continued

82 Staying in the Fight

Table 4.2. Sample of Senator Young's Record of Bill Sponsorship and Cosponsorship (*Continued*)

Label	Title	Introduced	Status
S.J.Res. 58	A joint resolution to require certifications regarding actions by Saudi Arabia in Yemen, and for other purposes	April 11, 2018	Out of Committee
S. 2757	National Economic Security Strategy Act of 2018	April 25, 2018	Introduced or Prefiled
S. 2656	Department of Veterans Affairs Oversight Enhancement Act of 2018	April 12, 2018	Introduced or Prefiled
S.J.Res. 55	A joint resolution to require certifications regarding actions by Saudi Arabia in Yemen, and for other purposes	March 8, 2018	Introduced or Prefiled
S. 2174	Veterans Crisis Line Study Act of 2017	November 30, 2017	Introduced or Prefiled
S.Res. 114	A resolution expressing the sense of the Senate on humanitarian crises in Nigeria, Somalia, South Sudan, and Yemen	April 5, 2017	Enacted
S. 1228	National Diplomacy and Development Strategy Act of 2017	May 24, 2017	Introduced or Prefiled
S.J.Res. 31	Authorization for Use of Military Force Against al-Qaeda, the Taliban, and the Islamic State of Iraq and Syria	March 2, 2017	Introduced or Prefiled
S. 418	Department of State and United States Agency for International Development Accountability Act of 2017	February 16, 2017	Introduced or Prefiled
H.R. 5910	Improving Economic Sanctions Act of 2016	July 14, 2016	Introduced or Prefiled
H.R. 5911	Countering Violent Extremism Task Force Oversight Act	July 14, 2016	Introduced or Prefiled
H.Res. 814	Calling on the North Atlantic Treaty Organization (NATO) to invoke Article 5 of the North Atlantic Treaty and conduct a military campaign against the Islamic State of Iraq and Syria (ISIS)	July 7, 2016	Introduced or Prefiled
H.R. 5170	Social Impact Partnerships to Pay for Results Act	May 6, 2016	Passed Original Chamber
H.Res. 571	Establishing the Select Committee on Oversight of the Joint Comprehensive Plan of Action	December 17, 2015	Introduced or Prefiled

Table 4.2. Sample of Senator Young's Record of Bill Sponsorship and
Cosponsorship (*Continued*)

Label	Title	Introduced	Status
H.R. 427	Regulations from the Executive in Need of Scrutiny Act of 2015	January 21, 2015	Passed Original Chamber
H.R. 367	Regulations From the Executive in Need of Scrutiny Act of 2013	January 23, 2013	Passed Original Chamber

Source: Quorum Federal Database 2022. Search terms: *Armed Forces and National Security*; *Foreign Trade and International Finance*; and *International Affairs*.

counterterrorism operations directed at al Qaeda or associated forces)" (Senate Resolution SJ 54 2018). In the end, Young and his Senate colleagues maintained pressure on the administration through a series of legislative maneuvers, including restrictions on foreign military assistance and even arms sales.

Advocacy Coalitions

Senator Young actively pursued an inside/outside strategy of influence on Saudi and Yemen policy, spurred on by the severity of the humanitarian challenges of the conflict. The United Nations began warning that millions of people in Yemen were facing immediate threats of harm without access to potable water and sanitation. There were thousands of new cases of cholera and malnutrition, and young children were seen as especially vulnerable to the conditions of the war. On the "inside," Young saw committee hearings as a particularly fruitful venue to try to raise questions and influence policy, and critically, his staff coordinated efforts with concerned groups before, during, and after these hearings (author's interview, October 15, 2021). For example, in an SFRC hearing that his staff helped organize in early 2017 entitled "Flashing Red: The State of Global Humanitarian Affairs," Young built rapport with witnesses and groups that included the US Institute of Peace, the US Agency for International Development (USAID), and the International Committee of the Red Cross (US Senate Foreign Relations Committee 2017).

NGOs recognized Senator Young and other allies in Congress who could help them magnify their messages of concern. A spokesperson for the group Oxfam America described the importance of advocacy coalitions and of Young's work, in particular. They stated, "If you talk to folks in the administration . . . they say the single biggest force moving the conflict in a positive direction has been congressional pressure. And Senator Young has been at the heart of that" (quoted in Shesgreen 2018). Other NGOs worked with Young and his staff on public relations campaigns, helping create broad pressure that might overcome

84   Staying in the Fight

some traditional lines of resistance. Again, this was an especially noteworthy campaign because Saudi Arabia had traditionally maintained very strong lobbying influence in Congress that helped it avoid negative impacts on policies following serious criticisms in the past (Demirjian 2016).

Young also worked closely with other NGOs, including Human Rights Watch (HRW), to stop selling high-technology weapons systems to Saudi Arabia. Among their targets was the prevention of sales of precision-guided munitions (PGMs) to the Saudi regime. HRW experts had concluded that there were serious threats from the use of PGMs in Saudi attacks. HRW also coordinated data gathering with another nonprofit, the Yemen Data Project, which cataloged airstrikes and operations conducted by Saudi Arabia. Their dataset illustrated the highs and lows of the actions and civilian casualties. Taken together, these efforts were noteworthy. Summing up the political climate at the time, expert Bruce Riedel of the Brookings Institution said, "We haven't seen this much anti-Saudi activity on the Hill in a quarter of a century. Criticism of Saudi Arabia has come out of the closet, and I don't think it's going to go back in" (quoted in Demirjian 2016).

Outcome: Humanitarian Relief Operations and Export Bans

The foreign policy advocacy of Senator Todd Young and his colleagues appeared to gather momentum and influence executive branch decisions. Once again, this was especially noteworthy because Young was considered an important ally of the Trump administration and a reliable Republican vote on many initiatives. But in the case of Saudi Arabia and Yemen, Young clearly decided to draw the line. The senator articulated many connections between his experiences and training in the military and his activism on Yemen policy, and he sought better coordination between the executive and legislative branches on a circumscribed foreign policy agenda.

Young and his colleagues were able to insert stronger congressional oversight authority on actions. For example, he leveraged challenges to Trump administration policies focused on the legality of support for Saudi Arabia's actions that harmed noncombatants. His goal was to provide limits and guardrails on Saudi actions in the hopes that they would improve the security situation (Levine 2019). The case of the Saudis blocking the delivery of cranes for the port of Hudaydah and continued airstrikes became focal points in his challenge. The evidence also suggests that Young's office was especially effective at coordinating a coalition of advocates who supported changes in US foreign policy (author's interview, October 15, 2021). By 2020, the Trump administration had ceased aerial refueling operations for Saudi jets and increased its reporting to Congress on operations in the region, including acknowledging that a small number of the United States military personnel were deployed to Yemen to conduct operations against AQAP and ISIS.

Meanwhile, the level of congressional scrutiny steadily intensified, and in February 2021, the new Biden administration announced that it was formally ending US support for Saudi-led military operations in Yemen. The Biden administration said it would stop supporting the coalition's offensive and announced the appointment of a US special envoy for Yemen. Biden said that the war in Yemen had created "a humanitarian and strategic catastrophe" and called for a strategic rethinking of operations in the region. Congressional pressure had helped the White House to see the limits of executive branch authority and, potentially, the limits of US interventionism in contemporary international relations (Hanna and Salisbury 2021).

5

Veterans and Afghanistan

Ending America's Longest War

This chapter explores how two decorated combat veterans of the Afghanistan War pursued their goals in Congress to shape Afghanistan policy and help end the war. Representatives Michael Waltz (R-FL) and Jason Crow (D-CO) confronted the Trump and Biden administrations on Afghanistan policy and strove to shape an honorable withdrawal from America's longest war. While they have ideological differences, these two members of Congress share many common concerns regarding defense policy. They were both elected to office for the first time in 2018 and assigned seats on the powerful House Armed Services Committee. Crow and Waltz identified common problems based on their experiences in the Middle East, and they set out to challenge the executive branch at critical junctures. Both veterans tried to drive the US government to expand its Special Immigrant Visa (SIV) programs for Afghan allies and their families, and they challenged the Trump administration's efforts to broker a peace deal with the Taliban that was meant to permanently end US engagement in Afghanistan. Their coordination with other veterans in Congress and actors across the government also directly influenced the development of Afghanistan policies and refugee policies during a critical period. In short, this chapter nicely illustrates some of the dynamics of the larger study, including veterans' motivations, strategies, and engagement to resolve difficult policy issues.[1]

The Challenge: Ending the Afghanistan War

The war in Afghanistan began just weeks after the September 11, 2001, terror attacks and continued until the withdrawal of the last troops from the country in the summer of 2021. President George W. Bush launched the war with resolve, heady optimism, and strong support from Congress, the public, and

86

the international community. The goal of the US-led invasion of Afghanistan was to overthrow the Taliban and capture or kill al-Qaeda terrorists. Special operations soldiers and intelligence community operatives worked in concert with local forces who opposed Taliban rule in Afghanistan, and they quickly took control of parts of the country and marched on Kabul. By December 2001, direct combat in the war in Afghanistan seemed nearly over, though Osama bin Laden and other top leaders of al-Qaeda remained at large.

With its commanding position in Afghanistan and with the support of the United Nations (UN) and its allies, the Bush administration shifted its focus to stabilizing the country and promoting a transition to democracy. The UN sponsored a meeting in December 2001 in which key Afghan groups agreed to a power-sharing government and installed Hamid Karzai as the leader of an interim administration. The UN Security Council passed resolutions supporting this transition, including the establishment of a new International Security Assistance Force (ISAF) for peacekeeping operations in Afghanistan. The United States also helped train and equip a new Afghanistan Army that included more than 300,000 soldiers. By shifting from armed invasion to stabilization and reconstruction missions, the US government remained vested in the fate of Afghanistan. It called for the establishment of democracy along with liberalization in the country that included free media, business deals with the West, and greatly expanded rights and opportunities for women. The ISAF mission supported reconstruction assistance, emergency food aid, and stabilization forces. By 2021, the United States had spent over $1 trillion in the Afghanistan War and civic projects (Malkasian 2021).

However, the war never really ended: the new Afghanistan government and military faced near continuous challenges from a Taliban-backed insurgency during stabilization operations. A number of key Taliban leaders either fled across the Pakistan border or remained ensconced in rural strongholds and each spring the fighting would begin anew. It was during this period, in the years after the original invasion, that US troops suffered the highest casualties. Soldiers on the front lines deployed to forward operating bases in Taliban-controlled territory or those who met with local tribal leaders inevitably became targets in the broader war. More than 2,400 US soldiers were killed and 24,000 injured during the twenty-year military operation; thousands of private military contractors and foreign troops in the NATO stabilization mission were also killed.

President Donald Trump was resolved to change the US policy toward Afghanistan. During the 2016 presidential campaign, he criticized the government's commitment to seemingly endless wars, and he pledged to pull back on commitments in the Middle East. The Trump administration also reached out to Taliban leaders beginning in 2017 to pursue negotiations to end the Afghanistan war, and back-channel talks led to formal discussions in 2019. However, congressional resistance to White House efforts grew much louder against any negotiations with what many believed was a terrorist organization. WoT veteran lawmakers were especially critical of the idea of offering concessions to the Taliban to end the war; they set out to block White House progress using different strategies and a public advocacy campaign. For example, when the Trump administration proposed to negotiate with Taliban leaders at Camp David in 2019 during the anniversary of the September 11 attacks, concerned members of Congress joined with vocal critics from across the political spectrum to stop those plans and delay progress on a peace deal.

Another important set of government decisions related to US involvement in the Afghanistan War focused on supporting Afghan citizens who served as translators and worked on military bases during the twenty-year conflict. Because of the shadow of the insurgency and threats from the Taliban, any Afghan who did so knew that they and their families could become targets for reprisal. It was in this context that the Bush administration and Congress advanced the first US Special Immigrant Visa (SIV) program for Iraq and Afghanistan that became law in 2006.[2] Under Section 1059 of the 2006 National Defense Authorization Act (NDAA), those nationals who had worked directly with the US armed forces could apply for lawful permanent resident status in the United States (Micinski 2018). The government later expanded the SIV programs for Iraq and Afghanistan in 2008 and 2009 (respectively) to create pathways for thousands more people who supported US operations to attain lawful permanent residence. Among the features of these programs was a promise: if Iraqi or Afghan citizens worked directly for the US military effort to stabilize the country for one year or longer, typically as translators for civil affairs and military operations, larger groups of them could apply for lawful permanent residency and a pathway to citizenship (Bruno 2015). These programs were clearly political: they would help those who had sacrificed their own well-being to support causes the United States believed in for Afghanistan, including democracy and the rights of women and minorities. They were also humanitarian in nature: the SIV programs offered direct assistance and protection for groups of people in both countries who faced possible persecution (Payne 2018).

On the surface, the SIV programs offered a pathway out of the chaos of Afghanistan. In reality, though, the executive branch established application processes that were complicated, drawn-out, and expensive (Payne 2018). As the conflict in Afghanistan intensified and the United States reduced its force presence, the number of Afghans applying for the SIV programs increased significantly (Radford and Krogstad 2017). At the same time, however, the Trump administration acted to slow the processing of SIV applications. These tensions came to a head after President Joe Biden ordered the withdrawal of US troops from Afghanistan in the spring and summer of 2021. The Taliban seized the initiative with troop drawdowns and began taking over large portions of the country and marching toward Kabul. This created chaos and uncertainty for US troops as well as for the thousands of SIV applicants who sought asylum (Shear et al. 2021). Thousands of desperate Afghans rushed to the Hamid Karzai International Airport in Kabul and tried to gain entry and get on remaining commercial and military flights out of the country (Seligman 2021). The events around the Kabul airport in August 2021 cast US policies in Afghanistan—and the refugee resettlement program in particular—in a very harsh light, and concerned WoT veterans in Congress became powerful advocates for refugee resettlement at critical junctures, including during and after the chaotic drawdown in Kabul in 2021.

Congressman Mike Waltz (R-FL) and Afghanistan Peace Initiatives

US engagement in Afghanistan has a long and storied history. As noted, what began as an invasion in October 2001 to overthrow the Taliban regime and transform Afghanistan into a democracy eventually turned into an extended counterinsurgency struggle. By 2021, America's longest war had been incredibly costly in terms of expense and the sacrifices of its troops and private contractors (McCarthy 2019). When President Donald Trump took office in 2017, he vowed to stop US involvement in the "endless wars" of the post-9/11 era, raising the prospect of a fundamental policy change. This case study tells the story of the struggle between the executive and legislative branches to shape Afghanistan policy, which was greatly influenced by outspoken WoT veterans who served as powerful foreign policy advocates.

Distinctive Motivations

Representative Mike Waltz (R-FL) was a graduate of the Virginia Military Institute and a twenty-four-year veteran of the Army who served two combat tours as a Green Beret in Afghanistan (Lantis 2021). Waltz was a commander in a US Army Special Forces reserve unit that operated in some of the most dangerous provinces of Afghanistan near the border with Pakistan. He was also deployed to counterterrorism operations in several other areas in and near the Middle East (Waltz 2014). In addition, Waltz gained Washington experience during secondment to serve in the Office of the Secretary of Defense in the Pentagon and, later, to work for Vice President Dick Cheney as a special adviser for counterterrorism and South Asia affairs. Waltz played an important role in a White House strategic review of counterterrorism operations in Afghanistan and Pakistan, and he recommended greater resources and attention to the fight. Taken together, these postings gave Waltz a very strong base of experience,

90 *Staying in the Fight*

knowledge, and perspective that he would later apply in his new public service role as a member of Congress after he was elected in 2018 (author's interview, October 2, 2021).

Following an honorable discharge from active-duty service in 2010, Waltz established a defense contracting company called Metis Solutions, which fulfilled government contracts for training units in the new Afghan Army. This addressed a need that Waltz had seen up close for stronger training and service support in Afghanistan. Metis also consulted with the government for stabilization operations in the Middle East on contract, providing strategic analysis, intelligence support, policy guidance, and foreign commercial development programs.[3] Waltz was also a cofounder and partner in Askari Associates, a consulting firm that provided strategic advice and consulting services to foreign governments and commercial entities, particularly in the Middle East and North Africa. At the same time, Waltz continued to serve as an officer in the Florida National Guard.

In 2018, Waltz campaigned to represent the Sixth Congressional District of Florida in the House of Representatives, running as a Republican and emphasizing his military veteran status and combat experience during the election. Waltz won the election by a significant margin and took office in 2019 (PBS NewsHour 2018). Like many other veterans in public service, Waltz said that his military experience was critical and formative for his approach to work in Congress. He said that serving had taught him that "in the foxhole, nobody cares about race, religion, party, social economic background. It's about mission, it's about country, it's about getting things done. I could tell you, from my perspective, compromise is not a dirty word" (PBS NewsHour 2018). Waltz's (2019) congressional website stated he would employ his "warrior attitude" in this new public service posting and focus on "accomplishing missions for his country." Waltz's strong campaign win and professional military experience also drew attention on Capitol Hill, and party leaders assigned him to serve in the House Armed Services Committee as a freshman member. He was also posted to the Committee on Science, Space, and Technology, reflecting Florida's interests in government and commercial space operations.

Afghanistan was one of Waltz's most important foreign policy priorities from the start of his time in Washington (author's interview, October 19, 2021). In his 2014 autobiography, *Warrior Diplomat*, he outlines his concerns that the United States lacked "a broader strategy in fighting the current wars that we need to fight . . . a broader strategy on how to undermine the ideology of extremism, much as we did against communism and fascism" (226). Too often, he said, he witnessed short-term thinking and a lack of clarity about the future of engagement. And just one month into his first term, Waltz and other veterans in Congress were jolted by news that President Trump was fed up with the war in Afghanistan and that officials had reached out to the Taliban

Veterans and Afghanistan *91*

for negotiations on withdrawing all fourteen thousand US troops from that country (Lantis 2021). Despite his freshman status, Waltz launched a campaign to try to warn the Trump administration against trusting the Taliban as reliable negotiating partners, and he sought out allies among fellow former service members on the Hill. Waltz believed that significant concessions to the Taliban could be dangerous for US national security (author's interview, October 20, 2021). Waltz set the bar high: He wanted the Taliban to renounce its ideology, agree to become partners with the United States in counterterrorism operations in Afghanistan and Pakistan, support the legitimacy of Afghan Constitution, and commit to protecting the rights of women and girls (Powers 2019).

Issue Framing through Personal Narratives

Congressman Waltz and many of his fellow WoT veterans were alarmed that the Trump administration would negotiate with the Taliban without close congressional oversight. Indeed, they worried that the president was pressuring US envoy Zalmay Khalilzad to find a deal with the Taliban even if it meant significant concessions (Baker, Mashal, and Crowley 2019). For example, there were reports that the president was considering an agreement that would immediately draw down seven thousand US troops, or half the size of the occupation force at the time (De Luce and Yusufzai 2019). In return for the reduction, the Taliban would renounce ties with al-Qaeda and guarantee Afghanistan would not be used to plot operations against the United States or its allies (Ramani 2019). The State Department also became more directly involved in the process, and Secretary of State Mike Pompeo met with Taliban leaders during negotiations in Doha, Qatar.

WoT veterans in Congress took news of these developments personally, and they were instrumental in slowly ramping up congressional oversight in 2019 and 2020. Waltz had long been on record expressing concerns about policy disconnects in the wars in Afghanistan and Iraq based on what he had seen in combat and learned through work in the Bush White House (author's interview, October 19, 2021). Waltz said that during his deployments to Afghanistan, he had observed the anticipation that the Taliban displayed when it appeared the US commitment to the region was waning years before (Nelson 2019). They planned to simply wait out the American presence, he believed, and then take back control of the country. Meanwhile, he believed the US government was simply not focused enough on the underlying causes of instability in Afghanistan, including the warlord structure of society, extreme poverty, ethnic strife, and a lack of governance and border controls.

Waltz drew these perspectives to challenge the negotiations by framing the problem in two ways: First, Waltz warned that if the United States withdrew

92   *Staying in the Fight*

from Afghanistan, terrorists would "follow us home." "We cannot just wish these wars away, unfortunately," he said (Lantis 2021). Waltz seized on similar arguments from inside the government, including a Pentagon report in June 2019 that warned that even if a deal was reached, the al-Qaeda terrorist group and the Taliban would remain a "substantial threat" (Landay and Holland 2019). In such circumstances, Waltz said, "I don't think we have a choice but to remain engaged, because half of the world's terrorist organizations reside in the Afghan-Pakistan border region" (PBS NewsHour 2018). He called for a comprehensive strategy for engagement in the country to avoid the resurgence of ISIS 2.0 or the Taliban. The United States needed to stay on the offense, Waltz said, adding, "We can fight these wars in Kabul and in places like Damascus, or we can fight them in places like Kansas City. I prefer the former" (quoted in O'Dowd 2019; Lantis 2021).

Second, Waltz called for real engagement and consultations across the federal government to develop a long-term Afghanistan strategy. Drawing directly on his past experiences in the military and during his secondments to the White House and the Pentagon, he argued that a comprehensive strategy toward any negotiations—really a prenegotiation dialogue—would have to include the imposition of serious requirements on the Taliban, including ending any associations with al-Qaeda or any group affiliated with it. He said, "We need to worry about terrorism in Iraq and Afghanistan, and especially about how foreign intervention then was fueling more violence. We need a strong forward presence in the Middle East. The whole reason we have had any success is because of our forward presence" (author's interview, October 19, 2021). More specifically, he believed that a broader strategy would require engagement by the Afghan government and that the Taliban would have to accept the legitimacy of Afghan Constitution. This would include a commitment to protect the rights of women and girls, the elimination of incoming foreign funds and military support from non-Afghan organizations, and assistance and active partnership with the United States and Afghanistan in future counterterrorism operations.

Waltz felt very strongly that a lack of strategy would be the undoing of America's commitment to Afghanistan. He continually referenced what he believed was President Obama's strategic misstep in Iraq in 2011. He maintained, "A counterterrorism strategy must be nested within a broader counterinsurgency strategy" (Waltz 2014, 351). Waltz doubted that the Taliban would offer such sweeping promises, and he believed it was the duty of the United States to maintain order. Short of that, he worried, "historians would look back on the war and contribute its malaise to a handful of key strategic flaws" (Waltz 2014, 349). He was particularly incensed that the Trump administration had conducted negotiations that excluded the Afghan government, calling it a "strategic mistake" (author's interview, October 19, 2021).

Bill Cosponsorship and Bipartisanship

Mike Waltz's challenges to the Trump administration's Afghanistan policy resonated with other lawmakers on the political left and right. He acknowledged that there was a strong bond among fellow veterans on Capitol Hill, saying, "We know who has served in Iraq and Afghanistan, and we know that that colors our experiences for how we approach policy issues" (author's interview, October 19, 2021). He found support from Democrats who believed that the president might just be selling out the country and its US-backed government in the negotiations. They argued that the negotiations themselves were structured in favor of the Taliban, as Afghan government representatives were not invited to many meetings. Waltz also shared the views of many conservatives who believed that the unfavorable terms would erode America's standing in the world. Among Trump's critics on Afghanistan policy on the right was Senator Lindsey Graham (R-SC), also a WoT veteran, who argued, "Any peace agreement which denies the U.S. a robust counter-terrorism capability in Afghanistan is not a peace deal. Instead, it is paving the way for another attack on the American homeland and attacks against American interests around the world." Graham added, "Any agreement which denies the U.S. the ability to have a meaningful counter-terrorism force capability—based on conditions on the ground for as long as needed—is a recipe for disaster" (quoted in Shinkman 2019).

Perhaps one of the clearest examples of Waltz's bipartisanship was his role in founding a new caucus on Capitol Hill, the "For Country Caucus," made up primarily of military veterans in Congress. Waltz helped establish this new bipartisan group early in his first term. Members included Representatives Jimmy Panetta (D-CA), Don Bacon (R-NE), and Chrissy Houlahan (D-PA), all of whom served during the WoT and who sought to promote bipartisan support for the military (Riley-Topping 2019). One of the early projects that the group promoted was a legislative package to benefit Gold Star veterans' families by increasing benefits and support. Several members also supported the creation of the Honor Action political action committee as an extension of their commitments (Riley-Topping 2019). In an opinion piece celebrating the creation of the group, former congressional leaders Richard Lugar and Tom Daschle argued that the For Country Caucus would "provide principled military veteran members a platform to work in a nonpartisan way and create a more productive government." They would pursue an agenda that was less politicized and instead would be "driven by integrity, civility and courage" to always "put their country first" (Lugar and Daschle 2019).

During his first years in office, from 2019 to 2022, Waltz sponsored or cosponsored nearly six hundred bills. The majority of those bills were related to the armed forces, international affairs, veterans' affairs, and national security, and some bills were specifically targeted at Afghanistan and counterterrorism policy (see table 5.1).

94   *Staying in the Fight*

Table 5.1. Sample of Representative Waltz's Record of Bill Sponsorship and Cosponsorship

Label	Title	Introduced	Status
H.R. 8081	Wounded Warrior Bill of Rights Act	June 15, 2022	Introduced or Prefiled
H.R. 8056	Maritime Border Security Technology Improvement Act	June 14, 2022	Introduced or Prefiled
H.R. 7991	KREMLIN Act	June 8, 2022	Introduced or Prefiled
H.R. 7916	Protecting American Sovereignty Act	May 31, 2022	Introduced or Prefiled
H.R. 7611	Ukraine Democracy Defense Lend-Lease Act of 2022	April 27, 2022	Introduced or Prefiled
H.R. 7325	Countering Chinese Espionage Reporting Act	March 31, 2022	Introduced or Prefiled
H.Res. 990	Opposing engaging Russia for reviving any form of the Joint Comprehensive Plan of Action (JCPOA) with Iran	March 17, 2022	Introduced or Prefiled
H.R. 6969	No Oil from Terrorists Act	March 8, 2022	Introduced or Prefiled
H.R. 6940	Israel Anti-Boycott Act	March 3, 2022	Introduced or Prefiled
H.R. 6894	No Energy Revenues for Russian Hostilities Act of 2022	March 2, 2022	Introduced or Prefiled
H.R. 6879	Task Force Pineapple Congressional Gold Medal Act	March 1, 2022	Introduced or Prefiled
H.R. 6876	Ukraine Democracy Defense Lend-Lease Act of 2022	February 28, 2022	Introduced or Prefiled
H.R. 6422	Putin Accountability Act	January 19, 2022	Introduced or Prefiled
H.R. 6367	Guaranteeing Ukrainian Autonomy by Reinforcing Its Defense (GUARD) Act of 2022	January 10, 2022	Introduced or Prefiled
H.R. 5946	Valor Earned Not Stolen Act of 2021	November 9, 2021	Introduced or Prefiled
H.R. 1448	PAWS for Veterans Therapy Act	March 1, 2021	Enacted
H.Res. 607	Condemns President Biden's failure to heed the advice of military and intelligence advisers about the Taliban offensive, leading to a disorganized, chaotic, and abrupt evacuation of United States personnel and Afghan allies	August 24, 2021	Introduced or Prefiled

Table 5.1. Sample of Representative Waltz's Record of Bill Sponsorship and Cosponsorship (*Continued*)

Label	Title	Introduced	Status
H.Res. 604	Expressing the sense of the House of Representatives that Congress disapproves of United States recognition of the Taliban and supports an Afghan government-in-exile and the efforts to resist the Taliban in the Panjshir Valley	August 24, 2021	Introduced or Prefiled
H.R. 5071	To direct the Secretary of Defense to submit to Congress daily reports on the evacuation of citizens and permanent residents of the United States from Afghanistan, and for other purposes	August 23, 2021	Introduced or Prefiled
H.R. 4300	Alexander Lofgren Veterans in Parks (VIP) Act	July 1, 2021	Passed Original Chamber
H.R. 4471	Improving Veterans Access to Congressional Services Act of 2021	July 16, 2021	Introduced or Prefiled
H.R. 3385	HOPE for Afghan SIVs Act of 2021	May 20, 2021	Passed Original Chamber
H.R. 2225	National Science Foundation for the Future Act	March 26, 2021	Passed Original Chamber
H.R. 3513	Afghan Allies Protection Act of 2021	May 25, 2021	Introduced or Prefiled
H.R. 3367	Gold Star Children Act	May 20, 2021	Introduced or Prefiled
H.R. 2637	American Critical Mineral Independence Act of 2021	April 16, 2021	Introduced or Prefiled
H.R. 2409	US-Israel Cooperation Expansion Act	April 8, 2021	Introduced or Prefiled
H.R. 2214	Military Retiree Survivor Comfort Act	March 26, 2021	Introduced or Prefiled
H.R. 1699	Iran Sanctions Relief Review Act of 2021	March 9, 2021	Introduced or Prefiled
H.R. 1695	TRICARE Reserve Select Improvement Act	March 9, 2021	Introduced or Prefiled
H.R. 1115	Global War on Terrorism Memorial Location Act	February 18, 2021	Introduced or Prefiled
H.R. 1173	Taiwan Invasion Prevention Act	February 18, 2021	Introduced or Prefiled

Continued

96 Staying in the Fight

Table 5.1. Sample of Representative Waltz's Record of Bill Sponsorship and Cosponsorship (*Continued*)

Label	Title	Introduced	Status
H.R. 1022	PAWS Act of 2021	February 11, 2021	Introduced or Prefiled
H.R. 886	Veteran Treatment Court Coordination Act of 2019	January 30, 2019	Enacted
H.R. 7212	Military HOMES Act	June 15, 2020	Introduced or Prefiled
H.R. 7061	American Critical Mineral Exploration and Innovation Act of 2020	May 28, 2020	Introduced or Prefiled
H.R. 6863	COVID-19 Accountability Act	May 14, 2020	Introduced or Prefiled
H.R. 748	CARES Act	January 24, 2019	Enacted
H.R. 6392	Secure United States Bases Act	March 25, 2020	Introduced or Prefiled
H.R. 6393	Strengthening America's Supply Chain and National Security Act	March 25, 2020	Introduced or Prefiled
H.R. 3749	Legal Services for Homeless Veterans Act	July 12, 2019	Passed Original Chamber
H.R. 5284	Vet OUTREACH Act	December 3, 2019	Introduced or Prefiled
H.R. 4695	PACT Act	October 16, 2019	Passed Original Chamber
H.R. 4873	Syrian Partner Protection Act	October 28, 2019	Introduced or Prefiled
H.R. 3938	Gold Star Children Act	July 24, 2019	Introduced or Prefiled
H.R. 3266	JROTC Cyber Training Act	June 13, 2019	Introduced or Prefiled
H.R. 2811	Better Military Housing Act of 2019	May 16, 2019	Introduced or Prefiled
H.R. 2796	Afghan Allies Protection Act of 2019	May 16, 2019	Introduced or Prefiled
H.R. 2707	New START Treaty Improvement Act of 2019	May 14, 2019	Introduced or Prefiled
H.Res. 374	Condemning Iranian state-sponsored terrorism and expressing support for the Iranian people	May 10, 2019	Introduced or Prefiled

Table 5.1. Sample of Representative Waltz's Record of Bill Sponsorship and Cosponsorship (*Continued*)

Label	Title	Introduced	Status
H.R. 2512	Protecting NATO Skies Act of 2019	May 2, 2019	Introduced or Prefiled
H.R. 2481	Gold Star Family Tax Relief Act	May 2, 2019	Introduced or Prefiled
H.R. 1746	To direct the President to establish a unified United States Space Command	March 13, 2019	Introduced or Prefiled
H.Res. 222	Emphasizing the importance of alliances and partnerships	March 13, 2019	Introduced or Prefiled
H.R. 1674	Veterans Improved Access and Care Act of 2019	March 11, 2019	Introduced or Prefiled
H.R. 553	Military Surviving Spouses Equity Act	January 15, 2019	Introduced or Prefiled
H.R. 563	DD-214 Modernization Act	January 15, 2019	Introduced or Prefiled

Source: Quorum Federal Database 2022. Search terms: *Armed Forces and National Security*; *Foreign Trade and International Finance*; and *International Affairs*.

Waltz introduced a number of bills in the 116th Congress. For instance, he joined with members of the For Country Caucus and other military veterans in the spring of 2019 to cosponsor legislation entitled the "Ensuring a Secure Afghanistan Act," which would place requirements on the Taliban before a peace deal could be reached (Powers 2019). This bill adopted a frame consistent with his stance that the group would have to transform to ever become a trusted partner. It called for the Taliban to end any associations with al-Qaeda or any group affiliated with it, support the legitimacy of Afghan Constitution, commit to protect the rights of women and girls, and eliminate income from foreign funds and military support from non-Afghan organizations. In a statement accompanying the legislation, Waltz said, "We must stay on offense and negotiate from a position of strength.... [This act] provides necessary oversight over the current negotiations and set benchmarks for any major US reduction of military force" (Powers 2019). The WoT veterans also knew that Afghanistan policy also enjoyed bipartisan support. One poll conducted by the University of Michigan and the Nielsen Survey Group found that both Democrats and Republicans favored maintaining a modest troop presence in Afghanistan for the future (Telhami and Kopchick 2020).

This bipartisan group of lawmakers came together again in response to perceived weaknesses in the Trump and Biden administrations. In response to reports in the summer of 2019 that President Trump was threatening to immediately withdraw all troops from Afghanistan and to shut down the US embassy in Kabul, Waltz cosponsored a bill designed to create stronger congressional oversight on White House actions. Trump's complaints reportedly centered on the size and cost of maintaining the embassy compound, along with general frustration about the war. According to one former US official, "He was fed up with hearing that the U.S. was not winning there. . . . It was no secret he wanted out, but deciding to pull out of the embassy, too, was a shock" (quoted in Kube and Lee 2019). Waltz did not hesitate to challenge the Biden administration, either. He cosponsored a resolution in August 2021 that severely criticized the new president's approach to withdrawal from Afghanistan. Waltz said,

> President Biden has embarrassed the United States on the world stage and created the worst foreign policy blunder in our modern history. Rather than heeding the advice of military leaders and lawmakers, President Biden created a humanitarian crisis in Afghanistan that he alone owns—all for the sake of seeking a headline that he would withdraw our troops prior to the 20th anniversary of September 11th. Now, we will have shamefully given away the freedoms of Afghans, our military equipment and infrastructure, and countless other resources to the hands of Taliban terrorists because of the President's cluelessness and stubbornness. Additionally, it is growing more likely by the day we will have broken our promise to thousands of Afghan allies who stood should-to-shoulder with our troops on the battlefield that have now been handed a death sentence for our failure to safely evacuate them in a timely fashion. (Quoted in Carney 2021)

Advocacy Coalitions

Congressman Waltz worked with other veterans and policy research institutes to quickly build an advocacy coalition that favored continued engagement in Afghanistan. Indeed, he found ready allies among think tanks and the wider community of foreign policy experts who favored maintaining a solid, if modest, troop deployment in Afghanistan. Some of the most active were groups like the Council on Foreign Relations and the Center for Strategic and International Studies, whose experts believed that the United States should continue to pursue an activist agenda in global politics. This perspective was widely shared by many veterans serving in the US government, along with editorial teams at influential newspapers like the *Wall Street Journal* and the *Washington Post*. Choosing isolationism as an alternative to engagement, many experts warned at the time, would lead directly to the resurgence of terrorist groups like al-Qaeda and possibly another 9/11-style attack. Any withdrawal should be approached "responsibly" and in alignment with the particular security situation in country. By leaving small contingents of US troops or an active footprint in countries in the Middle East, many believed, the West would have protection against the rapid rise of dangerous groups (Lyall 2021). One leader of the advocacy group VoteVets said they opposed a rapid withdrawal from Afghanistan, too, and "when the peace negotiations with the Taliban were proceeding, we joined with veterans on the Hill who challenged the idea that the Taliban would negotiate in Camp David on the anniversary of 9/11. That was contrary to US national security interests, and we let people in the administration know it" (author's interview, November 16, 2021).

It was in this context that Waltz and others supported a new commission, the Afghanistan Study Group (ASG), that would evaluate strategic options and offer recommendations to the United States for continuing stabilization operations (author's interview, October 2, 2021). The ASG would be led by retired four-star Marine General Joseph Dunford Jr., past chairman of the Joint Chiefs of Staff and a former top commander in Afghanistan. The group began its work in the spring of 2020, after the United States and the Taliban had signed the Doha agreement that expanded negotiations between the Taliban and the Afghan government. It concluded a report at the start of the Biden administration that recommended a reversal in Trump administration policies. The ASG report called for abandoning the May 1, 2021, withdrawal deadline established between Trump and the Taliban and instead slowing the withdrawal of troops from Afghanistan (Lyall 2021). The United States should maintain strategic bases in the country, including the massive Bagram airfield, and only commit to reductions in force presence in calibration with improvements in the security situation in the country over time.

Waltz applauded the efforts of the ASG as a reflection of a more strategic approach to the situation. But this also represented an expression of Washington politics and the continuation of a large, informal network of actors and groups that favored remaining in countries in the Middle East. The investment of US troops in country, they argued, reaped incredible dividends in terms of stability and access to a critical, strategic region (Barnes and Gibbons-Neff 2021). This message was echoed on editorial pages and in regular seminars and meetings sponsored by the RAND Corporation, the Brookings Institution, the Center for Strategic and International Studies, and other organizations (Jones 2018). The Brookings Institution held panels that incorporated the view of lawmakers and experts on prospects for success, warning that there were many pitfalls to try to overcome (O'Hanlon 2019). Waltz and other lawmakers were concerned about counterterrorism operations and intelligence in the region. They argued that Afghanistan was collapsing in 2021 and that the pullout of American troops, intelligence, and contractor resources were likely to lead to the collapse of the US-supported Afghan government. Indeed, up to the final

100 Staying in the Fight

weeks of the US withdrawal, Waltz was still arguing for action, calling for a reversal of plans and even carrying out air strikes to halt the Taliban advance on major cities.

Outcome: A Pyrrhic Victory in Afghanistan?

After nearly a year of negotiations, President Trump announced abruptly in September 2019 that planned talks with the Taliban in the United States had been canceled. Once again, this came after revelations that the administration wanted leaders of the Taliban and the Afghan government to meet President Trump at Camp David in the United States to finalize the peace deal. While there were conflicting accounts regarding what actually led to the cancellation of the meeting and the suspension of the US-Taliban negotiations, news reports revealed deep splits among Trump administration advisers over the issue (DeYoung 2019). On one side stood the president, Secretary of State Mike Pompeo, and the US chief negotiator, Zalmay Khalilzad, who all believed that they had reached agreement "in principle" and that the United States could begin withdrawing troops soon. The president pushed hard for a Camp David meeting that could become a historic televised event. Trump believed that his personal style could persuade anyone to make final concessions, and he believed that a substantial Afghan withdrawal could be a key pillar of his reelection campaign.

Meanwhile, on the other side of the debate stood vocal critics in Congress and their allies in the administration, including National Security Adviser John Bolton. Indeed, many members of the national security establishment, including leading voices in Congress and think tanks, questioned the potential value of any deal with the Taliban. Opponents were also deeply troubled by the suggested timetable for the talks that would bring Taliban leaders to Camp David during the week of the eighteenth anniversary of the September 11, 2001, terror attacks. Appearing on CNN's Sunday news program after the announcement, for example, Representative Waltz doubled down, saying, "As we head into the anniversary of 9/11, I do not ever want to see these terrorists step foot on the United States soil. Period." He said that he recognized public frustration about Afghanistan but believed the United States should stay the course: "This war has been long, hard and costly," he concluded, "but that doesn't mean that we can just walk away or just wish away these wars" (quoted in LeBlanc 2019). Similarly, Representative Liz Cheney (R-WY) said, "Camp David is where America's leaders met to plan our response after al-Qaeda, supported by the Taliban, killed 3000 Americans on 9/11. No member of the Taliban should ever set foot there. Ever."

However, even though concerned lawmakers helped stall negotiations with the Taliban, they were ultimately unable to block White House progress on a final deal. The Trump administration progressed toward the arrangement that would ultimately be implemented by President Biden—and that deal included the planned withdrawal of US troops from the country. Despite steady challenges from WoT veterans in Congress on both sides of the aisle, the new president carried forward with the plans that contributed to the collapse of Western stabilization efforts in Afghanistan. America's longest war ended in scenes of chaos and the deaths of even more US soldiers, coupled with a massive refugee and humanitarian crisis. Congressman Waltz and others launched a firestorm of criticism but could not in the end help the United States to avert a perceived military defeat and foreign policy debacle. Congressional policy advocacy in this case seemed to produce only a Pyrrhic victory.

Congressman Jason Crow (D-CO) and the Afghanistan Special Immigrant Visa Programs

From the start of his first term in Washington in 2019, Congressman Jason Crow (D-CO) was dedicated to issues that related back to his wartime experiences in Afghanistan and Iraq. One of the pressing matters facing the US government when he entered office was negotiating a withdrawal from Afghanistan and developing a strategy for stability and long-term success in that country. Crow strongly supported immigration policy reforms. His home state of Colorado was actually one of the largest hosts of refugees from Middle East conflicts resettled in the United States after those programs were expanded in 2008 and 2009.[4] Crow believed in the humanitarian and political commitments at the core of the programs and that their status as refugees should ensure they have social welfare support assistance.

Even before Crow took office, he was personally aware of the problem with backlogs and challenges with the Special Immigrant Visa (SIV) programs for Afghanistan. Crow was also sensitive to the ebbs and flows of federal policies regarding refugee access and support, and he knew from friends and colleagues that the application processes for SIVs were complicated, drawn-out, and expensive (author's interview, October 26, 2021). Crow believed that the Trump administration was directly responsible for some of the roadblocks on the SIV programs, and his concerns became more acute when President Trump announced that he had negotiated a peace deal with the Taliban that promised the withdrawal of all US troops from Afghanistan by May 2021. President Joe Biden announced that he would honor the deal with the Taliban to end the war, though he would move back the departure date for troops to September 2021. Biden made clear that he expected a gradual drawdown and peaceful turnover of bases to the Afghan Army and the US-backed regime would continue to govern. However, what occurred instead was the rapid collapse of the Afghanistan government and Taliban advances on Kabul. Thousands of SIV applicants

102 Staying in the Fight

joined a crowd of desperate Afghans outside the Hamid Karzai International Airport in August 2021, and thirteen US soldiers and dozens of Afghan citizens were killed in a suicide attack at an airport gate. Members of Congress who were WoT veterans leapt into action to try to provide assistance and to right the wrongs they saw in decisions by the executive branch.

Distinctive Motivations

Jason Crow was born in Madison, Wisconsin, in 1979 and grew up in a working-class family. He joined the National Guard after graduating high school, in part as a way to assist with college expenses at the University of Wisconsin; he then switched to the Reserve Officers' Training Corps (ROTC) program in his sophomore year. Following the September 11, 2001, terror attacks during his senior year, he was approved to enter active duty after graduation. Reflecting back on his decision, Crow said he was eager to serve: "We were at war, and I didn't like the idea of other people doing my fighting for me" (quoted in Cordell 2020).

Crow activated at a time when operations were ramping up in the WoT, and he chose to serve in the infantry and signed up for Airborne School to become a paratrooper. Crow's personal commitment to service and his leadership qualities allowed him to rise quickly in the military. Within a year, he was a platoon leader in the Eighty-Second Airborne during the 2003 invasion of Iraq. He engaged in combat in operations in the six-day battle of Samawah, as US and allied forces tried to clear that city during the invasion, and he earned a Bronze Star for his role in the battle. One officer who fought with Crow observed, "With all that chaos, you look for a cool head . . . someone who is solid, thoughtful, clear and concise and can execute what they need to do. That's how you build trust. That's Jason" (Justin DeVantier, quoted in Cordell 2020). Crow later entered Ranger School and joined the elite Army Seventy-Fifth Ranger Regiment for two tours of duty in Afghanistan that included patrols in dangerous provinces along the Pakistan border searching for al-Qaeda and Taliban leaders.

Crow personally acknowledges that his upbringing helped prepare him to address the challenges that he faced in battle and in the rest of his public life (author's interview, October 26, 2021). For example, he said that his family's limited means helped motivate him to work hard and find his own challenges and adventures. As a teenager, he loved Civil War history and hunting, and he took a variety of odd jobs to help with family expenses, from working construction to capturing turtles for a Department of Natural Resources study to running the drive-through window at an Arby's restaurant (Cordell 2020). He regularly cites those experiences as formative for his life that gave him an understanding of the challenges of working-class voters as well as the experiences of veterans. Notably, Crow was also raised in a very diverse community where encounters with people from different nationalities, race, and ethnicity was part of his daily experience.

Crow was honorably discharged from the Army as a captain in 2006 and became active in state and local veterans initiatives. He joined the Colorado Board of Veterans Affairs and helped organize veterans' affairs programs across the state. Crow attended law school at the University of Denver and made partner with the Holland & Hart Law Firm in Denver. His firm addressed business and regulatory issues, and he also worked on criminal litigation and legal compliance. Meanwhile, he remained politically active in his community in the Denver suburbs, including working with his wife, Dr. Deserai Anderson Crow, an associate professor at the University of Colorado–Denver, on environmental programs (Cordell 2020).

If the September 11 attacks helped motivate Crow for active-duty military service, the election of Donald Trump to the presidency inspired him to consider a new type of public service: just a few months after Trump's inauguration, Crow announced his candidacy for Congress, running as a Democrat in his Colorado district against a five-term Republican, Mike Coffman. This would be Crow's first run for elected office. Throughout the campaign, Crow pursued a campaign strategy that emphasized his military record and reached out to key communities, including African American voters, young voters, and members of the Ethiopian diaspora in his district. Crow also demonstrated a real commitment to grassroots politicking, personally knocking on thousands of doors throughout the district. Coffman's support seemed to erode quickly though, and the Republican Party even withdrew some funding from the campaign in the final stretch. In the end, Crow won by an 11 percent point margin, earning more than 54 percent of the popular vote.

During his first term, Crow and his staff prioritized its focus on national security issues, gun control, and fighting the power of money in US politics as well as challenging the legitimacy of the Trump presidency. And he often acknowledged the power of his military experience in shaping his approaches. In an interview, Crow stated that "military experience affects the way that I see things and the way that I lead—and combat experience was also critical: it means that I have learned to be goal oriented and even tempered" (author's interview, October 26, 2021). It is thus unsurprising that Crow quickly became a Democratic Party stalwart, offering strong support to Speaker Pelosi and the Democratic Party leadership, and he supported the impeachment proceedings for Donald Trump in 2019 and 2021. Crow had a seat on the powerful House Armed Services Committee and was a member of subcommittees on Intelligence, Emerging Threats and Capabilities, and on Readiness. Crow also became cochair of the National Security Task Force in the Democratic Caucus, which provided yet another opportunity for professional advancement and

104 *Staying in the Fight*

leadership, and he became a member of the bipartisan For Country Caucus, the Refugee Caucus, the Military Veterans Caucus, and many others (author's interview, September 22, 2021). Even in years of increasing acrimony and polarization in national politics, Crow stood out for his personal engagement on the issues, whether it be appearing for a press conference at the US-Mexico border to challenge Trump's immigration policies or asking tough questions of the administration at congressional hearings. Crow also focused on US foreign policy in the Middle East, drawing on his personal experiences to articulate his policy rationales on questions like troop deployments and operations in Syria, Iraq, and Afghanistan (Baran, Horton, and Dwoskin 2021).

Issue Framing: Linking Personal and Policy Narratives

Jason Crow appeared determined to change the course of US immigration policy and Afghanistan policy. The congressman was rather vocal about connections that he saw between his own experience and policy circumstances. For example, he argued that immigration policy needed major reform, stating, "As a combat veteran, I know what it feels like when you're not getting enough resources from Washington and I've been on the receiving end of those decisions" (Crow 2019). In one of his first major pieces of legislation, Crow introduced a bill that would guarantee that members of Congress and their staffs could gain access to US Immigration and Customs Enforcement (ICE) facilities. This initiative was a direct outcome of his personal commitment to immigration issues and the experiences that he and his staff had when they tried to visit the Aurora Contract Detention Facility for ICE early in his first term but was turned away. Crow and his staff remained focused on mismanagement and failures by ICE during a period when the Trump administration faced blistering criticism for its "child separation" policies and for its treatment of unaccompanied minors seeking asylum at the US-Mexico border (author's interview, August 16, 2021). Crow's bill was quickly enacted into law.

Crow has acknowledged that his military experiences directly shaped his approach to Afghanistan policy. In an interview, he stated, "I was profoundly affected by my military service, and I really see my leadership style as a mix of strategies and public service and private and active duty. . . . It completely changed my outlook" (author's interview, October 26, 2021). Throughout his first year in office, he became increasingly concerned that the Trump administration might abandon US interests in the country and its people by negotiating a deal that would be favorable to the Taliban. Crow and his staff also tracked the quiet but steady drawdown in thousands of US troops that was underway from that country. In October 2019, Crow led a bipartisan congressional delegation visit to Afghanistan where US lawmakers met with Afghan government

Veterans and Afghanistan   105

ministers and visited troops and bases with General Scott Miller, commander of the NATO mission and US troops in Afghanistan. Crow, fellow veterans on the trip, and staffers became even more focused through this experience on the potential terms of a peace deal and how to maintain support and stabilization operations for Afghanistan after such an agreement came into force (author's interview, October 26, 2021). Reflecting on the experience, he said, "Now that I'm in Washington, helping to oversee that policy, I always think about the impact on the ground. I remember what life was like as a lieutenant and thinking, 'the things I'm seeing in the news don't match my reality on the ground' and that's why it's important to go right to the front and talk directly to the soldiers on the ground and get their perspectives" (quoted in Mason 2019). He added, "On a personal level, flying over Kabul and the mountains for the first time in over 14 years was challenging to some extent," Crow said. "I thought about the battles I had, the people I served with and the friends I lost. It made me reflect in a way that I hadn't in a long time . . . I'm still reflecting and processing what I saw and my conversations and my meetings about this challenge and not really having any good options left . . . how it is we do the right thing" (quoted in Mason 2019).

These concerns intensified upon his return home to the news that President Trump had ordered the immediate withdrawal of all US troops from Syria, another country where Crow believed that a modest commitment of forces had lent needed stability. Crow lamented at the time, "What's very clear to me is that President Trump doesn't know what he's doing with national security and our military policy. There is no policy right now and, in fact, there are top commanders in the region that have told us that . . . our military is just kind of holding ground right now, waiting for some direction" (quoted in Mason 2019).

When the Trump administration announced the completion of a peace deal with the Taliban in February 2020, concerned members of Congress were determined to pressure the Trump administration to change course. It is important to note that Crow's personal position at the time was not a dogged determination to maintain US forces in Afghanistan at any cost (author's interview, October 26, 2021); rather, he seemed to recognize the practicalities on the ground: The combat mission for the United States in Afghanistan should come to a close, he believed, in part because the strategic situation seemed to be unwinnable. But the United States should continue to provide strong backing for the Afghan government and military, and there should be a clear and managed plan for the withdrawal of troops and Afghan civilians who supported the US military mission.

Lawmakers were also concerned about Afghan refugees if that country should fall to the Taliban. When President Biden announced that the United States would honor its agreement to withdraw from Afghanistan by September 2021, Crow and his staff knew that those plans would have dramatic implications for US foreign policy and for Afghans who supported military operations in that country. The lawmaker was particularly concerned about SIV program applicants, and his office began to reach out to the State Department to investigate the status of its review pipeline and visa application processing (author's interview, September 22, 2021). For Crow, this issue was both political and personal. He had worked directly with Afghan interpreters and knew about their lives and situations. He even credited an interpreter for saving his life, warning him during one patrol that the Afghans they were speaking with were lying to the soldiers and even possibly preparing to attack them (author's interview, October 26, 2021).

Crow knew that the SIV programs for Iraq and Afghanistan were designed to create pathways for thousands more people who supported US operations to attain lawful permanent residence in the United States. But he and his staff also knew that the actual bureaucratic process was plagued with difficulties (Payne 2018). Annual caps on the number of applicants that might be processed and accepted quickly clogged the bureaucratic process, and many applications were delayed for years. From 2001 to 2016, the number of SIV refugees resettled in the United States from Afghanistan totaled only thirty thousand (Micinski 2018). Furthermore, the process required that applicants had to apply in person through the US embassy and consulate offices, which was both expensive and dangerous, and applicants would have to offer proof of US government employment along with evidence of imminent threats due to their work. Conditions only got worse as the conflict in Afghanistan intensified and the United States reduced its troop presence (Radford and Krogstad 2017).

Crow and his colleagues watched with great concern as US forces withdrew from key locations, such as the Bagram airfield, in July 2021, and the Taliban made rapid gains across the country. Even as US leaders attempted to keep up the image of an orderly withdrawal of its own troops, the Afghan Army, who Crow had worked closely with during his deployments in Afghanistan, was collapsing. Afghan soldiers were putting up little fight, and some units were simply switching allegiance to the Taliban. US-supplied military equipment was falling into the hands of the Taliban, while US forces were deployed only to bases in Kabul. By August, even that force posture had changed: troops were exfiltrated through flights out of Karzai International Airport, and the mission became providing support for continued embassy operations. But even that would change rapidly in the first few weeks of August (Shear et al. 2021, A1).

Again, Crow and his fellow veterans on Capitol Hill took these developments very personally. For example, Representative Seth Moulton (D-MA) was an Iraq War veteran with combat experience who joined with Crow's office to promote rapid vetting of SIV applicants and other Afghans who wanted to flee the country (Shear et al. 2021). But at the time, what Crow and Moulton called for that summer seemed to be beyond the conception of some Biden administration officials. They attempted to stay the course of orderly withdrawal, even while trying to speed up visa processing and preparing American citizens in Afghanistan and their supporters to prepare to leave (Baran, Horton, and Dwoskin 2021). Afghan president Ghani traveled to Washington in late June, where Biden again tried to convince him to promote the perception of stability and an orderly transition. Again in early July, Biden described US activity in Afghanistan as "a rational drawdown with our allies" and insisted "there's nothing unusual about it" (quoted in Shear et al. 2021). But what Crow and other concerned members of Congress saw in Afghanistan, instead, was chaos and instability (author's interview, September 22, 2021).

Bill Cosponsorship and Bipartisanship

Crow appeared to demonstrate strong commitments to bill cosponsorship and bipartisanship on foreign and defense policy matters. Indeed, he managed to embrace the spirit of teamwork and camaraderie on Capitol Hill even as polarization and ideological clashes were on the rise. On a personal level, for example, he found friends with similar interests across the political aisle, including Representative Markwayne Mullin (R-OK) and Troy Balderson (R-OH). He and Balderson joined the new Civility & Respect Caucus together in 2019, a group that had been explicitly formed to promote bipartisan cooperation. In explaining his rationale, Crow said, "In the Army I learned to find common ground with people from different backgrounds and with different views. It's the same perspective I bring to Congress because you don't need to agree on everything to get things done. . . . We share the same goal of working together to end the gridlock in Washington and put the well-being of our communities over politics" (quoted in Special to Richland Source 2019). Crow also became a member of the bipartisan For Country Caucus, which included dozens of WoT veterans who were committed to cooperation and policy progress. When asked about his commitments, Crow said, "The era of the Donald Trump presidency will end at some point, and this country's going to have to move on. We're going to have to repair our divisions. We're going to have to come together. And I'm looking at that long game" (Cordell 2020).

Crow's commitment to bipartisanship continued in his legislative record. Indeed, nearly half of all the bills that Jason Crow advanced were cosponsored by Republicans. Among the many legislative items that Crow worked on were important bipartisan initiatives for veterans' affairs legislation. For example, in May 2021, Crow and Meijer introduced cosponsored bipartisan legislation ("Veterans Improved Access to Care Act") to address hiring shortages within the Veterans Affairs. The act would establish a pilot program to expedite onboarding of licensed medical professionals at understaffed VA facilities. In May 2021, Crow introduced the Securing a Strong Retirement Act of 2021 that would help military spouses save for retirement.

108   *Staying in the Fight*

Table 5.2. Sample of Representative Crow's Record of Bill Sponsorship and Cosponsorship

Label	Title	Introduced	Status
H.R. 8164	Resilient Defense Assistance Act of 2022	June 21, 2022	Introduced or Prefiled
H.R. 7991	KREMLIN Act	June 8, 2022	Introduced or Prefiled
H.R. 7945	MARCH for Military Servicemembers Act	June 3, 2022	Introduced or Prefiled
H.R. 7625	Protection of Civilians in Military Operations Act	April 28, 2022	Introduced or Prefiled
H.R. 7621	Department of Defense Civilian Harm Transparency Act	April 28, 2022	Introduced or Prefiled
H.R. 6930	Asset Seizure for Ukraine Reconstruction Act	March 3, 2022	Passed Original Chamber
H.R. 6968	Ending Importation of Russian Oil Act	March 8, 2022	Enacted
H.R. 6954	DICTATOR Act of 2022	March 7, 2022	Introduced or Prefiled
H.Res. 947	Supporting an independent and democratic Ukraine	February 25, 2022	Introduced or Prefiled
H.R. 6470	Defending Ukraine Sovereignty Act of 2022	January 21, 2022	Introduced or Prefiled
H.R. 5314	Protecting Our Democracy Act	September 21, 2021	Passed Original Chamber
H.R. 4996	Ocean Shipping Reform Act of 2021	August 10, 2021	Passed Original Chamber
H.R. 5788	SERVICE Act of 2021	October 28, 2021	Introduced or Prefiled
H.R. 5776	Serving Our LGBTQ Veterans Act	October 28, 2021	Introduced or Prefiled
H.R. 5709	Afghanistan Security Through Intelligence Act	October 25, 2021	Introduced or Prefiled
H.R. 5513	No Clearance for Terrorists Act	October 8, 2021	Introduced or Prefiled
H.R. 5159	Afghanistan Transparency Act	September 3, 2021	Introduced or Prefiled
H.R. 5112	Space National Guard Establishment Act	August 27, 2021	Introduced or Prefiled
H.R. 1448	PAWS for Veterans Therapy Act	March 1, 2021	Enacted

Table 5.2. Sample of Representative Crow's Record of Bill Sponsorship and Cosponsorship (*Continued*)

Label	Title	Introduced	Status
H.R. 5096	Afghan and Iraqi Allies Resettlement Improvement Act	August 24, 2021	Introduced or Prefiled
H.R. 4736	Improving Access for Afghan Refugees Act	July 28, 2021	Introduced or Prefiled
H.R. 3985	Averting Loss of Life and Injury by Expediting SIVs Act of 2021	June 17, 2021	Passed Original Chamber
H.R. 4628	Veterans Health Care Stamp Act	July 22, 2021	Introduced or Prefiled
H.R. 3385	HOPE for Afghan SIVs Act of 2021	May 20, 2021	Passed Original Chamber
H.Res. 505	Expressing support for the people of Afghanistan, condemning the Taliban's assault on human rights, and calling for the government to protect the Afghan citizens who bravely served alongside the Armed Forces of the United States	June 28, 2021	Introduced or Prefiled
H.R. 3672	Armed Forces Transgender Dependent Protection Act	June 1, 2021	Introduced or Prefiled
H.R. 3576	Reproductive Rights Are Human Rights Act of 2021	May 28, 2021	Introduced or Prefiled
H.R. 3577	United States Army Rangers Veterans of World War II Congressional Gold Medal Act	May 28, 2021	Introduced or Prefiled
H.R. 3512	Healthcare for Our Troops Act	May 25, 2021	Introduced or Prefiled
H.R. 3513	Afghan Allies Protection Act of 2021	May 25, 2021	Introduced or Prefiled
H.R. 3367	Gold Star Children Act	May 20, 2021	Introduced or Prefiled
H.R. 3224	I am Vanessa Guillén Act of 2021	May 13, 2021	Introduced or Prefiled
H.R. 3027	Veterans Improved Access to Care Act of 2021	May 7, 2021	Introduced or Prefiled

Continued

110   *Staying in the Fight*

Table 5.2. Sample of Representative Crow's Record of Bill Sponsorship and Cosponsorship (*Continued*)

Label	Title	Introduced	Status
H.R. 3000	Inspire to Serve Act of 2021	May 4, 2021	Introduced or Prefiled
H.R. 2974	Military Spouse Hiring Act	May 4, 2021	Introduced or Prefiled
H.R. 2838	Syrian Partner Protection Act	April 26, 2021	Introduced or Prefiled
H.R. 2436	Veterans Burn Pits Exposure Recognition Act of 2021	April 8, 2021	Introduced or Prefiled
H.R. 1808	Assault Weapons Ban of 2021	March 11, 2021	Introduced or Prefiled
H.R. 1022	PAWS Act of 2021	February 11, 2021	Introduced or Prefiled
H.R. 7433	Military Spouse Student Loan Deferment Act	June 30, 2020	Introduced or Prefiled
H.R. 7343	Afghanistan Partnership and Transparency Act	June 25, 2020	Introduced or Prefiled
H.R. 6957	National Guard COVID-19 Earned Benefits Guarantee Act	May 22, 2020	Introduced or Prefiled
H.R. 748	CARES Act	January 24, 2019	Enacted
H.R. 4305	PAWS for Veterans Therapy Act	September 12, 2019	Passed Original Chamber
H.R. 550	No War Against Iran Act	January 15, 2019	Passed Second Chamber
H.Con.Res. 83	Directing the President pursuant to section 5(c) of the War Powers Resolution to terminate the use of United States Armed Forces to engage in hostilities in or against Iran	January 8, 2020	Passed Original Chamber
H.R. 5210	Refugee Protection Act of 2019	November 21, 2019	Introduced or Prefiled
H.R. 4695	PACT Act	October 16, 2019	Passed Original Chamber
H.R. 4873	Syrian Partner Protection Act	October 28, 2019	Introduced or Prefiled
H.R. 95	Homeless Veteran Families Act	January 3, 2019	Passed Original Chamber
H.R. 299	Blue Water Navy Vietnam Veterans Act of 2019	January 8, 2019	Enacted

Table 5.2. Sample of Representative Crow's Record of Bill Sponsorship and Cosponsorship (*Continued*)

Label	Title	Introduced	Status
H.R. 2481	Gold Star Family Tax Relief Act	May 2, 2019	Introduced or Prefiled
H.R. 2456	To Repeal the Authorization for Use of Military Force Against Iraq Resolution of 2002	May 1, 2019	Introduced or Prefiled
H.R. 2435	Accelerating Veterans Recovery Outdoors Act	May 1, 2019	Introduced or Prefiled
H.R. 1585	Violence Against Women Reauthorization Act of 2019	March 7, 2019	Passed Original Chamber
H.R. 1896	Supporting Children of the National Guard and Reserve Act	March 27, 2019	Introduced or Prefiled
H.R. 1857	International Human Rights Defense Act of 2019	March 25, 2019	Introduced or Prefiled
H.Res. 220	Recognizing the interdependence of diplomacy, development, and defense as critical to effective national security	March 13, 2019	Introduced or Prefiled
H.R. 1674	Veterans Improved Access and Care Act of 2019	March 11, 2019	Introduced or Prefiled
H.R. 1581	Reproductive Rights Are Human Rights Act of 2019	March 7, 2019	Introduced or Prefiled
H.R. 1296	Assault Weapons Ban of 2019	February 15, 2019	Introduced or Prefiled
H.J.Res. 37	Directing the removal of United States Armed Forces from hostilities in the Republic of Yemen that have not been authorized by Congress	January 30, 2019	Passed Original Chamber
H.R. 1019	Full Military Honors Act of 2019	February 6, 2019	Introduced or Prefiled
H.R. 1030	Veteran Spouses Equal Treatment Act	February 6, 2019	Introduced or Prefiled
H.R. 712	VA Medicinal Cannabis Research Act of 2019	January 23, 2019	Introduced or Prefiled
H.R. 663	Burn Pits Accountability Act	January 17, 2019	Introduced or Prefiled

Source: Quorum Federal Database 2022. Search terms: *Armed Forces and National Security*; *Foreign Trade and International Finance*; and *International Affairs*.

112   Staying in the Fight

As the crisis in Afghanistan heated up in the summer of 2021, Crow and his staff began to focus on trying to alleviate the bottlenecks in the SIV application process. For example, they worked to overturn past legislation like an amendment in the 2016 NDAA that had required Afghans who worked for the US military to prove they had done so for two years rather than one and bureaucratic stipulations that applications include a letter from a human resources officer in the US military or government attesting to that person's service. The process also required that SIV applications be approved by the chief of mission at the US embassy in Kabul—an increasingly difficult challenge due to the backlog of applications and, later, the closure of the embassy during the Taliban takeover of the country (author's interview, October 26, 2021). Sadly, even after Trump's completion of a peace deal with the Taliban—and US officials knew that tens of thousands of Afghans who assisted the military by serving as interpreters or even driving fuel trucks could be in mortal peril from Taliban reprisals—there was no concerted effort to accelerate or improve the SIV application process (Date 2021).

One of the strongest examples of Crow's commitments to bipartisanship and Afghanistan policy came when he authored H.R. 7343, the Afghanistan Partnership and Transparency Act. This was a bipartisan initiative that was cosponsored by Crow and Mike Waltz (R-FL), along with other WoT veterans in Congress. This bill was designed to ensure that any reduction of troops from Afghanistan would be conducted in a strategic and thoughtful manner, subject to congressional oversight. Congress sought to assert its authority to help direct US national security policy while also ensuring protections for vulnerable populations in Afghanistan. The goal was to establish an oversight and monitoring program that would help counterbalance any plans developed by the Trump administration, including proposals for rapid troop withdrawal. Among its terms were requirements for reports and certifications to withdraw troops down to certain levels (including thresholds of eight thousand and five thousand troops). This would require assessments of issues ranging from the status of the Taliban to the potential impact on human rights and civil rights. Congress also sought greater transparency overall, both in communications among the branches of government and in providing information to the American people. The goal of the legislation was thus both substantive and political: A bipartisan consensus in Congress wanted the Trump administration to "own" any difficult developments in Afghanistan (author's interview, September 22, 2021).

In statements of support for the bill, Crow once again linked his own experiences with the legislation and drew direct connections between his military service and its goals. Crow said,

> I served in Afghanistan and I know firsthand what makes the U.S. military the strongest in the world, but I also know the limitations of

military power. If there was a military solution to the war in Afghanistan, we would've found it long ago. The war in Afghanistan must end, but we must do so in a way that ensures lasting peace. The world is watching to see whether America keeps its promises. This bill is transformative in its ability to ensure that we keep our promise—to the women and children of Afghanistan, to our partners and allies in peacekeeping, and to a safer, and more secure world order.

In the end, the bill was referred to both the House Armed Services Committee and the House Foreign Affairs Committee for consideration.

Throughout this activism, Crow stressed that he focused his energies on bipartisanship and cooperation, especially with fellow military veterans. He stated that he was "profoundly affected" by his military service. One gains a clarity of focus through military service and combat experiences, he argued, that allows them to see the value of cooperation with diverse individuals. Trust represents an essential quality for members of any organization to achieve their objectives, he said, and clarity of vision. He said, "I take time to pause and think about steps and realize the need to change course and develop creative policy options in response to challenges." Crow was very concerned about Trump's "irresponsible plan to end the war in Afghanistan," and he worked with members of Congress from both parties, including Republican Liz Cheney (R-WY) and Elissa Slotkin (D-MI), to challenge those policies. Crow also emphasized that relationships can be established behind the scenes with like-minded lawmakers, even if these ties are not as visible in public forums like committee hearings. Ultimately, he argued, leadership is about "building trust and relationships" (author's interview, October 26, 2021). "We just understand each other. We don't question each other's motivations. We instinctively know that there is a common commitment to national security. And even if we disagree 90 percent on issues from political ideological perspectives, we still find 10 percent that we agree on" (author's interview, October 26, 2021).

Advocacy Coalitions

Jason Crow was clearly committed to immigration issues and providing assistance to those fleeing violence or persecution. Crow campaigned in 2018 on the promise to represent the concerns of immigrant groups, and he garnered strong support from historically marginalized groups in the election. Crow knew that his district was diverse—indeed, more than 10 percent of voters there were naturalized citizens—and Crow leaned into the idea that he could represent their interests in Washington (Cordell 2020). He and his staff focused on immigrant and detainee challenges in Washington during his first term. For example, Crow joined a bipartisan coalition of lawmakers supporting the Dignity for Detained

114   Staying in the Fight

Immigrants Act. This bill was designed to end the use of private detention facilities for immigrants and improve transparency across the government. Drawing on experiences of refugees and immigrants in his district, plus particular frustrations with the privately run ICE detention facility in Aurora, Crow argued, "Our immigration system should reflect our values as a nation and affirm that all people deserve to be treated with dignity and decency. Instead, our immigration detention system is driven by corporate greed. Since taking office, I have fought for accountability and to bring an end to the for-profit immigration detention system. The Dignity for Detained Immigrants Act is a step forward towards reforming our broken immigrant system" (Cordell 2020).

When it came to Afghanistan policy, Crow was determined to build a broad advocacy network to pursue his foreign and security policy goals. In 2019, Crow and others attempted to pressure the Trump administration to consider retaining a modest deployment of several thousand US Special Forces and counterterrorism units in Afghanistan, with the goal of providing assistance to the Afghan government and stabilizing the region. But once the Trump administration completed its deal with the Taliban—and President Biden affirmed that he would honor its terms—Crow became even more committed to advocacy on behalf of SIV applicants. Crow and some of his fellow members of Congress formed the new Honoring Our Promises Working Group that was expressly bipartisan in nature. The group included ten Democrats and six Republicans at its founding, including a number of WoT veterans like Adam Kinzinger (R-IL), Mike Waltz (R-FL), Peter Meijer (R-MI), and others. Members adopted an aggressive advocacy posture, championing the cause of support for Afghans who had aided the US war effort. In one of the group's first letters to the president (and shared with the media), they emphasized the national security imperative of demonstrating support and resolve to support its local allies, promoting a whole of government plan to aid Afghanistan. And in particular, they focused on the SIV programs, arguing, "The current SIV process will not work. It takes an average of 800+ days, and we plan to withdraw in less than 100 days. . . . No U.S. entity—to include the Department of Defense, Department of State, USAID, et al—has the ability or authority to protect them in Afghanistan after our withdrawal." They concluded, "It would be a moral failure to transfer the responsibility to protect our Afghan partners onto the shoulders of the Afghan Government. The time is now to honor our promise and evacuate Afghan SIV applicants." In June 2021, Crow and members of the Honoring Our Promises Working Group introduced a new bill H.R. 3985 titled the Averting Loss of Life and Injury by Expediting SIVs (ALLIES) Act, which was designed to protect Afghan partners by expediting the Afghan Special Immigrant Visa (SIV) process as the US withdrew from Afghanistan (quoted in Simon 2021).

Crow's staff adopted an inside/outside advocacy strategy—working inside the government on legislation and pressure on the administration, while at the same time drumming up grassroots support from nongovernmental organizations for immigration policy reforms. Crow's office consciously constructed coalitions in support of policy reforms, drawing on statements and testimony from NGOs and prominent foreign policy and military authorities outside of government. This included regular outreach to dignitaries like former secretaries of defense Chuck Hagel and Robert Gates, and former National Security advisers Steven Hadley and H. R. McMaster. And they also networked with supportive NGOs who became engaged in rallying protections for Afghans were veterans organizations like the American Legion, Vets for American Ideals, the Military Chaplains Association of the United States of America (MCA), Military Order of the Purple Heart (MOPH), the Reserve Officers of America (ROA), VoteVets, and the Korean War Veterans Association. Other organizations that participated in the broader advocacy coalition were groups devoted to human rights and the plight of immigrants, including the group No One Left Behind and the National Immigration Forum (author's interview, October 26, 2021).

As the crisis in Afghanistan continued to unfold, Crow and his colleagues became much more focused on rescuing SIV applicants and other Afghan civilians who supported the US military mission and causes like human rights, women's rights, and democracy in that country. Supporters intensified their call on the Biden administration to expedite the visa process and protect SIV applicants and their families who face threats from the Taliban. Specifically, the ALLIES Act would streamline visa processing and evacuations from the country for supporting allies. It would immediately raise the SIV allotment by an additional eight thousand visas to cover all potentially eligible applicants, amend the "credible threat" requirement that involved paperwork to prove a threat to those who worked with the United States, strengthen protections for families, and expand eligibility to Afghans who worked for NGOs "performing critical democracy, human rights, and governance work." Crow strongly supported this initiative, arguing: "For twenty years, Afghan interpreters, guides, and other partners have served alongside U.S. forces, helping us complete our mission. I may not be here today were it not for the bravery and sacrifice of the Afghan men and women who worked with me during my service. As we withdraw from Afghanistan, we must honor our promises and protect those that protected us. The ALLIES Act increases the visa cap for our Afghan partners and improves the visa process so that we can process visas safely and efficiently. Time is running out for us to do the right thing and I am grateful for the support of my colleagues to pass this bill." The Biden administration also issued a Statement of Administration Policy on the ALLIES Act, calling the changes "critical to expediting the application process and helping us get more Afghan partners through the process and into safety." The bill passed the House on July 22, 2021, by a vote of 407 to 16.

116   Staying in the Fight

However, by July 2021, just as the legislative wheels of Washington were finally turning on Afghanistan policy, it became clear that this would not be enough. The Taliban were quickly advancing on Kabul while US forces departed from the country. Instead of a well-coordinated refugee resettlement program, a new form of advocacy campaign began: Congressman Crow and his fellow WoT veterans who were concerned about the situation on the ground in Afghanistan began hearing from their regular network of nongovernmental organizations (and brand-new ones that had sprung up overnight) that a massive ad hoc rescue operation had begun for SIV applicants and other Afghans who sought refuge from the Taliban. Veterans in Congress along with scores of civil society groups (including many veterans' organizations) launched into action with government-authorized and privately funded rescue operations for Afghan SIV applicants and other vulnerable populations. To military veterans in Congress, the reality of the situation quickly sank in: Afghans who supported the US military, including thousands with pending SIV applications, were facing imminent danger (Simon 2021).

Crow and his colleagues opened up a network for emergency communications, and the offices of at least eight members of Congress who were also members of the Honoring Our Promises group began to share data and information on circumstances on the ground (de Yoanna 2021). By opening a virtual command center the members and their staffs found common ground for trying to tackle some of the humanitarian and logistical challenges of the crisis in Kabul. They centered their attention on tracking SIV applicants and family members with connections to their districts who were attempting to pass through key gates at the airport in Kabul and join flights to freedom. The crisis escalated, though, as tens of thousands of Afghans flocked to the airport and tried to appeal to multinational forces there that they should be evacuated (author's interview, October 26, 2021). Crow expressed his frustration publicly, telling the press, "We didn't need to be seeing the scenes that we're seeing at Kabul Airport with our Afghan friends climbing aboard C-17s. That's why a very broad bipartisan group of us since April has been very clear that we should have started this evacuation months ago and had we done that, tens of thousands of folks could have been brought to safety." They continued to work with key advocacy groups, along with a virtual flotilla of rescue networks staffed by veterans themselves. This became a form of advocacy at the most fundamental level, with veterans on Capitol Hill determined to try to right what they saw were the wrongs of the Biden administration on Afghanistan withdrawal (Baran, Horton, and Dwoskin 2021).

Outcome: Saving Lives in Afghanistan

Special Immigrant Visa programs for allies in Afghanistan and Iraq had been established for more than a decade when Jason Crow took office, but members of Congress were only slowly coming to terms with this difficult situation. In reality, there were few primary advocates for the SIV programs in Congress who personalized the issues and really championed the causes of Afghans and Iraqis early on, but this changed with the arrival of a larger group of WoT veterans in Congress who had direct connections to this situation. These veterans became critical advocates for expanding support for SIV applicants.

When President Biden ordered that all US troops should be withdrawn from Afghanistan before September 11, 2021, it soon became clear that protections for SIV applicants had not been thought through. The Biden administration's rapid timetable for withdrawal was certainly problematic, but experts have also noted that it was representative of deeper and long-term miscalculations in prior administrations. Indeed, the Trump administration officials had been purposefully obstructionist in their approaches to SIV programs. And US government predictions that it would take years for the Taliban to gain momentum in Afghanistan following the US withdrawal were wildly off the mark. The withdrawal of four thousand soldiers from the Bagram Air Base seemed to open the floodgates for the Taliban. In the weeks that followed, troops tried to keep the US embassy open and staffers processing SIV applications for those who wanted to leave the country, but that position became untenable (Shear et al. 2021). During this same period, the Taliban surrounded and then began to take control of the Afghan capital, Kabul, and concentrate its forces around the sole remaining US military position at the Hamid Karzai International Airport. Thousands of desperate Afghans rushed to the airport and tried to get on the remaining commercial and military flights out of the country.

Ironically, just as the legislative wheels of Washington were finally turning on Afghanistan policy, it became clear this would not be enough. The United States presence in that country was falling apart, and the government itself seemed unwilling to take major action that could further endanger US troops. Veterans on Capitol Hill and civil society actors leapt into that vacuum by sponsoring both government-authorized and privately funded rescue operations for Afghan SIV applicants and other vulnerable populations. Crow and other WoT veterans in Congress directed their staffs to track SIV applicants and family members with connections to their districts and find ways to help them pass through key gates at the airport in Kabul and join flights to freedom. They used both personal connections and pressure campaigns inside the government to influence bureaucratic decisions. Notably, Crow and other advocates said that when the State Department proved unresponsive in particular cases, they would simply go around them by using their direct contacts with US veterans and even active-duty troops on the ground. While there were some differences of opinion about how and where refugees should be processed (e.g., groups like No One Left Behind favored a mass evacuation to a US military base in Guam, while others favored regional processing centers), advocates shared a common commitment to achieve the goal of assisting Afghan refugees. In the

118   Staying in the Fight

end, the United States supported the rescue of almost 130,000 Afghans from Kabul in the final six weeks of airlift operations.

Finally, it is important to note that lawmakers have continued to debate protections for Afghan SIV applicants and refugees in the United States and other countries. About 70,000 Afghans have lived in the United States under temporary humanitarian parole status since 2021, but that provision was set to expire in 2023. Members of Congress advanced a series of bills and amendments to the 2023 NDAA, such as the Afghan Adjustment Act, which would have granted Afghans a pathway to legal permanent residency. Similarly, Mike Waltz cosponsored the Support Our Afghan Partners Act (H.R. 8628), which was designed to protect Afghans who still sought to flee Afghanistan through legal channels. However, these and other provisions that would have clarified the legal and political status of Afghan refugees in the United States failed to pass in the final version of the NDAA. At this writing (fall 2023), many Afghans are living in a precarious legal limbo.

6

War on Terror Veterans and Public Health

Military veterans in Congress have been concerned about the health, safety, and well-being of active-duty soldiers and veterans since the founding of the country. Lawmakers' focus on these issues, often motivated by personal experiences, has helped prompt the federal government to build stronger networks for care and benefits for veterans over time (Baker 2014). The government established the first veterans' hospitals during World War I, developed the GI Bill to promote college and vocational training during World War II, and created long-term care programs for disabled veterans. In 1989, the Department of Veterans Affairs (VA) was formally established as a cabinet-level bureaucracy in 1989, with a primary mission to serve US military veterans and provide for their health and well-being (Gordon 2018).[1] The VA bureaucracy employs hundreds of thousands of people who assist millions of military veterans and administer a wide range of policies and programs, from health care benefits (via the single largest integrated hospital system in the nation) to disability pensions, education benefits, job search services, tax codes, education, and life insurance, among others (Adler 2017; Ortiz 2015).

However, despite its many achievements, the VA has struggled over the years to provide sufficient care to meet demand—and especially to address certain types of illnesses and disabilities of soldiers that occurred during the WoT (Baker 2014). Two of the most significant health challenges for WoT veterans have been illnesses related to exposure to toxic plumes and particulates in the air around "burn pits" on military bases and post-traumatic stress disorder (Slatore et al. 2018). This chapter explores the advocacy of WoT veterans and Representatives Elaine Luria (D-VA) and Steve Stivers (R-OH) to promote needed reforms in VA care and treatment policies.

119

The Challenge: WoT Veterans Affairs and Public Health

As the scope of veterans' care has expanded considerably throughout the history of the United States, it is perhaps unsurprising that the government has faced many challenges. For example, the Continental Congress offered incentives for soldiers to fight in the American Revolution, including limited care and pension programs for disabled veterans; these were expanded in the years following the War of 1812 to create a separate and exclusive system for veterans (Stevens 1991; Weber and Schmeckebier 1934). During the Civil War, the Union government established a program with expanded pension benefits to all soldiers administered by the new Pension Bureau. The Union government also created its first system of hospitals for wounded veterans (Adler 2017; Lasker 1980). However, as the number of veterans in the United States grew, so, too, did their political voice as a lobby that could pressure the government for better care and assistance programs. Former soldiers of the Union Army began to organize as a group in the 1860s, for example, calling themselves the Grand Army of the Republic, and they lobbied the government for more benefits (Kinder 2015).

In the twentieth century, groups like the American Legion and the Veterans of Foreign Wars (VFW) were created to lobby against inequities in the system, and they challenged the federal government to improve its support for veterans (Lasker 1980). Veterans of World War I became increasingly dissatisfied with government attention to veterans affairs.[2] That war created a new cohort of veterans in a relatively short period of time (1917–19): nearly 300,000 veterans from the war could require medical care and financial support, and the federal government faltered in its response efforts (Adkins 1967; Stevens 1991). As pressure built for government protections, veterans groups also worked with sympathetic members of Congress, including fellow veterans on Capitol Hill, to achieve their goals. For example, the 1932 march on Washington by the Bonus Army involved more than 40,000 veterans of World War I who sought cash payments from the government for lost wages from their period of military service.[3] Sympathetic members of the House of Representatives, including World War I veteran Representative Wright Patman (D-TX), sponsored legislation to provide more payments to veterans at the time. Later, World War II produced the largest cohort of military veterans in US history, presenting new challenges for the federal government. While there were substantial debates in Congress over the scope of benefits for a new generation of veterans, lawmakers ultimately adopted a broader or more generous social safety net for them (Ortiz 2015; Sparrow 2011). Some of these initiatives were articulated in the 1944 Servicemen's Readjustment Act, which also became known as the GI Bill (Kinder 2015; Gordon 2018). Thirty years later, Vietnam War veterans received job assistance, disability support, and life insurance, for example, and the GI

War on Terror Veterans and Public Health   121

Bill helped thousands of veterans attain a college education or advanced job training. Meanwhile, the costs of those services continued to rise (Burtin 2020).

Veterans of the War on Terror and Burn Pit Exposure

Many members of a new generation of WoT veterans have required VA medical care and social services. As noted in chapter 1, WoT veterans experienced higher rates of disabilities and injuries from wartime service on average than previous cohorts. One study found that individuals who fought in the WoT had a 43 percent chance of suffering a service-related disability, and they also had a higher chance of surviving serious injuries than prior generations (Olenick, Flowers, and Diaz 2015; Goldberg 2010). WoT veterans also suffered a large number of illnesses that experts believed could be linked to their exposure to toxic plumes from burn pits during their service in Iraq and Afghanistan. Burn pits were typically large, open-air pits used as landfills for waste located on bases and outposts. Regulations drafted by the US Central Command (CENTCOM) called for camp environmental officers to dispose of solid waste through burn pits and landfill operations (author's interview, September 21, 2021). While official guidance called for proper methods for waste disposal that would protect the health and safety of coalition forces, the reality on the ground was that burn pits were often the first form of waste disposal created in new camps or base areas. They were set up hastily to accommodate needs, and jet fuel and other compounds were sometimes used as accelerants to maintain the fires (Coughlin and Szema 2019).

Hundreds or perhaps even thousands of open-air burn pits were used during operations in the WoT in the Middle East to dispose of garbage, medical waste, and other waste from military installations—including large quantities of plastics and polystyrene that could produce known carcinogens and hazardous pollutants in the air (Taylor, Rush, and Deck 2008; Poisson et al. 2020). Millions of soldiers were potentially exposed to toxic plumes, but the effects of that exposure could take time to manifest: Some WoT veterans who escaped direct injury in combat returned home ostensibly healthy, only later to find out they were suffering from lung diseases, cancers, and autoimmune diseases that they believed were caused by exposure to toxic military (author's interview, September 22, 2021). Unfortunately, though, the federal government was slow to acknowledge the scope of these dangers and to respond. The VA maintained that the burden of proof was on veterans to prove a direct connection between illnesses or disabilities and their military service—a particularly tough challenge when illnesses developed years after soldiers' initial deployments (Szema et al. 2017). Concerned veterans, advocacy groups, and members of Congress who began to champion the cause of burn pit victims found that even with the accumulating evidence, fighting the federal government was quite difficult

122 Staying in the Fight

(Tam and Lee 2021; Sharkey, Schickedanz, and Baird 2014). Finally, in the late 2010s, members of Congress began to build support for new and progressive legislative solutions along with executive policies designed to respond to the pressing challenge (author's interview, October 18, 2021).

Veterans and Post-Traumatic Stress Disorder

Post-traumatic stress disorder (PTSD) is a mental health disorder typically associated with exposure to catastrophic circumstances or life events, whether for civilians or military veterans. Traumatic experiences may include anything from surviving natural disasters, pandemics, or personal injury in the civilian world to military deployments and exposure to combat. PTSD at its extremes can severely negatively affect mental and physical health, impair daily functioning, and reduce quality of life (Seal et al. 2009). According to the Department of Veterans Affairs, military veterans experience on average higher rates of prevalence of PTSD compared to their civilian counterparts. The disorder has received greater attention from the medical community (including revision of PTSD criteria in the *Diagnostic and Statistical Manual of Mental Disorders* [*DSM*] in the 2010s) (Aggarwal 2015).

Greater attention to the effects of PTSD in the veterans community has prompted improved awareness and health care measures (Cormack 2018). The VA has strengthened its regularized screening protocols among veterans' populations over the past two decades and improved access to care and counseling in VA facilities during the WoT. Among the improvements has been the greater availability of in-patient psychiatric care and protection against veteran suicides. The Department of Defense has also worked to promote education and reduce the stigma associated with seeking mental health treatment (Rhidenour, Barrett, and Blackburn 2019). In 2019, Representative Seth Moulton (D-MA), a Marine veteran who was running for president, disclosed that he sought treatment for PTSD after his combat deployments during the Iraq War (Thompson 2019). In 2021, Marine veteran and Democrat congressman from Arizona Ruben Gallego disclosed that he and many fellow members from his unit who served in Iraq suffered from PTSD. He hoped that the American public would recognize and respect the challenges, saying, "Veterans aren't this scared individual that's just hiding out in his house or a violent man ready to explode," he said. "We are people that are walking around every day, living our lives and still carrying this burden on our shoulders" (Gallego 2021, 161).

Similar to the burn pits issue, members of Congress and concerned organizations like the American Legion and IAVA have also pushed for significant reforms in mental health care access. They have called on the VA to do even more to promote mental health care and suicide prevention programs and to establish ready resources for injured soldiers. In one government response in the mid-2010s, for example, the VA expanded access for veterans to hospitals and mental health organizations technically outside their network (Stroupe et al. 2019). It also authorized more study of government mental health care programs and expanded access to counseling and support through telehealth programs (Vest et al. 2018). In 2019, President Trump signed new legislation from Congress that would expand the Veterans Choice Program by allowing greater access to immediate care in the public system for veterans in need. Nevertheless, the scope of the problem would demand even more creative responses from Congress and the executive branch.

Representative Elaine Luria (D-VA): Bipartisan Advocacy for Veterans' Health Care

Lawmakers in Washington were alarmed by mounting evidence that veterans from the WoT were suffering from unexpected, specific illnesses that might be associated with their deployments to Iraq and Afghanistan. For Democrat representative Elaine Luria from Virginia, these circumstances were all too real. She had commanded naval vessels for two decades and had extensive training in the nuclear-powered fleet. Luria was well aware of the severity of health risks associated with military operations, and she was deeply committed to veterans' health and safety concerns as a delegate from the district with the single highest concentration of veterans anywhere in the United States. The most prudent way to manage this situation, Luria believed, was to balance the inquiry on burn pits with public pressure and a call for transparency in public health measures. Luria joined with like-minded colleagues, including WoT veterans, to promote a more cohesive VA response both through traditional channels and public advocacy. This case study also details the achievements of this campaign, including the presumptive shift in the burden of proof away from veterans and to deployment conditions, legislation, and additional executive branch actions.

Distinctive Motivations

Elaine Luria was born in 1975 and grew up in Birmingham, Alabama. Luria attended high school at Birmingham's Indian Springs School and then earned an appointment to the US Naval Academy ("Another Way to Serve" 2018). Luria graduated in 1997 as a commissioned officer and then attended the US Naval Nuclear Power School in South Carolina. She also earned her master's in engineering management from Old Dominion University in Norfolk in 2004 (Luria 2019).[4] Luria was an active-duty member of the US Navy from 1997 to 2017,

124 *Staying in the Fight*

serving for twenty years as a surface warfare officer and nuclear engineer. Luria was one of the first women in the Navy's nuclear power program and one of the few to serve her entire career on combat ships. Luria commanded ships stationed in Japan twice in addition to serving as an officer on destroyers, cruisers, and aircraft carriers based in the Middle East and western Pacific. During the last three years of her active-duty service (2014–17), she ranked as commander of the Assault Craft Unit 2, working with hundreds of sailors seconded to the Marine Corps. Throughout her service as a naval commander, Luria was known for her keen intellect and moderated leadership style (Portnoy 2019b).

Following her retirement from military service, Luria returned home to Norfolk, Virginia, and managed small businesses in the area. She announced that she would run for the House of Representatives in 2018 to represent the Virginia Second District, which includes Hampton Roads and the region around the Norfolk US Navy base (Bartel 2018). This is a purple district, in that it includes equal proportions of voters who identified as Democrats and Republicans. It also remains notable for its high concentration of active-duty military personnel and military veterans, including roughly eighty thousand veterans under the age of sixty-five. One in five residents of the district were either active-duty military, veterans, or their relatives. Luria ran a successful campaign in 2018 and flipped the seat from Republican control by defeating incumbent Scott Taylor by just two percentage points (Goldberg 2020).

When Luria arrived in Washington, she was awarded by leadership with a seat on the House Committee on Armed Service and in the subcommittees on Seapower and Projection Forces and Readiness. She was also named to the Committee on Veterans' Affairs, and she became chair of the Subcommittee on Disability Assistance and Memorial Affairs and a member of the Subcommittee on Oversight and Investigations. Luria quickly became known in Congress for her bipartisan and pragmatic approach, and she joined the Problem Solvers Caucus and the New Democrat Coalition. Luria championed veterans' causes from the start of her time in Washington. She and her staff became interested in the burn pits issue almost immediately, researching the results from some of the early studies by groups like the Armed Forces Health Surveillance Center and the Naval Health Research Center that found no conclusive links between exposure and health effects (Poisson et al. 2020). But Luria and her staff suspected that there was more to the story, and her early advocacy was also informed by news of lawsuits filed by veterans in federal courts alleging that the private military contractors, including Kellogg Brown & Root Services Inc. and Halliburton Company, which ran the burn pit operations, were negligent and responsible for health disorders. In 2013, a consolidated package of lawsuits was considered by the US District Court in Maryland, but the court dismissed the claim.[5]

Issue Framing through Personal Narratives

Two of the issues that Luria championed on Capitol Hill were boosting defense spending and veterans' health care. Luria supported higher defense spending by the federal government, with particular attention to spending for the Navy (author's interview, October 18, 2021). One of the rationales for more spending, Luria argued, was the critical need to adopt a more assertive posture against China's expanding influence by deploying more naval and air assets in the Asia-Pacific theater (Weissert 2021). She was also willing to speak truth to power and to ask tough questions. During a visit to her district by Chairman of the Joint Chiefs of Staff Mark Milley in 2021, for example, he said that Luria "asks tough questions all the time, pins my ears against the wall on many, many topics" (Weissert 2021). In the years that followed, Luria would also be named to the House Homeland Security Committee and, later, to the high-profile Select Committee on the January 6 Attack (Hickey 2022).

As chair of the Subcommittee on Disability Assistance and Memorial Affairs, Luria also had a strong platform to draw connections between her personal and political narratives around veterans' health care and the burn pit controversy. She argued, "There is no higher priority to me than fighting for those who chose to serve their country in uniform. As a 20-year Navy veteran, I know firsthand the unique challenges and opportunities that our veterans face as they transition out of service" (Luria 2020b). The congresswoman made strong arguments in support of veterans' care, and she argued that any question of health effects of toxic plume exposure during deployments should be handled responsibly by the VA (author's interview, October 18, 2021). In 2019, Luria championed H.R. 299, the Blue Water Navy Vietnam Veterans Act by leading a subcommittee hearing on the issue and speaking on the House floor in favor of action. This bill was designed to extend and provide additional veterans' benefits for Vietnam War veterans who served at sea off the shore in the so-called Blue Water Navy (within twelve miles of the coastline) but who were exposed to defoliants and herbicides used in the war. For decades, claims to the VA of linked illnesses had been held up in a series of court challenges. Luria said on the House floor, "As a Navy veteran myself, this issue hits close to home, specifically in Coastal Virginia." "The goal of the bill," she said, was to "correct an injustice for veterans who are suffering and dying from conditions related to Agent Orange exposure, and who have been unfairly denied VA disability and health benefits for more than four decades." The bill was very popular; it drew more than three hundred cosponsors and was quickly passed into law.

Congresswoman Luria also led subcommittee and committee hearings on burn pit exposure for WoT veterans in the fall of 2020, focused on understanding health effects and probing ways to enhance government provisions of medical assistance. Witnesses represented a mix of civil society groups and medical experts. Luria opened the first hearing with a statement that tried to validate some of those claims. She stated, for soldiers deployed to the Middle East, their "environment was filled with dust and debris brought by sandstorms and exacerbated by burn pits, which indiscriminately exposed our service-members to hazards" (House Committee on Veterans' Affairs Hearing Report #116-698 2020). Lawmakers and witnesses cited a report from the Congressional Research Service that found that 78 percent of veterans who have applied for service connection due to toxic exposures have been denied since 2007 (Transcript of Hearing 2020). Luria repeatedly made connections between personal and political narratives, arguing, "I don't understand why everyone here is so content with the status quo because I really do think the VA is letting down our veterans, especially in the area of toxic exposures. We should work to break down barriers and take the burden off the veteran to fight for that health care" (Luria 2020a).

Bill Cosponsorship and Bipartisanship

From the start of her time in Congress, Luria made clear that she was committed to cosponsoring bills across the political aisle. She joined the bipartisan Problem Solvers Caucus and the New Democrat Coalition, and she also began cosponsoring legislation with Republicans in the caucus within months of taking office (Weissert 2021; Flynn 2021). Explaining her decision to seek a middle ground, Luria said that in the Navy, she "didn't think much about political party. I voted for the guy in '16 who I ran against in '18 . . . I think of myself as really moderate," she added (Weissert 2021). Luria also moved very rapidly to support legislation related to veterans' affairs. By the spring of 2021, with just two full years in office, Luria had actually sponsored or cosponsored over one hundred pieces of veteran legislation (see table 6.1). Once again, she knew not only that would this offer a pragmatic way to find solutions to policy challenges but also that the makeup of her district effectively demanded such an approach. As Mary Kaszynski of VoteVets described it, it is veterans like Luria who try to solve problems and forge bipartisan coalitions to keep issues on the agenda. Whenever other members of Congress "might try to 'punt' on an issue, veterans of Iraq and Afghanistan try to hold them to the issue and want to maintain focus when needed to solve problems" (author's interview, November 16, 2021). They do so out of both shared commitments and concerns and a level of "mutual respect that comes from having served," she added.

In the spring of 2021, Luria built on this momentum by introducing H.R. #2368, the Conceding Our Veterans' Exposure Now and Necessitating Training Act (COVENANT Act), which was designed to secure additional medical care for soldiers who were exposed to toxic plumes during deployments in the

Table 6.1. Sample of Representative Luria's Record of Bill Sponsorship and Cosponsorship

Label	Title	Introduced	Status
H.R. 5776	Serving Our LGBTQ Veterans Act	October 28, 2021	Introduced in House
H.R. 5543	Vet CENTERS for Mental Health Act of 2021	October 8, 2021	Introduced in House
H.R. 1448	Puppies Assisting Wounded Servicemembers for Veterans Therapy Act	March 1, 2021	Became Public Law
H.R. 5073	REACH for Veterans Act	August 23, 2021	Introduced in House
H.R. 4104	Vanessa Guillén Military Justice Improvement and Increasing Prevention Act	June 23, 2021	Introduced in House
H.R. 4021	Representation for Exceptional Military Families Act	June 17, 2021	Introduced in House
H.R. 3909	Veterans' Compensation Cost-of-Living Adjustment Act of 2021	June 15, 2021	Introduced in House
H.R. 3674	Vet Center Support Act	June 1, 2021	Introduced in House
H.R. 3367	Gold Star Children Act	May 20, 2021	Introduced in House
H.R. 3121	Military Child Care Expansion Act of 2021	May 11, 2021	Introduced in House
H.R. 2916	VA Medicinal Cannabis Research Act of 2021	April 30, 2021	Introduced in House
H.R. 2806	Honoring All Veterans Act	April 22, 2021	Introduced in House
H.R. 2368	COVENANT Act of 2021	April 5, 2021	Introduced in House
H.R. 2339	Military Hunger Prevention Act	April 1, 2021	Introduced in House
H.R. 1948	VA Employee Fairness Act of 2021	March 16, 2021	Introduced in House
H.R. 1695	TRICARE Reserve Select Improvement Act	March 9, 2021	Introduced in House
H.R. 1453	Military Spouses Retirement Security Act	March 1, 2021	Introduced in House
H.R. 852	United States–Israel PTSD Collaborative Research Act	February 4, 2021	Introduced in House

Continued

128   *Staying in the Fight*

Table 6.1. Sample of Representative Luria's Record of Bill Sponsorship and Cosponsorship (*Continued*)

Label	Title	Introduced	Status
H.R. 475	Health Care Fairness for Military Families Act of 2021	January 25, 2021	Introduced in House
H.R. 148	Jobs and Childcare for Military Families Act of 2021	January 4, 2021	Introduced in House
H.R. 4861	Effective Suicide Screening and Assessment in the Emergency Department Act of 2020	October 28, 2019	Passed House
H.R. 3010	Honoring All Veterans Act	May 23, 2019	Passed House
H.R. 3228	VA Mission Telehealth Clarification Act	June 12, 2019	Passed House
H.R. 4864	Global Child Thrive Act of 2020	October 28, 2019	Passed House
H.R. 7795	Veterans Benefits Fairness and Transparency Act of 2020	July 27, 2020	Passed House
H.R. 8172	VA Research Technology Act	September 4, 2020	Introduced in House
H.R. 8144	VA Mental Health Staffing Act	September 1, 2020	Introduced in House
H.R. 8130	VA Peer Specialists Act	August 28, 2020	Introduced in House
H.R. 8015	Delivering for America Act	August 11, 2020	Passed House
H.R. 7927	Military Spouses Retirement Security Act	August 4, 2020	Introduced in House
H.R. 7176	Health Care Fairness for Military Families Act of 2020	June 11, 2020	Introduced in House
H.R. 7111	Veterans Economic Recovery Act of 2020	June 4, 2020	Introduced in House
H.R. 7048	Nursing Home Pandemic Protection Act	May 28, 2020	Introduced in House
H.R. 6990	Homeless Veterans CREDIT Act	May 22, 2020	Introduced in House
H.R. 748	CARES Act	January 24, 2019	Debate
H.R. 3598	FREED Vets Act	June 28, 2019	Passed House
H.R. 6141	Protecting Moms Who Served Act	March 9, 2020	Introduced in House
H.R. 6148	TRICARE ECHO Improvement Act	March 9, 2020	Introduced in House

Table 6.1. Sample of Representative Luria's Record of Bill Sponsorship and Cosponsorship (*Continued*)

Label	Title	Introduced	Status
H.R. 6142	Black Maternal Health Momnibus Act of 2020	March 9, 2020	Introduced in House
H.R. 6157	Transparency for Student Veterans Act	March 9, 2020	Introduced in House
H.R. 5697	Veterans' ACCESS Act of 2020	January 28, 2020	Introduced in House
H.R. 5689	Every Veteran Counts Act	January 28, 2020	Introduced in House
H.R. 4817	VA Directly Returning Opioid Prescriptions Act	October 23, 2019	Introduced in House
H.R. 4748	Justice for ALS Veterans Act of 2019	October 18, 2019	Introduced in House
H.R. 95	Homeless Veteran Families Act	January 3, 2019	Passed House
H.R. 1199	VA Website Accessibility Act of 2019	February 13, 2019	Passed House
H.R. 2557	Get Veterans a Doctor Now Act	May 7, 2019	Introduced in House
H.R. 2481	Gold Star Family Tax Relief Act	May 2, 2019	Introduced in House
H.R. 2184	Reach Every Veteran in Crisis Act	April 9, 2019	Introduced in House

Source: Quorum Federal Database 2021. Search terms: *Armed Forces and National Security*; *Health*.

Middle East from 1990 to the present. This act became a focal point for her championing of personal and policy narratives. Luria cosponsored the legislation and spoke on the floor of the House in strong support of the COVENANT Act, further articulating connections between her personal experiences in the military and the toxic plumes issue. She called the act the "first bill addressing toxic exposure to include both a comprehensive list of overseas locations that would qualify a veteran for earned benefits, as well as a comprehensive list of presumptive illnesses contracted as a result of airborne exposure." It was designed to offer very broad coverage for veterans from the Persian Gulf War era in the 1990s to the WoT. Critically, the bill would cover more than fifteen presumptive disabilities, including respiratory conditions such as asthma, chronic obstructive pulmonary disease, chronic bronchitis, and several different types of cancers and ensures qualifying veterans are granted Priority Group

6 VHA health care (Tam and Lee 2021; Luria 2021). Ultimately, Luria said, "We cannot allow history to repeat itself. Veterans like myself watched our peers who served in Vietnam wait decades for the benefits they deserve. The recent veterans who served in the Middle East, Southwest Asia, East Africa, and the Philippines need our help today. They are hurting, and in some cases dying. Congress must not neglect them in their time of need" (Luria 2021).

Luria was quite successful at garnering support for bipartisan veteran legislation, and some bills that she cosponsored advanced rather quickly into law. For example, Luria sponsored the Veterans' Compensation Cost-of-Living Adjustment Act of 2020, which increased compensation for veterans with disabilities. Luria also cosponsored the Johnny Isakson and David P. Roe, MD Veterans Health Care and Benefits Improvement Act of 2020. This bill was designed to provide support for homeless veterans during COVID. It assisted with transportation, telehealth service access, and other basic necessities during the pandemic. It was signed into law in January 2021 (Clark 2021). Luria continued her activism on the part of disabled veterans. She cosponsored the Identifying Barriers and Best Practices Study Act, bipartisan legislation requiring that the Government Accountability Office study disability and pension benefits to members of the National Guard and members of reserve components of the armed forces. Luria was also involved as a supporter of the omnibus CARES Act, a massive federal COVID-19 relief package that included appropriations to the Department of Veterans Affairs for assistance with medical services and many other expenses.

Advocacy Coalitions

Congresswoman Luria and her staff maintained high levels of coordination with advocacy coalitions on issues related to veterans' affairs and health care. She entered office with a clear understanding that she was representing important points of view for veterans and had responsibilities to her constituents and the broader military community. Luria's work also appeared to be well coordinated with concerned groups. Her staff identified a strong advocacy agenda based on pending legislation, and her office "coordinated very closely" with interest groups and even the families of those made ill by exposure to these issues (author's interview, November 16, 2021).

The congresswoman worked closely with other advocacy organizations to promote a strong government response on the burn pits issue. Luria's office both shared government reports with and gathered information from advocacy groups in order to make the strongest case possible. Luria and her staff contended that there was clear evidence that millions of troops were exposed carcinogenic toxic fumes released by burn pits in the Middle East and that the government should be responsive to related health and benefit claims. They cited the fact that the Burn Pits Registry Act passed into law in 2012 had already gathered hundreds of thousands of individual claim information, and there were simply too many possible links to exposure to be ignored. Advocacy groups challenged the high threshold of proof demanded by the VA that exposure-related illnesses had a direct service connection. The onus of truth, they argued, should not be on individuals with limited means (author's interview, November 8, 2021). Her office worked especially closely with the legislative liaisons from the American Legion and the Iraq and Afghanistan Veterans of America (IAVA). In committee and subcommittee hearings in 2020, for example, Luria's staff drew together strong witness lists and letters of support for the case. Among the speakers at the hearings were the National Legislative Director for Disabled American Veterans and the American Legion and the Veterans Health Administration. The committees also read statements into the record from groups like the Military Officers Association of America, the Wounded Warrior Project, and the Veterans Healthcare Policy Institute.

Together, this broad coalition of activists, both inside and outside the government, advanced the argument that millions of veterans might have been exposed to burn pits and suffer rare cancers and respiratory illnesses, but the VA continued to deny many claims. By the winter of 2021, Luria's office was working even more closely with advocacy groups on legislation like the Honoring Our Promise to Address Comprehensive Toxics (PACT) Act. These groups included the nonprofit group Disabled American Veterans (DAV), the Military Officers Association of America, Iraq and Afghanistan Veterans of America, the Wounded Warrior Project, Burn Pits 360, and the Veterans of Foreign Wars. Their collective goal was to promote legislation that would provide health care, shift the burden of proof away from veterans by establishing a list of diseases presumed to be linked to toxic plume exposure and to create a better framework for treatment and support. Through significant inside-outside advocacy initiatives, the House passed the PACT Act on March 3, 2022, and groups expected that the issue would be voted on in the Senate by the end of May.

Outcome: Changes for Veterans' Health Care

Representative Luria was very successful at advocacy for veterans through pressure for executive branch policy changes and legislation. By the spring of 2021, Luria had actually sponsored or cosponsored more than one hundred pieces of legislation on veterans' affairs. She was especially active in promoting executive actions to respond to burn pits exposure, including the expansion of the VA's Airborne Hazards and Open Burn Pit registry to include a wider range of veterans who might have been exposed to different types of toxins. She and her fellow veterans on Capitol Hill produced legislation for a fast track to disability compensation for certain veterans who developed asthma, rhinitis, or sinusitis

132   Staying in the Fight

because of their exposure to burn pits during overseas deployments. She also helped pressure the Biden administration to change VA policies to process disability claims for certain conditions on a presumptive basis. In the spring of 2021, new VA secretary Denis McDonough initiated a federal rulemaking process to create a fast track to health care and disability compensation for some veterans suffering from respiratory illnesses.[6]

By 2020, Luria's bill on health care for toxic plume exposure had joined a field of more than a dozen similar bills trying to make the case for concerned government action. One of the dominant pieces of legislation that emerged in this mix was the Senate bill titled the Presumptive Benefits for War Fighters Exposed to Burn Pits and Other Toxins Act, cosponsored by Kirsten Gillibrand (D-NY) and Marco Rubio (R-FL). This bill—which had companion legislation advanced in the House by Representative Raul Ruiz (D-CA), a member of the House Committee on Veterans' Affairs—was more narrow in scope than the one favored by Luria. A primary concern driving Senate approaches was the projected cost of legislation, with the Congressional Budget Office estimate putting the bill's cost at over $300 billion over the next decade (Tasolides 2022). Like Luria's bill, their proposed legislation was designed to remove the "burden of proof" from the veteran to provide enough evidence to establish a direct service connection between their health condition and exposure, but criteria and coverage were to be more limited. Ultimately, some of the core items in Luria's bill were incorporated into the bipartisan Honoring Our Promise to Address Comprehensive Toxins Act (or the Honoring Our PACT Act), which was passed by the House in March 2022. The bill would expand VA coverage to millions of Iraq and Afghanistan veterans who might have been exposed to toxins and would establish a presumption of service connection for two dozen different respiratory illnesses and cancers (Associated Press 2022). Supporters gathered for a rally on Capitol Hill to celebrate passage of the legislation, and they urged the Senate to take it up as soon as possible (American Legion 2022).

As congressional debate on competing forms of legislation dragged on, the Biden administration announced that it was ordering the VA to begin a pilot program that would affect policy changes. The Department of Veterans Affairs began processing claims for veterans suffering from asthma, rhinitis, and sinusitis that were presumed to be linked to exposure to the pits. The president also directed the VA to conduct a comprehensive study of rare cancers and other conditions and report back in ninety days. In support of these actions, VA secretary Denis McDonough said publicly that the United States needed to do more on the matter. While he acknowledged that the "biggest challenge there is proving the scientific connection between those chemicals and that cancer," he said VA policies would change: "If it's a close call, we're going to resolve those in favor of the vet" (quoted in Kube 2021). President Biden also devoted time to the issue during his State of the Union address. The president said that he would expand VA disability and health care benefits to veterans suffering from nine rare respiratory cancers. He said, "We can and must do more to address the harms that come from hazardous exposures, which have gone unaddressed for far too long. We learned a horrible lesson after Vietnam, when the harmful effects of exposure to Agent Orange sometimes took years to manifest, and too many veterans were left unable to access the care they needed. I refuse to repeat that mistake when it comes to veterans of our wars in Iraq and Afghanistan." Those orders took effect in April 2022 (Saenz 2022).

Finally, the activism of Luria and other concerned veterans helped to build momentum for Senate consideration of the Honoring Our PACT Act in the summer of 2022. Hundreds of supporters, including wounded veterans, gathered in late July 2022 in the Senate chamber and outside the Capitol for what they expected to be a celebration of the passage of burn pits legislation, but in a last-minute set of parliamentary maneuvers, dozens of Republicans voted against it. This time, though, the Senate's failure to act sparked widespread national outrage, with protests extending around the country. One of Luria's allies in the fight, comedian and activist Jon Stewart, expressed just how upsetting the Senate's maneuver was in a press conference that went viral. Stewart demanded that the Senate act, stating, "It is despicable to continue to use Americans, men and women who are fighting for this country, as a political cause for anger you have about separate issues. . . . I'm used to the hypocrisy; I'm used to all of it. But I am not used to the cruelty. This is an embarrassment to the Senate, to the country, to the founders and all that they profess and hold dear." Days later, thanks to the steadfast support from many WoT veterans in Congress and a grassroots lobbying campaign, Luria and other sponsors of similar legislation were able to force the Senate's hand. The PACT Act was passed by the Senate and signed into law by President Biden in August 2022.

Representative Steve Stivers (R-OH): The PAWS Act and Veterans' Health Care for Post-Traumatic Stress Disorder

Representative Steve Stivers was a Republican from the Fifteenth Congressional District of Ohio who served in Congress from 2011 to 2021—a time period when Stivers was also promoted to the rank of Major General in the Ohio National Guard. In addition to his regular responsibilities with the Guard, Stivers was called up for active duty for a deployment to Kuwait and Iraq during Operation Iraqi Freedom in 2004–5, along with others. Stivers has acknowledged that he drew heavily on his experiences in the military as he began to focus his legislative agenda in Congress on veterans affairs, and he became especially interested in promoting better treatment of post-traumatic stress disorder (PTSD) by the VA. One of Stivers's capstone legislative initiatives was to create a work-therapy program through the VA for veterans to learn the art and

Staying in the Fight

science of training dogs for service. He first sponsored the bipartisan bill titled "Puppies Assisting Wounded Servicemembers (PAWS) for Veterans Therapy Act" (or the PAWS Act) in 2016. However, the VA was reluctant to endorse the program then, and Stivers had to advocate for the program for five years by networking with civil society groups and building broad bipartisan support. That bill was finally signed into law in the spring of 2021, at nearly the same time that Stivers retired from Congress to become the president and chief executive officer for the Ohio Chamber of Commerce (Freking 2021). This case study examines the commitment of WoT veterans to promote bipartisan solutions for treatments for PTSD during an era of polarized politics.

Distinctive Motivations

Steve Stivers was born in Cincinnati, Ohio, and graduated from Ohio State University in 1989 with a bachelor's degree in economics and international relations. Stivers joined the Ohio National Guard in 1988 and continued to serve in Quartermaster and Sustainment Battalions throughout his career. He went on to earn a master's in business administration (MBA) degree at Ohio State and another in strategic services from the US Army War College (Congressional Veterans Caucus 2021). Stivers participated in additional Army officer training programs, including classes at the Army Command and General Staff College, the Army Senior Leader Development Seminar, and the NORTHCOM Joint Task Force Commanders Course (author's interview, December 6, 2021).

Stivers continued his National Guard service while pursuing careers in the private sector and state politics. He worked as a manager in banking and finance in the 1990s, and he became the finance director for the Franklin County Republican Party in Columbus and as a staff member in the Ohio Senate. He ran successfully for an Ohio Senate seat, where he served from 2003 to 2008. During his time in that office, Stivers drew on his banking and finance experiences in service on the Insurance, Commerce and Labor Committee (where he became chair), the Finance and Financial Institutions Committee (vice-chair), the Ways and Means Committee, Judiciary Committees, and the Controlling Board (author's interview, December 6, 2021).

Stivers and his National Guard unit were called up to active duty during Operation Iraqi Freedom, and he had formative experiences there that shaped his political priorities. Stivers served as the battalion commander for the deployment, and his unit was based in Kuwait and completed service rotations in Iraq, Qatar, and Djibouti. Stivers received the Bronze Star Medal, the Global War on Terrorism Service Medal, and other decorations for his military service and experience in a war zone. When he returned home, Stivers decided to run for Congress in 2008 in the Fifteenth District of Ohio against Democrat Mary Jo Kilroy and several conservative third-party candidates. Stivers

War on Terror Veterans and Public Health   135

campaigned on his experience in the banking and financial services sector and military record but lost the election by little more than two thousand votes. In 2010, Stivers doubled down on his military service record and his commitment to small government in his campaign for the seat. His candidacy was further buoyed by a nationwide wave of Tea Party conservativism. Stivers won the 2010 election and joined the new Republican majority in the House. During his time in Washington, Stivers served on the Financial Services Committee and was the ranking member of the Housing, Community Development, and Insurance Subcommittee. Stivers was also very active in sponsoring and cosponsoring legislation to promote veterans' health care, including numerous bills related to veterans' health care and support services. At the same time, Stivers continued to serve in the Ohio National Guard and was promoted to the rank of Major General (author's interview, December 6, 2021).[7]

Issue Framing: Linking Personal and Policy Narratives

Stivers's commitment to veterans health care seems to epitomize the links between personal and professional military experience and policy advocacy. In an interview, Stivers said that in Congress he wanted to "focus on the things that matter, like cutting taxes, improving health care, or ensuring our veterans have the care that they deserve." Not only did Stivers's experiences help inform his approach, the congressman actually said the quiet part out loud: he made a point of publicly drawing these connections on many occasions. He said, "Being a member of the Ohio Army National Guard has given me countless lessons that I rely on every day as a Member of Congress, particularly when it comes to paying it forward for our veterans. Focusing on the mission and never losing sight of the people at the heart of that mission, I believe, makes me a more effective legislator. I am confident that the veterans across the country lean on the lessons they learned in the service, making them assets in every company and community they are a part of" (quoted in Roth 2021).

Stivers clearly described his experiences as helping frame his understanding about veterans' health care. He said, "As a representative for 43,000 veterans, and as a Major General in the Ohio Army National Guard, I know the struggle of the invisible wounds of war." Stivers became a vocal advocate for veterans' health concerns, with a special interest in helping soldiers suffering PTSD. In a personal interview, Stivers said that he focused on post-traumatic stress because the condition had often been marginalized or stigmatized as a dimension of veterans' health care. He said, "My goal in Congress was to draw on my experience and help educate colleagues, and this was an area where I knew I could make a difference. After all, the majority of members around me had never served in the military, so I saw an opportunity to help them understand the challenges" (author's interview, December 6, 2021). Stivers said that he had met "numerous veterans

136 *Staying in the Fight*

struggling with 'the invisible wounds of war'" (quoted in Eaton 2021). On a personal level, he said, "simple interventions can save lives. As a Brigadier General in the Ohio Army National Guard, I understand the sacrifices made by our men and women in uniform, and we owe it to them to explore every possibility that could curb the suicide epidemic facing our veterans" (quoted in Ripon 2020).

The congressman championed a canine therapy program for PTSD treatment beginning in 2016. His goal was to create a work-therapy program through the VA for veterans to learn the art and science of training dogs for service. However, he also knew that there were two primary concerns about the initiative at the time: First, clinical studies of the impact of canine therapy for PTSD treatment were limited and inconclusive at that point. Second, such a program could be very expensive. The VA already authorized the use of assistance animals for veterans with physical mobility issues such as a lost limb, paralysis, or blindness, but they still required nonprofit organizations to pay for them. Program costs could add up quickly: organizations that adopted and trained dogs and prepared them for assisting veterans estimated the cost for individual service dogs at $25,000 each. Preliminary scoring by the Congressional Budget Office for expanded canine therapy for veterans with PTSD estimated that the program could cost the federal government about $19 million per year, even if the VA itself did not pay for the dogs. In addition to concerns about costs, government officials still maintained that the evidence was limited and that service dogs really could help veterans suffering from PTSD (O'Neill 2021).

In the face of such challenges, Stivers shifted focus to build a broader base of cosponsors and tap into grassroots support for VA reforms. He acknowledged that one of the key lessons that he had learned from the military and state level politics was that one "had to be willing to vary your tactics to achieve your goals" (author's interview, December 6, 2021). He knew that studies showed that around 20 percent of veterans were diagnosed with PTSD but only about half sought treatment. Compounding the problem was that nearly half of those who did seek care later dropped out of treatment programs (O'Haire 2010). This was an issue that would require creativity and resolve (Roth 2021). He said, "I believe that the lessons I learned as a soldier have made me a more effective legislator, particularly when it comes to advocating for our veterans." In that spirit, he said that one of his core missions was to find ways to help soldiers "ease the transition from military service to civilian life, especially when it comes to their mental health" (Roth 2021). The congressman also directly referenced his deployments in the WoT, as well as his longtime service in the Guard, as formative (author's interview, December 6, 2021).

Bipartisanship and Legislation

Similar to the level of legislative activism of Representative Luria, Stivers sponsored or cosponsored nearly two hundred bills related to veterans' affairs during his ten years in Congress. Stivers regularly drew connections between the concerns of veterans and the legislative initiatives that he was pursuing. In the spirit of what he called "paying it forward for our veterans," Stivers encouraged his fellow lawmakers to advance programs that were proven to aid and assist those who had sacrificed for the nation (Stivers 2021).

Stivers advanced a series of initiatives to assist with veterans' health care. For example, Stivers cosponsored the Fast Care for Veterans Act of 2016, which directed the VA to pilot an eighteen-month program to provide mobile applications to medical facilities, providing veterans with faster care. This legislation was very popular and drew broad bipartisan support, and it became law on December 16, 2016. During the COVID-19 pandemic, Stivers was a cosponsor of the omnibus CARES Act, which included federal appropriations for the Department of Veterans Affairs in assisting veterans during the pandemic. Stivers also cosponsored the bipartisan Blue Water Navy Vietnam Veterans Act of 2019, recognizing the right of Blue Water Navy veterans to health care compensation related to possible exposure to toxic chemicals. This bill eventually generated an impressive 334 cosponsors in the House and was passed into law in June 2019 (Lutz and Mazzarino 2019; author's interview, November 8, 2021). The congressman also pursued bipartisan veterans programs for the workforce and criminal justice system. In one of his first pieces of legislation, for example, Stivers cosponsored the bipartisan 3 percent Withholding Repeal and Job Creation Act, which was designed to help the transition for veterans returning home and provides support for veterans. The bill was widely popular, and it became law in November 2011. Later, Stivers cosponsored the 2014 Workforce Innovation and Opportunity Act, which required that local employment offices have at least one veteran employment specialist to assist veterans. Stivers also cosponsored the Veterans Treatment Court Improvement Act of 2018 that required the VA to hire dozens of "Veterans Justice Outreach Specialists" to advocate for veterans caught up in state and local court systems for crimes that could be related to the effects of their military service. That bipartisan bill, with fifty-four cosponsors, became law in September 2018 (Stivers 2021).

When Stivers first introduced the PAWS Act in 2016, he acknowledged that the bill did not enjoy broad support. Looking back, he said, "There just wasn't a lot of interest, and the VA argued that the science was still 'out' on whether these programs would help with stress management" (author's interview, December 6, 2021). But Stivers did find cosponsors for his bill among Democrats, including an early supporter and fellow veteran Representative Tim Walz (D-MN). Stivers argued that the program would effectively give veterans a new mission in training therapy dogs that would have the added benefit of helping alleviate their symptoms of post-traumatic stress (PTS) or traumatic brain injury (TBI). Citing evidence from the mental health community and past VA programs, Stivers asserted, "These programs work. They reduce the amount of psychotropic

138 *Staying in the Fight*

drugs that these veterans are on. They reduce suicide. They improve overall mental health. . . . We can't afford to wait any longer" (quoted in Eaton 2021). Stivers's office also promoted results from a VA study that showed pairing service dogs with veterans with post-traumatic stress reduces PTSD symptoms and suicide as well as research from Purdue University and Kaiser Permanente that showed how working with service dogs decreased reported amounts of depression and led to better interpersonal relationships, lower risk of substance abuse, and overall better mental health (Rodriguez et al. 2021). After three years of advocacy, Stivers's legislation first passed the House in 2019, but it stalled out in the Senate.

After several years of persistence pushing against a very crowded legislative agenda and seeming congressional deadlock, Stivers was able to gain renewed momentum with the bill by bringing freshman Congresswoman Mikie Sherrill (D-NJ) on board (author's interview, November 8, 2021). Sherill was a graduate of the US Naval Academy and veteran of active-duty operations in Europe and the Middle East. She had earned her degree from Georgetown University Law School after leaving the Navy and worked in the US Attorney's Office in New Jersey before running for Congress. With Stivers's encouragement, Sherrill quickly adopted this as one of her first legislative campaigns. "Too many of the men and women who serve our country return home with unseen trauma," the former Navy pilot said. "Service dogs soothe the invisible wounds of war," she added. "Researchers, doctors, and veterans report the same thing: service dogs are a transformational form of therapy for our veterans with PTSD." Sherrill further stated, "Service dogs help create bonds of trust and love with veterans, soothing the invisible wounds of war. Right now, it is incredibly expensive and difficult for veterans to access the care that service dogs can provide" (Sherrill 2020). Ultimately, the Stivers-Sherrill partnership helped create more momentum for the bill, and they eventually generated 290 cosponsors for the legislation.[8]

Finally, Stivers also worked in a bipartisan fashion to generate support for federal funding of the new National Veterans Memorial and Museum in Columbus, Ohio. Early efforts to establish the institution were initiated in 2013 by former NASA astronaut and Ohio senator John Glenn (D-OH) and Republican Governor John Kasich. The plan was to be funded with a large donation from billionaire Les Wexner and his family foundation. When Stivers joined the project, it was designed to be an Ohio museum to honor the 900,000 veterans living in Ohio (the sixth-largest concentration of veterans in the United States), but the scope of the project expanded over time. In 2017, Stivers joined Representative Pat Tiberi (R-OH) and their Democrat counterpart representing the Columbus area, Representative Joyce Beatty (D-OH), to introduce H.R. 1900, the National Veterans Memorial and Museum Act, which was then referred to the Veterans' Affairs Subcommittee on Disability Assistance and Memorial

War on Terror Veterans and Public Health 139

Table 6.2. Sample of Representative Stivers's Record of Bill Sponsorship and Cosponsorship

Label	Title	Introduced	Status
H.R. 1029	Free Veterans from Fees Act	February 11, 2021	Passed House
H.R. 1448	Puppies Assisting Wounded Servicemembers for Veterans Therapy Act	March 1, 2021	Became Public Law
H.R. 2806	Honoring All Veterans Act	April 22, 2021	Introduced in House
H.R. 2368	COVENANT Act of 2021	April 5, 2021	Introduced in House
H.R. 2050	Huntington's Disease Disability Insurance Access Act of 2021	March 18, 2021	Introduced in House
H.R. 1695	TRICARE Reserve Select Improvement Act	March 9, 2021	Introduced in House
H.R. 892	Preexisting Conditions Protection Act of 2021	February 5, 2021	Introduced in House
H.R. 2328	Reauthorizing and Extending America's Community Health Act	April 15, 2019	Union Calendar assignment
H.R. 3414	Opioid Workforce Act of 2019	June 21, 2019	Reported by House Committee
H.R. 3010	Honoring All Veterans Act	May 23, 2019	Passed House
H.R. 8345	Air Carrier Worker Support Extension Act of 2020	September 22, 2020	Introduced in House
H.R. 4564	Suicide Prevention Lifeline Improvement Act of 2020	September 27, 2019	Passed House
H.R. 8125	Military Suicide Prevention in the 21st Century Act	August 28, 2020	Introduced in House
H.R. 8107	VA Emergency Department Safety Planning Act	August 25, 2020	Introduced in House
H.R. 8094	Dr. Lorna Breen Health Care Provider Protection Act	August 22, 2020	Introduced in House
H.R. 8004	To amend the Head Start Act to extend the duration of grants under such act, and for other purposes	August 11, 2020	Introduced in House
H.R. 7927	Military Spouses Retirement Security Act	August 4, 2020	Introduced in House

Continued

140 *Staying in the Fight*

Table 6.2. Sample of Representative Stivers's Record of Bill Sponsorship and Cosponsorship (*Continued*)

Label	Title	Introduced	Status
H.R. 7278	JUSTICE Act	June 18, 2020	Introduced in House
H.R. 497	BRAVE Act of 2019	January 11, 2019	Debate
H.R. 5887	Guard and Reserve Hazard Duty Pay Equity Act	February 13, 2020	Introduced in House
H.R. 4817	VA Directly Returning Opioid Prescriptions Act	October 23, 2019	Introduced in House
H.R. 1019	Full Military Honors Act of 2019	February 6, 2019	Introduced in House
H.R. 553	Military Surviving Spouses Equity Act	January 15, 2019	Introduced in House
H.R. 566	Agent Orange Exposure Fairness Act	January 15, 2019	Introduced in House
H.R. 2683	Protecting Veterans Credit Act of 2018	May 25, 2017	Reported by House Committee
H.R. 6	SUPPORT for Patients and Communities Act	June 13, 2018	Became Public Law
H.R. 4252	Foreclosure Relief and Extension for Servicemembers Act	December 15, 2015	Introduced in House
H.R. 313	Wounded Warriors Federal Leave Act of 2015	January 13, 2015	Became Public Law
H.R. 3958	Veterans Health Care Stamp Act	November 5, 2015	Introduced in House
H.R. 3970	Housing Our Heroes Act	November 5, 2015	Introduced in House
H.Res. 631	Supporting the goals and ideals of Posttraumatic Stress Disorder Awareness Month	June 19, 2014	Introduced in House
H.R. 3717	Helping Families in Mental Health Crisis Act of 2013	December 12, 2013	Referred to Committee
H.R. 635	HEALTHY Vets Act of 2013	February 13, 2013	Referred to Committee
H.R. 5948	Veterans Fiduciary Reform and Honoring Noble Service Act	June 12, 2012	Passed House
H.R. 3612	Blue Water Navy Vietnam Veterans Act of 2011	December 8, 2011	Referred to Committee

Source: Quorum Federal Database 2021. Search terms: *Armed Forces and National Security*; *Health*.

Affairs (author's interview, December 6, 2021). Unlike many projects, the goal of the legislation was not to secure federal funding but rather to establish a "national" museum designation. But even this required substantial effort: Stivers drew on his own military experience and testified in committee hearings in favor of it. "It was not something that just flew through the committee," Beatty said at the time. "We put a lot of sweat equity into it." In Stivers's appeals to Congress, he described the project as a bipartisan initiative and an "incredible landmark where we can honor and remember all of our nation's veterans. I am proud to work with Representative Beatty and the countless community leaders who understand the importance of this museum to our veterans, their families, and our entire nation" (quoted in Wehrman 2017). The bill was passed by the House in the fall of 2017, the Senate in the spring of 2018, and signed into law by President Trump that summer. The project, which ultimately cost $75 million, was opened to great fanfare in October 2018 (author's interview, December 6, 2021).

Advocacy Coalitions

Stivers and his staff worked closely with advocacy groups to advance proposals for veterans' affairs health legislation. In his efforts during the mid-2010s, for example, Stivers drew support for mental health initiatives regularly from groups like the VFW and the American Legion, including its office of National Veterans Affairs and Rehabilitation. These and other national organizations had begun to embrace health policy responses for PTSD and other illnesses associated with military service within a few years of the outbreak of the Iraq and Afghanistan Wars, and their lobbyists had found that these issues resonated widely with their own constituencies.

Stivers acknowledged that getting the support of advocacy groups was critical to the success of the PAWS Act and related legislation (author's interview, December 6, 2021). Many organizations became active in the 2000s and 2010s to address the physical and mental toll on soldiers who had served during the WoT. Beyond helping an unprecedented number of soldiers who survived serious injuries like traumatic brain injuries, for example, concerned medical professionals also began to focus more on mental health. The VA and interest groups promoted programs that helped WoT veterans transition from military to civilian life, suicide prevention, mental health care staffing and health care for women veterans. The VA also sponsored new research and initiatives designed to treat mental health care challenges such as depression and anxiety. They also began to develop alternative treatment programs for post-traumatic stress, including experimenting with animal therapy programs, agriculture therapy, sports and recreation therapy, art therapy and post-traumatic growth programs.[9]

142   *Staying in the Fight*

Stivers and his staff worked closely with civil society actors who promoted PTSD and mental health care legislation for veterans. These included groups like the Anxiety and Depression Association of America, the PTSD Foundation, and the National Military Family Association. Similar to the case of Representative Luria's focus on burn pits, Stivers and other WoT veterans in Congress received a significant amount of support from the Iraq and Afghanistan Veterans of America. This organization raised funds for lobbying in support of mental health treatment, and it sponsored its own programs designed to engage veterans across the United States (author's interview, November 9, 2021).

Stivers benefited from advocacy group support, and he sought to overcome traditional obstacles and move the PAWS legislative item up the agenda. Over time, he acknowledged, the PAWS legislation and related initiatives for the treatment of PTSD became "legacy issues" for him as a lawmaker. He maintained a focus on passing these bills right up to the end of his career in Congress, and he drew support from many different sectors. He and his staff reached out to key organizations that supported the development of veteran legislation and programs, including the American Legion and the VFW. Nonprofit groups that were already showing the value of service dogs for physical and mental health assistances, like K9s for Warriors and Canine Companions, also joined the campaign. In the end, Stivers said, he worked with these groups in a larger advocacy campaign that effectively applied pressure to every member of Congress, often including personal visits by therapists and their trained therapy animals to show their effects (author's interview, December 6, 2021).

Outcome: Progress in Veterans' Mental Health Care

Steve Stivers spent his career in Congress fighting for veterans. The Puppies Assisting Wounded Servicemembers (PAWS) for Veterans Therapy Act passed the House by a wide margin in the spring of 2021 and headed to the Senate and the president's desk for final approval. The PAWS Act was signed into law that August, and implementation of the program began in early 2022. The new program would provide free service dogs to veterans diagnosed with PTSD or related mental illness, and the treatments were also targeted at helping veterans. The goal was to promote recovery and wellness as well as to contribute to suicide prevention. Formally speaking, the PAWS Act, or Public Law 117-37, required the VA to conduct a five-year pilot program to provide canine training and therapy programs for all eligible veterans with certain diagnoses as part of a "complementary and integrative health program." The results of that pilot would inform future legislation (Pizzaro 2022).[10]

The PAWS Act helped fill a gap in traditional veterans care programs by providing assistance for those suffering mental health effects from service in the WoT. The expectation was that working with dogs would allow veterans to experience less anxiety and improve chemical and brain functions for veterans. The program would be administered at five VA medical centers nationwide (in Virginia, North Carolina, California, Texas, and Florida), and in close cooperation with nonprofit service dog training organizations. Supporters celebrated the passage of the PAWS Act. One advocate said that the outcome was a dramatic "win-win" across the board for the government, veterans, and advocacy organizations (O'Neill 2021).

7

The Ukraine War and the Fight for Democracy

The Russian invasion of Ukraine in 2022 fostered a rare modern instance of unity and resolve in Congress. Many lawmakers were concerned about the war, but WoT veterans in Congress seemed especially determined to help defend democracy and give Ukraine "a fighting chance." This group engaged strategically in the policy process to keep the issue high on the political agenda even as public support seemed to waver. Many veterans pushed the Biden administration to act more immediately and forcefully in the conflict, and when the White House appeared to drag its feet, they increased their inside/outside advocacy to expand US assistance. Veteran lawmakers who came from very different backgrounds and had different political ideologies—including Representatives Ruben Gallego (D-AZ) and Peter Meijer (R-MI)—demanded more from the administration. However, they also shared a sense of limits: most WoT veterans opposed direct intervention by US troops in the conflict. In the end, congressional advocacy efforts on behalf of Ukraine helped lead the policy process in 2022 rather than follow White House preferences. The United States would adopt a more proactive, but measured response that empowered the Ukrainian military to defend its country.

The Challenge: Responding to the War in Ukraine

Russia's invasion of Ukraine began on February 24, 2022, and the destruction and killings perpetrated by the Russian military in the early days of the conflict shocked the world. For many, the war invoked memories of the horrors of World War II. Not only did the invasion endanger a democratic state that was friendly with the West, it set off a mass evacuation of more than a quarter of Ukraine's civilian population of 44 million. The crisis also posed major

144

The Ukraine War and the Fight for Democracy   145

economic challenges. Before the war, Russia was a major exporter of oil and natural gas to Europe and even the United States, and Ukraine and Russia together produced agricultural goods like corn, wheat, and vegetable oils that were consumed around the world. But the war along with economic sanctions on Russian exports sparked steep rises in commodity costs and supply chain disruptions around the world (Nicas 2022).

The Biden administration was seemingly well prepared to assist Ukraine at the outset of this major war in Europe, but the conflict soon tested the boundaries and patience of the NATO alliance. For months prior to the invasion, the US government had actually warned Ukraine and the world that it was imminent, and officials signaled in advance how they would respond. The White House declassified an unprecedented amount of intelligence data collected on Russian intentions in an effort to effectively call out and warn that country against action (Naylor 2022). Most American diplomats and private citizens left Ukraine weeks in advance as Biden signaled to Russia that the United States would assist Ukraine with loans and defensive weapons systems. At the same time, US and European officials feared that more aggressive actions like the deployment of Western troops could be perceived as an existential threat to Russian security that might set Vladimir Putin on a path to World War III. The White House also was reluctant to provide weapons that could be seen as offensive systems to Ukraine for months at the start of the conflict, focusing instead on providing defensive weapons like hundreds of Javelin antitank missiles and Stinger antiaircraft missiles. US officials refused to authorize any NATO operations in Ukraine and rejected calls to establish a no-fly zone over Ukraine for protection of the civilian population (De Luce and Dilanian 2022).

The US government faced a cascade of decision points that generated significant domestic political deliberations in the first few months of the conflict. The Russian invasion itself sparked immediate policy responses, with many countries condemning the act as a violation of the United Nations Charter and international law and imposing economic sanctions on Russia.[1] Top administration officials, including Secretary of Defense Lloyd Austin and Secretary of State Blinken, cited evidence that the Russian military was targeting civilians, striking protected sites, and taking other actions that violated international law regulating the conduct of war (Congressional Research Service 2022). Yet, while members of Congress seemed unified in their support of assisting Ukraine at the outset of the war, questions about the actual nature and scope of aid soon generated debates on Capitol Hill. First, WoT veterans in Congress began to push for harsher economic sanctions than the Biden administration seemed to prefer early in the crisis. One such example was the debate about a US embargo of Russian oil and natural gas. The White House favored a gradual approach to sanctions, focusing on those that would help avoid harming the US economy and imposing direct costs to Americans like the price of gasoline at the pumps.

146   Staying in the Fight

For the first two weeks of the Ukraine War, the Biden administration held out against mounting pressure (Weisman 2022). But, in Congress, WoT veterans and many other lawmakers were hammering out bipartisan legislation that would ban the import of Russian commodities and suspend Russia's normalized trade status as a "most favored nation."[2] Nevertheless, concerned members of the US Congress pushed forward legislation that could achieve these goals. They also knew that they had backing from the American public: one survey conducted in early March found that nearly 70 percent of Americans said they supported harsh economic sanctions "even if they resulted in higher energy prices in the U.S." (Gittelson 2022). In these cases, congressional pressure led directly to executive branch actions.

Ukrainian President Volodymyr Zelenskyy's address to Congress on March 16, 2022, represented another pivotal moment in the debate about the US response. Zelenskyy called for greater military assistance, including the establishment of a no-fly zone and shipments of advanced military hardware. The early days of the war saw brazen attacks by Russian fighter jets, helicopters, and cruise missiles that struck deep into Ukraine at strategic targets, including government buildings, transportation hubs, and fuel depots. Zelenskyy used the opportunity in his address to Congress to press for greater assistance, but the idea that US or NATO planes would enforce a no-fly zone would mean likely combat with Russian aircraft. Some members of Congress, including WoT veterans like Congressman Adam Kinzinger (R-IL), called for this type of assistance. But others, including Senator Joni Ernst (R-IA), countered that such an action could lead to a major clash between the United States and Russia. In the end, despite significant pressure from Republicans and some Democrats, President Biden held the line on a major commitment of resources (Thiessen 2022).

Another decision point emerged over whether or not the United States should provide offensive weapons systems to Ukraine like fighter aircraft. Early in the war, the government of Poland announced that it was willing to transfer several dozen older Polish MiG-29 fighter jets to Ukraine for use in the war. President Zelenskyy of Ukraine argued at the time that if NATO would not institute a no-fly zone, then they would create one on their own using Ukrainian pilots and any aircraft that they could obtain, along with ground-based air defense systems. The Polish government claimed that it could send the MiGs to Ukraine if they could work out a deal with its allies to provide replacement aircraft to help "backfill" NATO defense in the Polish Air Force. This episode turned out to be much more complicated, though, and it generated a surprisingly complex political debate both in Washington and among NATO allies ("Ambassador Julianne Smith" 2022). Despite repeated public calls by Zelenskyy to send the jets, the Biden White House remained adamant that the transfer of the planes might cross a "red line" for Putin that would effectively bring NATO into the war. Nevertheless, Congress was unconvinced, and many WoT veterans in the House and Senate began to lobby heavily for the transfer of the MiGs.

For example, all fifty-eight members of the bipartisan Problem Solvers Caucus called on the White House to facilitate the fighter jet deal, and a poll at the time found that 81 percent of American voters called Ukraine a "friend" or "an ally," ranking it above longtime US partners like France and Japan (Weisman 2022). Veterans in Congress were instrumental in maintaining pressure on the Biden administration for action and influencing the path of US foreign policy.

Congressman Ruben Gallego (D-AZ): Finding Balance in Military Support for Ukraine

Congressman Ruben Gallego (D-AZ) was a Marine Corps combat veteran who supported strong economic sanctions against Russia for the invasion of Ukraine as well as military and humanitarian assistance. He believed that the Russian invasion was illegal and immoral, and he was an outspoken early advocate for US engagement. Indeed, Gallego's responses seemed almost visceral: he quickly adopted an aggressive tone on social media and in public statements toward Russia, and he cosponsored legislation designed to bolster Ukraine's defenses of its sovereign territory. However, like many of his fellow WoT veterans in Congress, Gallego also drew a firm line against the deployment of US soldiers to Ukraine. He supported the transfer of weapons systems to Ukraine but opposed the establishment of a no-fly zone over that country or any other actions that might draw US and NATO forces into direct conflict with Russia (author's interview, July 1, 2022).

Gallego's advocacy for Ukrainian defense appeared to be greatly influenced by his military experiences and socialization. As a Marine combat veteran from a unit that suffered a very high number of casualties, Gallego understood all too well the costs of war. Gallego believed that by adopting a position of providing military aid but stopping short of troop deployments, the United States could maintain a balance that would help it not get sucked into World War III. But that did not prevent Gallego from using harsh rhetoric in the confrontation. The congressman led two congressional delegation trips to Ukraine, in December 2021 before the war, and in December 2022, during the heat of the conflict. Explaining his commitment to aid Ukraine on the second trip to the region, Gallego said he was "moved to witness firsthand the resilience and drive of the Ukrainian people as they defend their homeland." He continued, "As we work to pass a Ukrainian aid package before the end of this Congress, I am more committed than ever to fight and ensure Ukraine gets the arms and resources it needs to protect its democracy" (Gallego 2022b).

Distinctive Motivations

Ruben Gallego is a first-generation American of Mexican and Colombian descent, born in Chicago on November 20, 1979. Gallego and his three sisters

148 *Staying in the Fight*

were raised by a single mother, and his family lived in Chihuahua, Mexico, during his childhood (Gamboa 2021). Gallego's parents divorced after his father was sentenced to prison for drug possession, and Gallego has acknowledged that his humble upbringing and his family's experiences living below the poverty line profoundly impacted his life. But he also knew that he would find a way: "I'm the guy who had a four-year plan to get into Harvard even though my family was dirt poor," he said in his autobiography (Gallego and DeFelice 2021, 8). And he did: Gallego was admitted to Harvard and earned a scholarship to support his academic work.

During his time in Cambridge, Massachusetts, Gallego also walked into a Marine Corps recruiting office and began his military and professional journey. The recruiter recommended the reserves to Gallego as a way for him to finish his degree, earn money, and train for military service. Gallego scored very high on a vocational aptitude test for service, and he was told that he could easily qualify to work on computers or serve as a law clerk. But Gallego insisted that he be allowed to join the infantry. He told the recruiter, "If I'm going to be a Marine, I want to be a *Marine* . . . on the front line, seeing action" (Gallego and DeFelice 2021, 11). Gallego went straight to boot camp at Parris Island and then returned to work toward his degree and graduated from Harvard in 2004.

Gallego joined the Marines as an enlisted soldier at the height of the WoT (Gamboa 2021). He was soon deployed to Iraq with the Lima Company of the Third Battalion of the Twenty-Fifth Marine Corps Regiment, and in 2005, the company suffered serious losses in Iraq, including the deaths of forty-eight soldiers and hundreds of injuries. Gallego described Lima as "the hardest hit unit in the Iraq War," and he was engaged in combat on multiple occasions. The events of the war had a strong impact on Gallego. He returned from military service as a veteran with a motivation to continue his public service in government. Gallego successfully ran for the Arizona House of Representatives in 2010, and the first bill that he sponsored there would grant in-state tuition status to veterans residing in the state. Gallego's policy activism and personal commitment drew praise, and a year later, he was named the assistant minority leader in the chamber, the first Latino representative to hold the post.[3] In 2014, Gallego announced his candidacy for US Congress in Arizona's Seventh Congressional District, a majority Latino district, and he gathered momentum through a crowded Democratic field in the primary. Gallego won the seat with an impressive 74 percent of the popular vote.

Congressman Gallego was sworn into office in January 2015, and he became a rising star on the left in the Democratic Party. Gallego joined the Congressional Progressive Caucus and was named to a seat on the House Armed Services Committee (HASC). He would later chair the HASC Subcommittee on Intelligence and Special Operations, providing him a platform to address critical veteran issues and military and security concerns. Some of the dominant

The Ukraine War and the Fight for Democracy   149

themes that played through his advocacy work in his early years in Congress included a commitment to service and sacrifice that was rooted in his own background and military service as well as a dedication to protect soldiers and veterans and to fight for vulnerable populations. Gallego embraced his distinctive identity as a proud Latino who sought to represent those concerns and interests in American politics and society. He called for greater consideration of the needs of minority populations in the country, including improved funding for schools, community health programs, and job opportunities. And, like many other WoT veterans in Congress, Gallego became even more active in the policymaking process when faced with President Donald Trump's new leadership style, rhetoric, and agenda.

Gallego's military training and experiences, coupled with his upbringing and concern for the plight of disadvantaged people, fed into his support for a strong response to Russia's invasion of Ukraine in early 2022 ("Rep. Ruben Gallego" 2022). Early in the war, there was near unanimity in Congress on the need to assist Ukraine through humanitarian and military assistance (Weisman 2022). Gallego and others also wanted to impose harsh sanctions on Russia. Indeed, Gallego championed even stronger sanctions than the White House favored, including a complete US embargo of Russian oil and natural gas. While the Biden administration favored a gradual approach to sanctions to try to forestall harm to the US economy, Gallego argued that a tougher stance would be worth it (Rainey 2022). He said, "Sending any conventional weaponry that they know how to use and can use effectively should be on the table, including the surface-to-air missiles they requested" (quoted in Hansen 2022). Gallego and other progressives in Congress agreed that there should be significant action, including providing support for sending all types of weapons to Ukraine.

However, Gallego also approached these questions as a military veteran—recognizing the need for limits on operations so as to protect US soldiers. He knew the emotional and psychological costs of war firsthand, and he was quite open about how those experiences affected him. Looking back on his deployment to Iraq, Gallego said that there were at least eleven times in which he felt that he had narrowly escaped injury or death during combat (Gallego and DeFelice 2021, 2). He also lost a good friend in his unit, Jonathan Grant, to an improvised explosive device attack. That experience hit him hard, and he reflected, "No matter what I achieved in life, I was already and forever a failure. I had let my best friend die." Gallego admitted that his combat experience gave him anger at "higher-ups" and that he turned to drinking as a way to try to manage the stress. But Gallego also found solace in therapy and talking with fellow veterans about losses from the war, and he said the experience "triggered a lot of memories I had suppressed." Once in Congress, Gallego also advocated for stronger mental health care for veterans and cosponsored a series of legislative items (discussed further in the paragraphs that follow) to provide

150 *Staying in the Fight*

better care for veterans and Gold Star families. He became a vocal advocate for confronting those challenges, saying that traumatic experiences were almost unavoidable and "war comes home with you, no matter what" (quoted in Gamboa 2021).

Finally, Gallego also gained national attention for his actions in Congress during the January 6, 2021, insurrection at the Capitol. Gallego was on the House floor when the rioters began to attack the chamber, and he recounted that he sprang into "Marine mode." Gallego jumped on a desk to shout orders to his fellow lawmakers urging calm and instructing them how to use their gas masks and move to safety. He said that the fear he saw on the faces of young staff members in the chamber "reminded me of the young men I served with and the faces I saw in combat. I had to do something." He quickly instructed fellow members of Congress and the staff to take off their jackets and recommended they use fountain pens as a weapon. He later acknowledged that he was prepared to "kill somebody that day" if it came to it, and he knew he would survive the insurrection. "Like, I survived a war," he said. "I was not going to die that day. I didn't give a fuck" (quoted in Rojas and Griffiths 2022).

Issue Framing through Personal Narratives

As the Ukraine War intensified, so, took, did Gallego's resolve to expand US assistance to the embattled country. Gallego took to Twitter to declare: "Russia go f**k yourself," which was accompanied by emojis of the American flag and a raised middle finger. He also acknowledged a perhaps surprising connection that he saw the conflict through the lens of his own experiences in Iraq: Gallego actually likened the Ukrainian struggle to the resolve that he saw among some Iraqis to try to drive out American occupiers in Iraq. But he also noted fundamental differences in terms of the scale of the conflict. The Russians, he said, were taking massive casualties in the first weeks of the war (far beyond US troops in Iraq or Afghanistan), and he believed the pace of the conflict would be unsustainable for Russia. Gallego said he believed the war would be "the end of Putin" (quoted in Arizona PBS 2022).

Gallego and other WoT veterans in Congress also praised the Ukrainian resistance and recommended that the United States dramatically increase its military assistance for the fighters. He said, "Sending any conventional weaponry that they know how to use and can use effectively should be on the table." In response to Ukrainian president Zelenskyy's call for aircraft and air defense systems, Gallego argued that surface-to-air missile systems should be sent. Gallego and other lawmakers, including both Republicans and Democrats, also called on the White House to facilitate the transfer of Polish MiG-29 jet fighters from Poland to Ukraine. Similarly, Senator Rob Portman (R-OH) argued, "The Ukrainians want the ability to have better control over the skies in order to give them a fighting chance. So, I don't understand why we're not doing it."

The Ukraine War and the Fight for Democracy 151

Providing military assistance to Ukraine was also broadly supported by the American public. Gallego similarly dismissed the risks that some had expressed that the transfer might draw NATO into the war, arguing, "I don't really care how we skin the cat as long as we get the MiGs over to them. The fear by the Biden White House that this is an escalatory move is just not true" (quoted in Hansen 2022).

However, Gallego drew a personal line against taking any actions in Ukraine that he believed might draw troops directly into the conflict (author's interview, July 1, 2022). His concerns manifested themselves in his opposition to a no-fly zone over Ukraine. He warned, "We need to be careful that while we're trying to help Ukraine we're not also hurting them by making the Russian resistance or will to fight even stronger." He added, "We don't want to find ourselves shooting down Russian planes or Russian planes shooting us down and finding ourselves escalating to something we can't control" (quoted in Arizona PBS 2022). Gallego recounted often his experiences with deployed to Iraq with the Lima Company of the Third Battalion of the Twenty-Fifth Marine Corps Regiment in 2005. Early in the war, that company had been known as "Lucky Lima" because the unit had the fewest casualties early in the war. But that luck would soon change: between 2005 and 2006, the Third Battalion suffered serious losses in Iraq during their deployment, including the deaths of forty-eight soldiers and hundreds of injuries. Gallego described Lima as "the hardest hit unit in the Iraq War" during his deployment in 2005, and he experienced combat firsthand on multiple occasions. The events of the war had a strong impact on Gallego. He reflected that one of the strongest lessons was the bitter reality of the situation: "It was the 18- and 19-year-olds going through heavy fighting led by young men in their 20s. That is war" (Gallego and DeFelice 2021, 62).

Gallego was willing to support sanctions on Russia, along with arming Ukraine and providing intelligence and logistics support, so long as there would not be direct involvement of the US military. There were many reasons for this, of course, both strategic and personal. For example, Gallego had publicly acknowledged just months earlier that he suffered from a kind of "low level" post-traumatic stress disorder (PTSD). He said, "Despite being in Congress, despite having a political career that I'm sure others would be envious of, I was still stuck emotionally in a darker space." He went on, "I had nightmares. I thought about my dead friends. I wonder why I was alive. I couldn't seem to find anything to cheer me up. . . . I saw danger in shadows constantly. Ten years after the war, my fears remained real" (Gallego and DeFelice 2021, 271). It was only after seeing therapists and testing that he was officially diagnosed with PTSD.

Bill Cosponsorship and Bipartisanship

Ruben Gallego's support for Ukraine resonated with a diverse group of lawmakers on the political left and right. Gallego actually led a bipartisan congressional

152 Staying in the Fight

delegation (CODEL) to the country in December 2021, just months before the outbreak of war, in order to "get an in-depth understanding of what's happening in Ukraine" (Williams 2021). Other lawmakers on the trip included members of the House Committee on Armed Services and fellow WoT veterans, such as Representatives Mike Waltz (R-FL) and Seth Moulton (D-MA). During their visit, Gallego said that the United States should impose "extreme sanctions" against Russia if they invaded and provide military assistance to Ukraine to "bring in weaponry that will actually put a toll on the Russian troop movements" (Williams 2021). The lawmakers also highlighted the fact that there was strong bipartisan resolve to back Ukraine, describing this as a unique issue area on which there seemed to be consensus (Yahoo News 2021).

Gallego adopted an active legislative agenda focused on pragmatic objectives. During his terms in office prior to the Ukraine War, for example, he sponsored or cosponsored a number of bills on veterans' affairs, international affairs, and national security (see table 7.1). Gallego regularly drew support for his bills from lawmakers across the spectrum. For example, he worked with Republican representative Don Bacon (R-NE) to secure $180 million in funding for the Baltic Security Initiative (BSI) in the FY 2022 National Defense Authorization Act. As the threats intensified to Western security, they cosponsored the Baltic Defense and Deterrence Act, designed to reinforce the US commitment to the defense of Baltic countries. Gallego said the bill was necessary since Russia's invasion of Ukraine showed Putin's "blatant disregard for democracy." He added, "That is why it is more important than ever to shore up a strong level of support for our Baltic allies in Latvia, Lithuania, and Estonia" (quoted in "Rep. Ruben Gallego" 2022). Gallego also strongly supported the Biden administration's $40 billion package for Ukraine relief in May 2022, the Additional Ukraine Supplemental Appropriations Act, which passed the House by a vote of 368 to 57. The bill included $15 billion to support US government purchases of weapons for Ukraine and a fund to effectively restock US military hardware that was being sent abroad, as well as funding for refugee and humanitarian assistance for Ukrainians displaced by the war (Edmondson 2022).

Critically, though, Gallego drew the line in support with the question of creating a NATO no-fly zone over Ukraine (author's interview, July 1, 2022). While recommending that the United States and its allies do what they can to support Ukraine against Russia, he said that he was not in favor of putting a no-fly zone over Ukraine. "We need to be careful that while we're trying to help Ukraine we're not also hurting them by making the Russian resistance or will to fight even stronger," Gallego said. "We don't want to find ourselves shooting down Russian planes or Russian planes shooting us down and finding ourselves escalating to something we can't control" (Arizona PBS, February 28, 2022) Measures that he did support centered on arming Ukraine's own forces, providing weapons and intelligence without direct involvement, along with maintaining the tough economic sanctions.

Table 7.1. Sample of Representative Gallego's Record of Bill Sponsorship and Cosponsorship

Label	Title	Introduced	Status
H.Res. 1130	Expressing support for the sovereign decision of Finland and Sweden to apply to join the North Atlantic Treaty Organization (NATO)	May 18, 2022	Introduced in House
H.R. 3344	Transatlantic Telecommunications Security Act	May 19, 2021	Passed House
H.R. 7290	Baltic Defense and Deterrence Act	March 30, 2022	Introduced in House
H.R. 7075	Ukrainian Independence Park Act of 2022	March 15, 2022	Introduced in House
H.R. 3967	Honoring Our PACT Act of 2021	June 17, 2021	Passed House
H.R. 5819	Autonomy for Disabled Veterans Act	November 2, 2021	Introduced in House
H.R. 5470	HOMES for our Veterans Act of 2021	September 30, 2021	Introduced in House
H.R. 5352	Military Suicide Prevention in the 21st Century Act	September 23, 2021	Introduced in House
H.R. 3985	Averting Loss of Life and Injury by Expediting SIVs Act of 2021	June 17, 2021	Passed House
H.R. 4398	Reducing Exposure to Burn Pits Act	July 9, 2021	Introduced in House
H.R. 4104	Vanessa Guillén Military Justice Improvement and Increasing Prevention Act	June 23, 2021	Introduced in House
H.R. 3946	Pell Grant Preservation and Expansion Act of 2021	June 16, 2021	Introduced in House
H.R. 3852	William Collins Jet Fuel Exposure Recognition Act	June 11, 2021	Introduced in House
H.R. 3513	Afghan Allies Protection Act of 2021	May 25, 2021	Introduced in House
H.R. 2588	Veterans Medical Marijuana Safe Harbor Act	April 15, 2021	Introduced in House
H.R. 2382	Veterans' Pathway to Citizenship Act of 2021	April 8, 2021	Introduced in House
H.R. 2372	Presumptive Benefits for War Fighters Exposed to Burn Pits and Other Toxins Act	April 5, 2021	Introduced in House

Continued

154 *Staying in the Fight*

Table 7.1. Sample of Representative Gallego's Record of Bill Sponsorship and Cosponsorship (*Continued*)

Label	Title	Introduced	Status
H.R. 8125	To direct the secretary of defense for a pilot program to preprogram suicide prevention resources into smart devices	August 28, 2020	Introduced in House
H.R. 5786	VA Quality Health Care Accountability and Transparency Act	February 6, 2020	Introduced in House
H.R. 4305	PAWS for Veterans Therapy Act	September 12, 2019	Passed House
H.R. 3806	Protecting Immigrant Gold Star and Military Families Act	July 17, 2019	Introduced in House
H.Res. 495	Expressing the sense of the House of Representatives regarding the prevention of Iran from obtaining or developing nuclear weapons	July 16, 2019	Introduced in House
H.R. 299	Blue Water Navy Vietnam Veterans Act of 2019	January 8, 2019	Became Public Law
H.R. 2907	Wounded Warrior Research Enhancement Act	May 22, 2019	Introduced in House
H.R. 2829	AUMF Clarification Act	May 17, 2019	Introduced in House
H.R. 2796	Afghan Allies Protection Act of 2019	May 16, 2019	Introduced in House
H.R. 2790	Our Obligation to Recognize American Heroes (OORAH) Act of 2019	May 16, 2019	Introduced in House
H.R. 2481	Gold Star Family Tax Relief Act	May 2, 2019	Introduced in House
H.R. 1714	Stop Militarizing Law Enforcement Act	March 13, 2019	Introduced in House
H.R. 186	Veterans Jobs Opportunity Act	January 3, 2019	Introduced in House
H.Con.Res. 138	Directing the President pursuant to the War Powers Resolution to remove US Armed Forces from hostilities in the Republic of Yemen	September 26, 2018	Introduced in House
H.R. 2345	National Suicide Hotline Improvement Act of 2018	May 3, 2017	Became Public Law

The Ukraine War and the Fight for Democracy   155

Table 7.1. Sample of Representative Gallego's Record of Bill Sponsorship and Cosponsorship (*Continued*)

Label	Title	Introduced	Status
H.R. 6437	Secure America from Russian Interference Act of 2018	July 19, 2018	Introduced in House
H.R. 6224	Protect European Energy Security Act	June 26, 2018	Introduced in House
H.R. 299	Blue Water Navy Vietnam Veterans Act of 2018	January 5, 2017	Passed House
H.R. 5671	Burn Pits Accountability Act	May 1, 2018	Introduced in House
H.R. 5087	Assault Weapons Ban of 2018	February 26, 2018	Introduced in House
H.R. 3897	Gold Star Family Support and Installation Access Act of 2017	October 2, 2017	Passed House
H.R. 3563	Veterans' Pathway to Citizenship Act of 2017	July 28, 2017	Introduced in House
H.R. 3440	Dream Act of 2017	July 26, 2017	Introduced in House
H.R. 3025	Fostering Unity Against Russian Aggression Act of 2017	June 22, 2017	Introduced in House
H.R. 1448	Reclamation of War Powers Act	March 9, 2017	Introduced in House
H.R. 1470	Restoring Respect for Immigrant Service in Uniform Act	March 9, 2017	Introduced in House
H.R. 1472	Military and Veteran Caregiver Services Improvement Act of 2017	March 9, 2017	Introduced in House
H.R. 411	Veteran Suicide Prevention Act	January 10, 2017	Introduced in House
H.R. 2493	Wounded Warrior Service Dog Act of 2015	May 21, 2015	Referred to Committee
H.R. 1247	Improving Veterans Access to Quality Care Act of 2015	March 4, 2015	Referred to Committee
H.R. 969	Blue Water Navy Vietnam Veterans Act of 2015	February 13, 2015	Introduced in House

Source: Quorum Federal Database 2022. Search terms: *Armed Forces and National Security*; *Foreign Trade and International Finance*; and *International Affairs*.

156 *Staying in the Fight*

Finally, there was substantial bipartisan agreement on the question of whether Congress should authorize any escalation of forces by the Biden administration. Once again, the issue of war powers authority raised its head in reaction to the challenges of the time. Early in the conflict, for example, House resolutions were advanced by a mix of lawmakers on the far-right and far-left of the ideological spectrum calling for limits on US troop engagement in the conflict. One resolution submitted by scores of lawmakers, including several WoT veterans, called for the president to not send US troops into Ukraine, or declare war, before receiving authorization from Congress. Democratic and Republican lawmakers acknowledged there's no intention now to place US troops in Ukraine. "However, if the ongoing situation compels you to introduce the brave men and women of our military into Ukraine, their lives would inherently be put at risk if Russia chooses to invade," the lawmakers said in the letter. "Therefore, we ask that your decisions comport with the Constitution and our nation's laws by consulting with Congress to receive authorization before any such deployment" (Pergram 2022). Gallego supported active congressional involvement in any decision related to hostilities and the possibility that US troops could be put in harm's way.

Advocacy Coalitions

Congressman Gallego deftly practiced inside/outside advocacy in his approach to policy development on the Ukraine War. He worked hard on the inside to challenge the expansion of the US operational footprint. As chairman of the HASC Subcommittee on Intelligence and Special Operations, Gallego had access to significant intelligence data in the months before the invasion that suggested Russia would be aggressive. He called on his fellow lawmakers to establish strong positions on economic sanctions in the leadup to the conflict to signal to Russia the West's intentions. His CODEL in December 2021 was another signal that he saw the signs of the impending challenge. Gallego argued that the United States should be prepared to impose serious sanctions as well as provide lethal aid to Ukraine (Yahoo News 2021).

Gallego was also quite willing to challenge Russia publicly and to work with like-minded groups and individuals on the outside of government who were ready to call out Russian aggression for violating international law and norms. Gallego's office also coordinated their efforts with veteran organizations that supported the defense of Ukraine, including the Veterans of Foreign Wars and the American Legion. One piece of legislation that illustrates this well was the April 2022 Ukraine Democracy Defense Lend-Lease Act. The goal of this legislation was to promote even stronger military assistance programs for Ukraine and to provide equipment through a modern version of the World War II Lend-Lease Act. The United States would deliver more aid to Ukraine for its own soldiers to take over and use during the war effort. But critically, the act would not require the deployment of US troops to the country. Gallego issued a statement of support, saying, "Two months into the Russian invasion, Ukraine continues to stand strong against Putin's unfathomable aggression and horrific crimes. But this war is far from over, and to ensure Ukraine remains a sovereign democracy, the United States cannot let up on providing the arms, intelligence, and aid Ukraine requires to defend its homeland. That is why I voted to pass the Democracy Defense Lend-Lease Act to cut through the red tape and quickly get Ukraine what it needs to keep up the pressure against Russia" (Gallego 2022a).

Notably, these efforts coincided with a period in which Gallego had actually begun to seek more national exposure in the possible run-up to a primary challenge against Senator Kyrsten Sinema. He began to appear in more forums and on cable channels and became a voice of opposition to the Russian invasion. Gallego was also able to multiply his appeal by drawing on resources from political action committees supporting Latino candidates. Gallego was the chair of BOLDPAC, the political arm of the Congressional Hispanic Caucus that provided millions of dollars to other candidates to run for Congress. When Sinema announced that she was leaving the Democrat Party in December 2022, experts recognized a new lane of opportunity for Gallego. His campaign touted his representation of Latinos in politics and his record of public service as a way to try to mobilize Latino voters through registration and fundraising drives (Rodriguez 2023).

Outcome

The US government steered a careful course on Ukraine with the close guidance of lawmakers like Gallego and other WoT veterans. In the first six months of the war, the United States provided billions of dollars' worth of military and humanitarian assistance, and it imposed heavy economic sanctions on Russia for its invasion. But members of Congress were also fairly unified on where to draw the line on this aid: Gallego and many others opposed the imposition of US troops into the war, either directly or indirectly, through actions like imposing a NATO no-fly zone. Gallego expressed his support for a clearly enunciated set of boundaries surrounding the Biden administration's actions, and for the first six months of the war, no US active-duty soldiers found themselves directly in harm's way. Gallego continued to support funding and weapons shipments in the months that followed. For example, he strongly supported the $40 billion aid package in May 2022, and he publicly criticized Republicans who voted against it ("House Member" 2022). As the war dragged on, Gallego also fought to keep Ukraine high on the public agenda and stress US responsibility to support that country and to stand up for democracy around the world.

Representative Peter Meijer (R-MI): Politics and Personal Responsibility in the Fight for Ukraine

Peter Meijer and Ruben Gallego had virtually nothing in common beyond their military experiences when they arrived in Congress. Meijer was the grandson of Fred Meijer, the billionaire superstore magnate who created a national chain of retail stores in the United States. He grew up in a family where many expected that he would take over corporate leadership someday. While Gallego had limited means and a humble background, Meijer arrived in Congress in 2021 as one of its wealthiest members with a blind family trust reportedly worth more than $50 million. Nevertheless, these two very different lawmakers shared a bond in their military service records and their dedication to the fight—Gallego as a Marine veteran and Meijer as an Army veteran of the Iraq War. On Capitol Hill, they found themselves in strong agreement on Ukraine policy.

At issue during the first months of the war was not the question of whether the United States would respond—the verdict for action was nearly unanimous across the US political spectrum—but rather just how much military assistance it would be willing to provide. President Zelenskyy's address to a joint session of Congress on March 16, 2022, represented a pivotal moment in the early formulation of US assistance policies for Ukraine. Zelenskyy used the occasion to call for greater military assistance, including the establishment of a no-fly zone and shipments of advanced military hardware. In his address, Zelenskyy compared the Russian invasion to the September 11, 2001, terror attacks, and argued that Ukraine needed "aircraft, powerful, strong . . . aviation to protect our people, our freedom, our land. . . . You have them, but I need them to protect our sky." He appealed directly to lawmakers in the speech, saying, "Members of Congress, please take the lead." The debate over a NATO no-fly zone also became intertwined with the question of whether the United States should endorse the transfer of several dozen older Polish MiG-29 fighter jets to Ukraine for use in the war. Here again, lawmakers were divided: a bipartisan group of members of Congress supported the shipment of US or NATO planes to the theater to enforce a no-fly zone, while others warned that it could be provocative and lead to direct combat with Russian aircraft (Weisman 2022).

The MiG debate also developed in a broader political context: At the outset of the war, many Republicans seemed to support military action, and some actually criticized the Biden administration for doing too little, too late, to help Ukraine. House Minority Leader Kevin McCarthy (R-CA) and other Republicans said the president had "consistently chosen appeasement and his tough talk on Russia was never followed by strong action" (quoted in Jackson 2022). But a growing number of conservative Republicans and think tanks began to take a different line as the conflict waged on: they argued that prioritizing

The Ukraine War and the Fight for Democracy   159

Ukraine at a time when US citizens were facing rampant inflation and supply chain disruptions at home represented misplaced priorities (Beals 2022). Dozens of conservative Republicans in the House voted against aid packages for Ukraine as the war dragged on (Edmondson 2022).

Meijer adopted a middle-ground position on these questions that was more similar to Democrat veterans of the WoT than that of many of his fellow Republicans. He believed that it was in the national security interest of the United States to provide limited, targeted assistance packages (author's interview, June 22, 2022). Meijer joined with his fellow military veterans in the For Country Caucus to promote bipartisan, measured responses to challenges to US and allied national security. Meijer was a voice for action on Ukraine but with clearly established limits. He publicly supported Biden administration policies, including shipments of defensive weapons systems like Javelin antitank missiles, Stinger antiaircraft missiles, Switchblade drones, and other equipment (Thiessen, March 17, 2022). Yet as the war continued, the political consensus behind US military support began to fray, raising new questions for concerned lawmakers.

Distinctive Motivations

In 2022, Peter Meijer was a freshman Republican congressman from the Michigan Third District and an Army veteran who served in Iraq as an intelligence specialist. Like many other veterans who were elected to Congress, he drew heavily on his military training and personal experiences to shape his political agenda. But the story of how he got there sets him apart: Meijer was an heir to the fortune of a national chain of retail stores in the United States who chose not to join the management of his family company and instead pursue a life of public service that included almost a decade in the Army Reserves. Meijer studied for a year at the US Military Academy at West Point but then transferred to Columbia University and joined the Army Reserve. He majored in cultural anthropology at Columbia, where he also became a public advocate for reinstating the Reserve Officers' Training Corps program on campus. Meijer volunteered for the emergency medical technician program for the university's medical services. Meijer's junior year of college was interrupted when his unit was activated for deployment to Iraq, and he served as an intelligence specialist in 2010 and 2011. Meijer actually completed some of his college assignments while on duty, and he returned to graduate in 2012 (McVicar 2019).[4]

Meijer was profoundly affected by his military service. Meijer volunteered with the nonprofit veterans group Project Rubicon after he returned from Iraq, and he spent two months working with Rubicon volunteers to run medical clinics in refugee camps in South Sudan during the summer after his graduation from Columbia. A few months later, Meijer joined a Rubicon project to

160 *Staying in the Fight*

help victims of Hurricane Sandy in 2012, including participating in search and rescue operations and setting up evacuation shelters. Next, he took on a dangerous assignment to work in Afghanistan as a director at the International Safety NGO Organization, an international charity that supports the safety of aid workers in conflict zones. Needless to say, these experiences at a relatively young age were quite formative (author's interview, June 14, 2022).

Meijer returned home to Michigan after these experiences and worked in a real estate development company for several years before announcing in 2019 that he would run for the Republican nomination to represent the Third District of Michigan in the US Congress. The lawmaker who occupied that seat at the time, Justin Amash, had declared that he was fed up with hyperpartisanship in Washington and was going to become an Independent.[5] Meijer declared his candidacy for the seat by describing himself as a war veteran and a Republican moderate who would represent an alternative to the volatile and deeply divided nature of Washington politics. He said, "The American people deserve better than political theater in the House of Representatives." Among his stated policy priorities as a candidate and early in office were to focus on strong immigration policy (arguing "we need to secure our borders") and protection of soldiers and veterans (including a call to "bring our troops home from senseless wars") (McVicar 2019).

Meijer would have certain advantages in his campaign for Congress, even as he downplayed any sense of entitlement. The Michigan Third District leaned conservative, but there was also a sizable Democratic vote. Meijer's centrism would appeal to a broad swath of voters. He also campaigned by touting his military service record and volunteerism, and he certainly benefited from name recognition (Cam 2021). Meijer won the 2020 election for the Third District with 53 percent of the popular vote, and he was sworn into office on January 3, 2021. Meijer was appointed to a seat on the powerful House Committee on Foreign Affairs (and its Subcommittee on Europe, Energy, the Environment and Cyber) and the Committee on Space Science and Technology and was appointed Ranking Member of the Subcommittee on Oversight, Management, and Accountability in the Committee on Homeland Security.

Unfortunately, though, Meijer's early days in Congress were also marred by the experience of the January 6, 2021, insurrection. Meijer was in the House gallery that day and was evacuated by armed law enforcement officers (Ford School Policy Talks 2021). Meijer reacted strongly to the events, stating publicly that what he saw that day convinced him that the president was "unfit for office." On January 13, Peter Meijer was one of only ten Republicans in the House to vote to impeach President Donald Trump (Cam 2021). In an interesting twist of fate, that decision to stand for the Constitution would ultimately lead to his loss of the seat in the Republican primary elections in Michigan in August 2022.

Finally, Meijer adopted a different tone than many of his fellow Republicans in Congress on the question of Ukraine. Some conservatives were ready to plaster criticisms on the Biden administration as events unfolded in early 2022, for example. As Congressman Steve Scalise (R-LA) said, "President Biden continues to have this attitude of, 'Well, I don't want to help Ukraine too much' because he might offend Putin." But Meijer and other veterans were concerned about the true costs of war and the potential spillover of any actions the US government might take. Meijer found a level of agreement on the question with many fellow WoT veterans, along with many Democrats in Congress (Weisman 2022). He believed that a centrist position of support and engagement with Ukraine, short of the deployment of US troops, was the most reasonable approach. In an interview, Meijer said the Ukraine War was "grounding . . . if you look at what's happening in Ukraine, and it's like a car accident, a near-death experience that snaps you back to reality" (quoted in Weisman 2022). That reality, he believed, was the need for bipartisanship and moderation, and this position was quite influential in the policy debates about Ukraine in the months that followed.

Issue Framing through Personal Narratives

Congressman Meijer displayed a personal commitment to try to help people in need that was rooted in both his family upbringing and his military experiences (author's interview, June 14, 2022). This is well illustrated by an episode that occurred before the Ukraine War: Meijer and a fellow WoT veteran in Congress, Representative Seth Moulton (D-MA), made an unauthorized trip to Kabul, Afghanistan, during the chaotic US pullout from that country in August 2021. They had been critical of the US response and claimed that they took the trip under the auspices of conducting congressional oversight (Linskey et al. 2021). The lawmakers took a commercial flight to the region and then found their way onto a military transport headed to Kabul. They spent time on the ground there talking to different groups and officials involved in the evacuation, and they left the country on a flight that also carried refugees. In reality, though, what appeared on its surface to be a congressional delegation visit was primarily a freelance affair: the representatives' trip had not been approved through normal channels by the House leadership or the US government, and many called the action reckless (Linskey et al. 2021).[6] But in their own statement, Meijer and Moulton defended their action, stating, "America has a moral obligation to our citizens and loyal allies, and we wanted to make sure that obligation is being kept." They added, "As members of Congress we have a duty to provide oversight on the executive branch. There is no place in the world right now where oversight matters more. We conducted this visit in secret to minimize the risk to the people on the ground" (quoted in Cole et al. 2021).

162 *Staying in the Fight*

When it came to the US response to the Russian invasion of Ukraine nine months later, Representative Meijer was initially similarly inclined to leap to the defense and assistance of another population in need. He believed that the United States had an obligation to assist a fellow democracy against direct aggression—and he acknowledged that this represented a natural extension of his past military and civilian experiences (author's interview, June 22, 2022). Meijer could draw on many experiences—from his deployment to Iraq to his time with Team Rubicon in South Sudan and in emergency response to Superstorm Sandy in 2012. Meijer said that throughout his life, he was driven in life by the mantra of his grandfather: "No matter where you are and what position you have, you can always try to do good" (quoted in Martinez 2012). His seat on the House Foreign Affairs Committee provided valuable perspective on the developments, and he publicly championed the provision of US assistance in the form of military hardware and humanitarian aid. At the same time, Meijer knew that he had to protect US troops and national security interests, so he sought to balance the demands and national security policy priorities the United States faced on the question. Economic sanctions on Russia and tranches of military and humanitarian assistance for Ukraine were one thing, but the concept of direct intervention through initiatives like enforcing a no-fly zone were absolutely opposed by Meijer.

Another issue that Meijer was especially interested in was the question of whether war crimes had been committed by Russians in Ukraine. Meijer knew well the laws of war and the importance of rules of engagement in military operations. Like many others, he was convinced that Russia had already violated international law through the invasion itself (*jus in bello*) and was closely monitoring the use of force and the conduct of hostilities (*jus ad bellum*) (Congressional Research Service 2022). Meijer's position on the HFAC Subcommittee on Europe, Energy, the Environment and Cyber allowed him direct access to intelligence reports on the war. He was aware that Russian actions had violated standards during the 2014 invasion of Crimea and subsequent occupation and low-intensity struggle in the Donbas region in eastern Ukraine. But he and other lawmakers watched closely how the war was conducted in the first weeks and months, and they periodically called out what they saw as war crimes, including violations of the Geneva Conventions like the failure to distinguish between civilians and combatants and the use of cluster munitions in civilian areas.

Determining war crimes was one thing, but the question of what exactly to do about them was quite another. Meijer's view on the question of whether the United States would deploy troops to Ukraine under any circumstances was strongly framed by his military and professional experiences. The evidence was clear that Russia was committing war crimes and paving a destructive path: it was targeting civilians, striking protected sites, and taking other actions that violated international law regulating the conduct of war. This was where Zelenskyy's speech to Congress on March 16, 2022, seemed to become another pivotal moment in the debate. Zelenskyy called for greater military assistance, including the establishment of a no-fly zone and shipments of advanced military hardware. Zelenskyy highlighted the damage and destruction and alleged war crimes in his speech to Congress, and he urged action to help end widespread slaughter and destruction. But the idea that US or NATO planes would enforce a no-fly zone would mean likely combat with Russian aircraft. Some members of Congress, including WoT veterans like Congressman Adam Kinzinger (R-IL), called for this type of assistance. But others, including Senator Joni Ernst (R-IA) countered that such an action could lead to a major clash between the United States and Russia. In the end, despite significant pressure from Republicans and some Democrats, President Biden held the line on a major commitment of resources.

Bill Cosponsorship and Bipartisanship

Representative Meijer's approach to legislative challenges and congressional oversight on Ukraine was bipartisan in nature, and he and his staff regularly pursued opportunities for bill cosponsorship (see table 7.2). Two strong foundations for this approach were in his collaborations with fellow WoT military veterans and through his work on the House Foreign Affairs Committee. Meijer signaled that he was dedicated to working with Democrats in multiple ways. As noted previously, he was one of only ten Republicans to vote to impeach President Trump for his actions associated with the January 6 insurrection. Meijer also signed on to a special letter from House Republican freshmen that was sent to President Biden on his inauguration day, saying that the group was looking forward to working with him on common concerns. Meijer and his colleagues wrote, "After two impeachments, lengthy inter-branch investigations, and most recently, the horrific attack on our nation's capital, it is clear that the partisan divide between Democrats and Republicans does not serve a single American." The Republicans signaled their intention to cooperate and that together, they hoped, the government could "rise above the partisan fray" (quoted in Roche 2021). Meijer also joined the Problem Solvers Caucus, a four-year-old bipartisan group on Capitol Hill dedicated to working across the aisle to achieve unity.

Meijer was deeply committed to bipartisanship on Ukraine, and all of his legislative initiatives on the issue were cosponsored with colleagues in the Democratic Party during the first six months of the war. Meijer was especially focused on legislation implementing economic sanctions and the seizure of Russian assets. Just weeks after the invasion, he cosponsored several bills designed to freeze Russian assets as a way to implement harsh sanctions. First, he introduced a bipartisan bill titled "Yachts for Ukraine Act," which was

164   Staying in the Fight

designed to authorize the seizure of Russian oligarch assets and their transfer to Ukraine in humanitarian efforts. Meijer cosponsored the bill with fellow WoT veterans Seth Moulton (D-MA), Mike Gallagher (R-WI), and Jake Auchincloss (D-MA). The plan was simple: wherever possible, the US government should seize Russian assets found in the West, sell them, and then reallocate the proceeds of their sale to assistance for Ukraine. Meijer said, "The United States must no longer turn a blind eye towards Russian oligarchs and any assets they have hidden in our country. I am proud to join this legislative effort to send yet another clear message that we intend to hold Vladimir Putin and his cronies accountable for their illegal invasion of Ukraine, and we will use every economic sanction available to economically isolate anyone who is complicit in Putin's terror around the world" (quoted in "Peter Meijer" 2022). Financial experts estimated that these actions could yield billions of dollars' worth of assistance for Ukraine.

In a related move, Meijer cosponsored bipartisan legislation entitled the "Stop Russian Government and Oligarchs from Limiting Democracy Gold Act of 2022," which was designed to freeze Moscow's access to tens of billions in gold. Specifically, the bill would close a loophole in the sanctions program that might allow Russia to access its gold reserves held abroad, valued at over $100 billion. This approach would have a number of advantages, Meijer staff members argued. First, it would effectively block the Russian government's access to gold reserves that it needed to prop up the value of the ruble. Second, the action would indirectly reduce government assets that might be used to prosecute the war. And third, the new law could create future opportunities for seizure (author's interview, June 22, 2022).

Meijer also supported military and humanitarian assistance packages for Ukraine. He and fellow WoT veterans offered early support for small aid packages early in the war and then intensified his support for a major new $40 billion aid package for Ukraine in May 2022, the "Additional Ukraine Supplemental Appropriations Act." This drew broader support and passed the House by a vote of 368 to 57. The bill would have a significant impact on national and international spending, especially because it included $15 billion to support US government purchases of weapons for Ukraine and a fund to effectively restock US military hardware that was being sent abroad. The bill also offered funding for refugee and humanitarian assistance for Ukrainians displaced by the war (Edmondson 2022).

In addition, Meijer also emerged as an early advocate for prosecuting Russian soldiers for war crimes. Meijer's HFAC Subcommittee on Europe held several virtual hearings to initiate investigations of war crimes, with the first one occurring just weeks after the onset of conflict. Committee hearings represented one of the first outlets of official (and public) hearings investigating the question, and the committee would hold hearings in March, April, and

Table 7.2. Sample of Representative Meijer's Record of Bill Sponsorship and Cosponsorship

Label	Title	Introduced	Status
H.R. 496	To oppose violations of religious freedom in Ukraine by Russia and armed groups commanded or otherwise supported by or acting on behalf of Russia	January 28, 2021	Passed House
H.Res. 336	Calling on the Government of the Russian Federation to provide evidence or to release United States citizen Paul Whelan	April 20, 2021	Passed House
H.R. 3344	Transatlantic Telecommunications Security Act	May 19, 2021	Passed House
H.R. 6089	Stop Iranian Drones Act	November 30, 2021	Passed House
H.Res. 833	Reaffirming support for strong United States and Moldova relations, Moldova's democracy, and its sovereignty and territorial integrity	December 2, 2021	Passed House
H.R. 6930	Asset Seizure for Ukraine Reconstruction Act	March 3, 2022	Passed House
H.R. 7372	Protecting Semiconductor Supply Chain Materials from Authoritarians Act	April 1, 2022	Passed House
H.R. 7108	Suspending Normal Trade Relations with Russia and Belarus Act	March 17, 2022	Became Public Law
H.R. 7276	To direct the President to submit to Congress a report related to war crimes and other atrocities committed during the full-scale Russian invasion of Ukraine	March 29, 2022	Passed House
H.R. 4476	DHS Trade and Economic Security Council Act of 2021	July 16, 2021	Passed House
H.R. 7312	To prohibit the use of federal funds to support or facilitate the participation of the Russian Federation in the Group of Seven, and for other purposes	March 31, 2022	Introduced in House
H.R. 7302	Cyber Deterrence and Response Act of 2022	March 30, 2022	Introduced in House

Continued

166 Staying in the Fight

Table 7.2. Sample of Representative Meijer's Record of Bill Sponsorship and Cosponsorship (*Continued*)

Label	Title	Introduced	Status
H.R. 7187	Yachts for Ukraine Act	March 21, 2022	Introduced in House
H.R. 7147	Cost of War Act of 2022	March 17, 2022	Introduced in House
H.Res. 991	Expressing the sense of the House of Representatives that the President should immediately support the transfer of requested fighter aircraft to Ukraine	March 17, 2022	Introduced in House
H.R. 7075	Ukrainian Independence Park Act of 2022	March 15, 2022	Introduced in House
H.R. 7068	Stop Russian GOLD Act of 2022	March 11, 2022	Introduced in House
H.R. 6954	DICTATOR Act of 2022	March 7, 2022	Introduced in House
H.R. 6951	Ban Russian Energy Imports Act	March 7, 2022	Introduced in House
H.Res. 966	Expressing the sense of the House of Representatives regarding the need for investigation and prosecution of the crime of aggression by Russia	March 7, 2022	Introduced in House
H.Res. 963	Expressing the sense of the House of Representatives condemning the Russian Federation, President Putin, members of the Russian Security Council, and others for aggression	March 7, 2022	Introduced in House
H.R. 6894	No Energy Revenues for Russian Hostilities Act of 2022	March 2, 2022	Introduced in House
H.R. 6858	American Energy Independence from Russia Act	February 28, 2022	Introduced in House
H.R. 6846	Corruption, Overthrowing Rule of Law, and Ruining Ukraine: Putin's Trifecta Act	February 25, 2022	Introduced in House
H.R. 6842	To impose sanctions on members of parliament of the Russian Federation	February 25, 2022	Introduced in House
H.R. 6748	Midland Over Moscow Act	February 15, 2022	Introduced in House
H.R. 6659	Health Care for Burn Pit Veterans Act	February 9, 2022	Introduced in House

The Ukraine War and the Fight for Democracy 167

Table 7.2. Sample of Representative Meijer's Record of Bill Sponsorship and Cosponsorship (*Continued*)

Label	Title	Introduced	Status
H.R. 6273	VA Zero Suicide Demonstration Project Act of 2021	December 14, 2021	Introduced in House
H.R. 6014	Afghanistan War Commission Act of 2021	November 18, 2021	Introduced in House
H.R. 5755	Veterans Patient Advocacy Act	October 27, 2021	Introduced in House
H.R. 5134	Showing American Values by Evacuating (SAVE) Afghan Partners Act of 2021	August 31, 2021	Introduced in House
H.R. 1448	PAWS for Veterans Therapy Act	March 1, 2021	Became Public Law
H.Res. 607	Condemns President Biden's failure to heed advice about the Taliban offensive, leading to disorganized, chaotic evacuation of US personnel and Afghan allies	August 24, 2021	Introduced in House
H.R. 3985	Averting Loss of Life and Injury by Expediting SIVs Act of 2021	June 17, 2021	Passed House
H.R. 4471	Improving Veterans Access to Congressional Services Act of 2021	July 16, 2021	Introduced in House
H.R. 4498	To make emergency appropriations to the National Guard	July 16, 2021	Introduced in House
H.Res. 529	Standing with the Cuban people and their struggle for freedom, democracy, and human rights	July 13, 2021	Introduced in House
H.R. 3261	To repeal the Authorization for Use of Military Force Against Iraq Resolution	May 14, 2021	Passed House
H.R. 3385	HOPE for Afghan SIVs Act of 2021	May 20, 2021	Passed House
H.R. 3601	Fully Informed Veteran Act of 2021	May 28, 2021	Introduced in House
H.Res. 426	Expressing opposition to removing sanctions with respect to the Nord Stream II pipeline	May 20, 2021	Introduced in House
H.R. 2932	Veterans CARE Act	April 30, 2021	Introduced in House
H.R. 2916	VA Medicinal Cannabis Research Act of 2021	April 30, 2021	Introduced in House

Continued

168   Staying in the Fight

Table 7.2. Sample of Representative Meijer's Record of Bill Sponsorship and Cosponsorship (*Continued*)

Label	Title	Introduced	Status
H.Res. 340	Condemning the Government of Russia's attempted assassination of Mr. Navalny and criminal acts to intimidate and silence Russian freedom defenders	April 21, 2021	Introduced in House
H.R. 2372	Presumptive Benefits for War Fighters Exposed to Burn Pits and Other Toxins Act of 2021	April 5, 2021	Introduced in House
H.R. 2014	Outdated AUMF Repeal Act	March 18, 2021	Introduced in House
H.R. 275	To establish the National Commission on the Domestic Terrorist Attack upon the United States Capitol	January 12, 2021	Sponsor intro. remarks on measure
H.Con. Res. 5	Censuring and condemning President Donald J. Trump for trying to unlawfully overturn the 2020 presidential election and violating his oath of office on January 6	January 12, 2021	Introduced in House

Source: Quorum Federal Database 2022. Search terms: *Armed Forces and National Security*; *Foreign Trade and International Finance*; and *International Affairs*.

May to promote broader consideration of Russian war crimes. Meijer was also a cosponsor of a broad bipartisan House bill, H.R. 7276, "To direct the President to submit to Congress a report on United States Government efforts to collect, analyze, and preserve evidence and information related to war crimes and other atrocities committed during the full-scale Russian invasion of Ukraine since February 24, 2022, and for other purposes." Members of Congress built on information they established through congressional hearings of the attacks on civilians and potential Russian accountability for war crimes. Experts argued that there were already thousands of possible instances of war crimes—and that this war could easily become one of the most documented cases in history given the prevalence of social media and significant coverage of the war by Western journalists. The goal of the bill, then, was to collect and analyze information so that they can promote accountability. This followed the news that the Organization for Security and Cooperation in Europe started reviewing possible cases of war crimes. The report found "clear patterns of international humanitarian law violations by the Russian forces," and it recommended additional investigations. The State Department was also reportedly supporting Ukrainian courts with resources for future legal proceedings. The bill was widely supported in the House, and it quickly passed the chamber by a vote of 418 to 7.

Finally, Meijer's bipartisanship on defense policy and Ukraine includes his commitment to provide careful congressional oversight on war funding. Finally, Meijer joined with several House Democrats, including Representatives Nikema Williams (D-GA), Sarah Jacobs (D-CA), and Barbara Lee (D-CA), to cosponsor HR 7147, the Cost of War Act, which would require the Pentagon to reveal the cost per taxpayer of any military operation since 9/11. The goal was accountability and balance—with an emphasis on transparency to the American people for the dramatic costs of military operations and defense spending. Meijer said, "With the rising costs Americans are facing right now, we owe our constituents clear information on government spending. When we invest in things like schools and infrastructure we use daily, we feel the impact in our communities. But it's much harder to grasp the costs and impacts of our military spending." He added, "This is a critical step forward in our bipartisan effort to restore congressional authority and oversight on matters of national security" (quoted in Rainey 2022).

Advocacy Coalitions

Meijer entered Congress in 2021 with a focus on teamwork that was influenced by his many past experiences. Meijer adopted a bipartisan approach to his work on Capitol Hill, and he recognized that coordination with advocacy groups could serve as a force multiplier in his own work. He "talked the talk" of leadership in networks, stating, "At every stage, I think it is important to serve and to be a part of a cause that is greater than yourself. I think to a family, to an individual, [a job] is a sense of agency, determination of being able to strike out and provide within a community. It's the uniting of individuals towards a common shared purpose so that the whole can be greater than just the sum of its parts" (quoted in US Chamber of Commerce 2021). But he also "walked the walk" of leadership through building advocacy solutions. He strove for legislative solutions that would benefit Americans in the long term, arguing against the passions of the electoral cycle. He said, "If there is one thing our government needs less of it is folks that are only prioritizing the best short term electoral interest rather than what is truly needed for our long term governance as a nation." This was one of the reasons that he said that he joined the Problem Solvers Caucus, in order to build bridges across the political aisle and find commonsense solutions to major problems.

170   Staying in the Fight

Meijer saw the value of advocacy coalitions through his efforts on Ukraine assistance legislation, especially as opposition to the aid emerged on the far-right of his own party and the battle intensified. The May 2022 package of $40 billion in military and humanitarian assistance served as a focal point of the advocacy and counteradvocacy pressures. Opponents of the bill adopted an America First lens toward the question, arguing that inflation and supply chain interruption at home should be addressed before the nation aided another. Dozens of Republicans in the House threatened to vote no on the legislation, and they found ready allies in conservative think tanks. The Heritage Foundation was one of the organizations leading the opposition at the time. Traditionally a fairly hawkish think tank, Heritage and its leadership had transformed during the Trump administration to support an America First agenda. The new president, Kevin Roberts, said that he believed endless pressure to expand US engagement in the world was misdirected. The $40 billion assistance package, he claimed, "puts America last." Other groups opposed to expanding US aid to Ukraine included Concerned Veterans for America, a conservative advocacy group funded by the Koch network (Edmondson 2022).

At the same time, Meijer saw great value in collaboration with other actors. For example, in the case of his bipartisan Cost of War Act that would require the Pentagon to reveal the cost per taxpayer of any military operation since 9/11. The bipartisan initiative received support from a number of moderate and left-wing civil society groups, including the NAACP and progressive groups like Just Foreign Policy, VoteVets, and Foreign Policy for America. Meijer was also used to working with interest groups during his campaign and early in his term of service. He enjoyed broad Main Street appeal related to his personal and family story, for example, earning endorsements from the US Chamber of Commerce, a powerful business lobby, and receiving support from large corporations such as auto manufacturers and retail companies. Meijer's moderate approach to problem-solving and his openness to bipartisanship allowed him to broaden his advocacy networks to help achieve key objectives.

Outcome

With support from Peter Meijer and others, the Biden administration was able to pass a dozen different assistance packages for Ukraine in the first six months of the war. US aid was framed as primarily defensive in nature and meant to prevent human rights abuses and the Russian seizure of more Ukrainian territory. At the same time, though, the programs were overtly positioned in ways that were designed not to antagonize Russia or promote a wider war. With strong pressure from WoT veterans and moderates, President Biden was able to maintain the middle ground and enjoy fairly broad support from liberals and conservatives.

Finally, Meijer's story of congressional activism came full circle when he lost in the primary election in August 2022. His home base in the Michigan Third was redistricted in 2021 to encompass more traditionally Democrat areas along Lake Michigan, presenting new opportunities for Meijer's challengers. But perhaps the most serious direct threat to his incumbency was an endorsement by former president Trump of his Republican challenger in the primary election, John Gibbs. Trump openly targeted Meijer as one of only ten Republicans in the House that voted to impeach him following the January 6, 2021, insurrection. Meanwhile, Meijer stood his ground, stating, "I'm not going to violate my conscience, my convictions or my principles. If [Gibbs] has to betray his principles in order to keep his job, that's not something I'm willing to do. I'm putting the trust in the voters rather than choosing the path of least resistance." On August 2, 2022, those voters chose John Gibbs in an upset victory over the incumbent war veteran.

8

Findings and Conclusion

WoT military veterans in Congress are making their presence known in the defense-policymaking process. This book highlights patterns in the ways that WoT veterans have framed their common experiences as part of a generational identity or distinct subculture in Congress. This study also goes beyond the numbers to provide insights into different personalities and their self-professed motivations, policy preferences, and advocacy work. For example, some WoT veterans in this study served multiple tours of duty, some experienced combat, and others performed intelligence work or legal services in support operations or commanded vessels in littoral waters or standoff positions near operations. Some subjects have also publicly revealed that they suffer from post-traumatic stress disorder (PTSD). Together, these narratives help paint a bigger picture of what WoT veterans often carry with them in their engagements in life and politics after active-duty service.

The theoretical model and in-depth case research in this book have addressed critical questions in the civil-military relations and foreign policy analysis literatures, including the following: What does the pattern of growth of WoT veteran representation on Capitol Hill mean for foreign policy advocacy? What strategies do these members pursue to influence executive branch policies, and how do these help to explain defense policy outcomes? This research has illuminated different processes of policy advocacy, or how distinct groups like military veterans employ creativity and intensity in the process of pursuing favorable changes, sheds light on their strategies of engagement. Finally, this study probes questions in civil-military relations related to public trust and political activism in the military ranks. Empirical evidence shows that Huntington's vision of an apolitical, professionalized military leadership can easily become blurred when ranking officers also become elected leaders. And with today's guard and reserve forces operating much more like an operational reserve called up regularly for active-duty operations than in the past,

172

Findings and Conclusion   173

the potential for crossover effects between civilian and military life increases (Blankshain 2020). This chapter concludes with reflections on the implications of these dynamics for national security and democracy.

Defining the New War on Terror Generation on Capitol Hill

Distinctive Motivations and Service Experiences

Veterans from the WoT generation have distinctive records of service and sacrifice. The ten lawmakers in this study demonstrated some common characteristics of this new generation of veterans. They are a mix of individuals with long service records in the active-duty military (like Elaine Luria) or the National Guard (Steve Stivers) as well as some who have experienced call-ups for more frequent activation periods and combat deployments (such as Adam Kinzinger). All but one (Ruben Gallego) became ranking officers during their time in the military—from Naval Unit Commander Luria and Lieutenant Colonels Gabbard and Kinzinger to the two captains: Jason Crow and Todd Young. Consistent with findings in the civil-military literature (Vespa 2020), WoT veterans in this study also had higher levels of education. Indeed, every lawmaker earned higher degrees or gained advanced specialized training in command through professional military education programs (or both).

Notably, these lawmakers are part of the first sizable cohort of war veterans in Congress who *volunteered* for their service and participated in prolonged major foreign conflicts. Five of the ten members of Congress in this study joined the military before September 11, 2001, and they have attributed their primary motivations to patriotism or a desire to give back. For example, Representative Steve Stivers joined the military through the Reserve Officers' Training Corps program at Ohio State University in 1985, and he continued to rise up the ranks of the National Guard, including an active-duty deployment to Iraq and Kuwait in 2004. Elaine Luria graduated from the Naval Academy in 1997 and was already an active-duty officer in the Navy on 9/11. She commanded naval groups that were deployed in the littoral waters around the Middle East. Representative Ted Lieu joined the Air Force in 1995 through an ROTC scholarship, and he successfully appealed to high-ranking officers for an exception to receive a commission after failing an eye exam.

The other five lawmakers in this study—Mike Waltz, Adam Kinzinger, Jason Crow, Tulsi Gabbard, and Peter Meijer—joined the military after 9/11 and cited a deep commitment to the global campaign against terrorist threats. In several cases, these members followed family or community traditions of military service. For example, Mike Waltz took this path, in part, because it was consistent with his family history: Waltz's father and grandfather were Navy officers who were professionally successful. Waltz's experience in the Special Forces in Afghanistan and his time as a military adviser in Washington helped him become the first Green Beret ever elected to Congress. Ruben Gallego said that he was partly motivated to serve by his community identity, stating that "among Latinos and Hispanics there is a strong tradition of joining the Marine Corps, and undoubtedly I absorbed that growing up" (Gallego and DeFelice 2021, 11).

Every subject interviewed for this study (which included dozens of experts, veteran members of Congress, and staff members) confirmed strong links between the patterns and processes of individual experiences and subsequent political activism and engagement in this context. They offered evidence of how veterans' experiences help create a sense of community among veterans (Robinson et al. 2020). Many described what they saw as observable difference between the values, goals, and strategies of veterans versus nonveterans, and they accepted the characterization of WoT veterans as a distinct subculture (Gambone 2021). As expert Jeremy Teigen (2018, 27) argues, in these kinds of stories we see "clear evidence that experience in the armed forces imbues veterans with a uniquely powerful bond." Broadly speaking, then, these results appear to corroborate assertions about the power of collective forms of political socialization that impact the attitudes of larger cohorts, or generations, on issues like political participation and efficacy (Burden 2007; DiCicco and Fordham 2018; Swers 2013; Kriner and Shen 2014).

At the same time, it is clear that many veteran lawmakers also personalize defense policy issues in ways that can add intensity to their policy activism. For example, one can see connections between Ted Lieu's training and service as a military lawyer in the JAG Corps and his commitment to legal standards and practices in defining US assistance to Saudi Arabia during the Yemen civil war. Tulsi Gabbard's concerns for the well-being of US soldiers were rooted not only in her core principles but also in her experience in medical and civil affairs units during the WoT. The intensity of Jason Crow's commitment to provide immediate relief for SIV applicants in Afghanistan who were desperate to leave the country can be seen as grounded in his own military deployment there, along with his personal support for human rights and refugee issues. In short, this pattern echoes findings from other studies, including that of Danny Sjursen (2017, 8), who argued that veterans often "rendered arguments in the context of military experiences and reached conclusions from a veteran's as much as a legislator's perspective."

Moderating Executive Authority and Military Force

This study also illustrates another important marker of this generation of veterans of the WoT in Congress: veteran lawmakers tend to challenge or resist the idea of unfettered military operations driven by the president, even if they support the surgical use of military force to achieve specific objectives. Many subjects in this study actively sought ways to curtail executive authority, particularly when it comes to decisions about deploying troops abroad in war zones. This speaks directly to the debate over whether elected veterans would be more or less likely to support the use of military force in conflicts abroad (Huntington 1957; Janowitz 1960; Kriner 2010): consistent with contemporary studies showing that veterans in Congress are more likely to practice careful oversight (e.g., Lupton 2022; Parker and Peters 2015; Sjursen 2017), this study shows that most WoT veterans in Congress believe in significant congressional oversight over the disposition and care of American armed forces. Critically, it also examines the process by which lawmakers seek to curtail executive dominance regarding the use of force.

This research also reinforces arguments from the civil-military literature that generational effects may have "direct relevance for how leaders evaluate issues" like the utility of using military force (Horowitz and Stam 2014, 527; Klingler and Chatagnier 2016; Leal and Teigen 2015). This study finds that nearly all six veterans with combat experience that it investigated appeared less likely to advocate for the use of force abroad (Horowitz, Stam, and Ellis 2015): Representatives Tulsi Gabbard, Adam Kinzinger, Jason Crow, Mike Waltz, Ruben Gallego, and Peter Meijer. These findings are consistent with more nuanced contemporary analyses that the effects of military service are strongest where the experience is highly salient: the oversight of war operations (Lupton 2017). Indeed, the subjects of this study demonstrated a readiness, even an eagerness, to more carefully scrutinize war operations, to take responsibility for foreign and security policy legislation, and to monitor the implementation of relevant legislation (Lowande, Ritchie, and Lauterbach 2019).

At this writing (in the fall of 2023), veterans in Congress are also leading a new charge to moderate or limit executive authority by calling for the repeal of the past Authorizations to Use Military Force (AUMFs). This research found surprising momentum on questions about reform of the AUMFs, as lawmakers called for fundamental changes when it comes to expanded executive authority. For example, H.R. 256, principally authored by Congresswoman Barbara Lee (D-CA), called for the repeal of the Authorization for Use of Military Force Against Iraq Resolution of 2002 (2002 AUMF). Introduced on the first day of the Biden administration in 2021, the bill was cosponsored by dozens of veterans in Congress, as well as Chairman of the House Armed Services Committee Mark Takano (D-CA). The bill was designed to repeal or terminate the statutory authorization for the use of military force against Iraq. H.R. 256 was passed by the US House of Representatives in a bipartisan vote of 268 to 161 and moved on to the Senate. If this bill became law, it would be the first time in decades that a use of force authorization had been terminated by Congress

176 Staying in the Fight

(with the Gulf of Tonkin Resolution repeal the only prior example). Veterans in both parties spoke out in support of the legislation because they believe in more focused, targeted, and limited future authorizations, as well as an important voice for Congress in foreign policy decision-making.

Creativity and Clarity of Purpose

Many WoT veterans appear to have a clarity of purpose when it comes to key defense policy issues and they demonstrate creativity in their strategies of engagement and policy activism. This study shows how they were able to successfully frame, develop, and advance their ideas through both the formal legislative process and through congressional oversight and activism. Lawmakers in this study supported concrete changes in the treatment of PTSD, for example, as well as improvements in the SIV programs for refugees from Afghanistan and Iraq. Representative Peter Meijer was so committed to respond to the chaos in Afghanistan in the summer of 2021 that he and a fellow WoT veteran, Democrat Seth Moulton (D-MA), took a secret and highly controversial trip to Kabul that they claimed was to monitor operations. Similarly, Representatives Steve Stivers and Mikie Sherill (D-NJ) established a strong bond of cooperation on veterans' affairs issues, and they appeared together in multiple venues to promote improved treatment programs for PTSD.

All ten of the members of Congress examined for this study exhibited commitments to pursue their goals that clearly went beyond the bounds of their service as mere delegates or trustees. This reinforces arguments from the advocacy literature and civil-military studies that suggest military veterans are most engaged in issues that are highly salient to them, such as war fighting, veterans' affairs, or congressional oversight of military operations (Parker and Peters 2015; Sjursen 2017; Cormack 2018; Lupton 2017). WoT veteran representatives identified particular challenges and sought to become agents and advocates for key issues. Several members of Congress stated directly that their common experiences of military training and deployments also combined socialization processes as components of the physical and mental preparation for the potential rigors of service (Jackson et al. 2012). This meant that while they would quickly learn the norms of Congress, they were also attuned to how to rise up to the challenge and stand out.

Veterans Affairs and Public Health

WoT veterans in Congress in this study all appeared to be deeply committed to providing high-quality benefits that would support their fellow veterans. Congresswoman Luria's advocacy on behalf of victims of exposure to burn pits is a classic example of this linkage. Evidence that deployment proximity to burn

Findings and Conclusion   177

pits could lead to higher rates of rare forms of cancer and respiratory illnesses for soldiers serve to catalyze support for action on Capitol Hill. This became a bipartisan concern that drew support from fellow veterans in both the House and Senate. More than a dozen companion bills were drafted and introduced in Congress over a five-year period, resulting in bipartisan legislation that was backed heavily by WoT veterans in Congress, health care advocates, and many civil society groups. Similarly, Steve Stivers found ready bipartisan support for legislation to promote better care and treatment of veterans' mental health challenges. Stivers's program for therapy dogs was the capstone of what had been years of work to support veterans from inside the government. The achievement of substantial, yet relatively inexpensive, legislative packages with bipartisan support is noteworthy. Stivers told me that he found it relatively easy to build a network of support among his colleagues for most veteran health care programs and promoted activism to address concerns (author's interview, December 6, 2021).

Summary of Findings

The results of this study appear to provide robust evidence that WoT veterans employed multidimensional strategies to achieve policy objectives. Evidence from a structured, focused comparison of cases presented in table 8.1 captures the significance of these actors and strategies in defense policy outcomes.

These data illustrate how successful advocacy processes often require creative combinations of strategies along with persistence. The motivations that guided WoT veterans in Congress to consider issues like humanitarian concerns in Yemen or illnesses among veterans of the wars in Iraq and Afghanistan appeared quite deep—and they helped propel lawmakers through a series of steps taken both inside and outside the government to achieve their goals. Veterans interviewed for this study repeatedly asserted that wartime experiences in theaters of conflict provided both motivations and lessons about perseverance in the face of obstacles. As noted previously, these often included efforts to curtail executive authority over the use of force and to protect vital national security interests. Each of these themes is articulated further in this section.

Issue Framing: Linking Personal and Policy Narratives

This study provides substantial support for the proposition that newer members of Congress who are veterans have learned the value of issue framing and problem definition to help shape policy issues. Consistent with the public policy theories, lawmakers often tried to frame issues using policy narratives to advocate for preferred foreign policy outcomes in the public arena (Shanahan et al. 2018; Ertas 2015; Nelson 2011). Many of these connections began in their

178　Staying in the Fight

Table 8.1. Summary of Findings

Member of Congress	Issue Framing	Bipartisanship	Advocacy Coalitions	Outcome
Representative Jason Crow (D-CO)	High	High	High	Success: Expanded Afghan SIVs Support
Representative Peter Meijer (R-MI)	High	High	Moderate	Success: Moderated Support for Ukraine
Representative Tulsi Gabbard (D-HI)	Moderate	High	High	Failed: US Maintained Support for Syrian Rebels
Senator Todd Young (R-IN)	High	High	High	Success: Changed US-Saudi Policies
Representative Mike Waltz (R-FL)	High	High	High	Success: Expanded Afghan SIVs Support
Representative Elaine Luria (D-VA)	High	High	High	Success: Passed Legislation to Aid Veterans
Representative Adam Kinzinger (R-IL)	High	High	Moderate	Success: Maintained Support for Syrian Operations
Representative Ruben Gallego (R-AZ)	High	High	High	Success: Moderated Support for Ukraine
Representative Steve Stivers (R-OH)	High	High	High	Success: Passed Legislation to Aid Veterans
Representative Ted Lieu (D-CA)	High	High	High	Success: Changed US-Saudi Policies

political campaigns, where veterans featured their military service and articulated specific policy concerns. When successful, those WoT veterans arrived at Capitol Hill "primed" to work on salient or significant issues. These results again complement civil-military studies suggesting a link between issue salience and policy advocacy (Parker and Peters 2015; Sjursen 2017; Cormack 2018).

WoT veterans have also found value in framing problems as analytical constructs; policymakers could associate themselves with preferred solutions (Nelson, Oxley, and Clawson 1997). Numerous representatives studied for this book—including Seth Moulton, Jason Crow, Tulsi Gabbard, Adam Kinzinger, and Todd Young—had strong feelings about the use of armed forces in conflicts. Many of them were drawn to the issues because of their personal connection, and they often used their own experiences to create policy narratives around problems. For example, Mike Waltz and Jason Crow publicly stated their concerns about delays in the Special Immigrant Visa programs for Afghanistan, and they made clear their personal connections to Afghan interpreters and guides who had supported allied military operations. Tulsi Gabbard drew on her own experiences in a war zone to argue that US soldiers should not be risked in operations in Syria and that a preferred solution would be for the United States to remain disengaged as President Assad consolidated power. In contrast, Adam Kinzinger drew on his own experiences with counterterrorism operations to argue that a modest US investment of force in Syria and the region would help counterbalance Syrian, Russian, and Iranian interests. Senator Young similarly seized on the challenge of delivering humanitarian relief supplies to the Yemeni people, and he used the question of opening the port of Hudaydah as a wedge in his campaign to pressure the Trump administration to change its policies.

Teamwork, Bipartisanship, and Cosponsorship of Legislation

WoT veterans in Congress also adopted traditional tools for policy advocacy, including development, sponsorship, and cosponsorship of legislation, to try to achieve their goals. Veterans interviewed for this study said that bill cosponsorship represents a significant tool for agenda-setting and policy influence, allowing both an expression of policy preferences and actions and is not beholden to party leadership control (Swers 2002; Binder 2003; Harbridge 2015; Sulkin 2011). Indeed, most of the WoT veterans in this study had active legislative records, often with a primary focus on defense policy and veterans affairs. Some of them, including Congressmen Ted Lieu and Elaine Luria, had some of the highest rates of bill sponsorship and cosponsorship among their peers in a term-by-term comparison. They served as primary authors and sponsors of some legislation, but they also readily cosponsored bills that reflected their particular concerns. For example, Lieu and his staff worked closely with other veterans in Congress to advance legislation related to war powers and support for Saudi Arabia's involvement in Yemen, and Luria found that many issues related to veterans affairs and public health offered her a chance to serve her constituency and fellow veterans while also making an impact legislatively. Luria's support for an iterated series of bills related to veterans' health care was noteworthy examples.

Time and again, subjects interviewed for this study acknowledged that military veterans seem to especially be predisposed or likely to work with their fellow veteran lawmakers in Congress. Consistent with civil-military relations literature arguments that veteran bill cosponsorship also often reflects a combination of bipartisanship and a degree of homophily, or the tendency of individuals to be drawn to others similar to themselves, these veterans work together toward common objectives. This is not unique to the WoT cohort,

180   *Staying in the Fight*

of course, but rather reinforces arguments that ties between veterans in Congress have historically been quite strong, and lawmakers have established social networks through relationships grounded on similar experiences (Guerrero and Jason 2020; Lowande, Ritchie, and Lauterbach 2019; Best and Vonnahme 2019). There are many examples of these dynamics at work in these case studies. Representatives Mike Waltz and Jason Crow completely disagreed about most policies, but they cooperated on some as a direct function of their common experiences. In separate interviews, both lawmakers easily identified a series of examples of their cooperation and comradeship, grounded in similar military experiences. Not only did they advance congressional oversight in the case of SIV program reform for Afghanistan policy, but they also participated in many informal and quiet ways of cooperation. Together, they trained for an airborne jump to celebrate the seventy-fifth anniversary of D-Day in 2019, and they regularly volunteered with veterans groups clean national memorials in the DC area. Representative Steve Stivers demonstrated strong commitment to veterans in the military through his legislative efforts on mental health policies, and he found common ground on issues like protection of veterans exposed to toxic burn pits during the Iraq and Afghanistan wars with Elaine Luria. Stivers also described a very strong relationship between him and his Democrat counterpart in the House, Representative Tim Walz (D-MN), in promoting critical issues (author's interview, December 6, 2021).

Advocacy Coalitions

As illustrated in table 8.1, this study also provides ample evidence in support of the proposition that veterans gain leverage through outreach to policy advocacy coalitions. This study found high levels of coordination between congressional offices and nongovernmental organizations, and these connections were often significant in promoting policy development or change. Staffers, members of Congress, and policy experts described how regular networking with concerned groups and individuals helped provide them leverage to influence policy outcomes by intensifying inside/outside pressure networks. Several members of Congress articulated the rationale clearly: working with grassroots organizations provide advantages by simultaneously raising attention to issues on the agenda and putting pressure on their colleagues for policy development, reforms, or change. For example, Steve Stivers described how his office's coordination with veterans' organizations effectively reached out to constituents in nearly all congressional districts around the country and encouraged them to contact their representatives to promote legislation that would improve veterans' health care (author's interview, December 6, 2021). Senior congressional staff members also described the power of advocacy networks as leverage to help convince other lawmakers and executive branch agencies of the need for change.

Findings and Conclusion   181

Advocacy coalitions were also critical to the policy activism of Representatives Kinzinger and Gabbard toward US involvement in the Syrian Civil War. For example, as it became clear that President Trump was intent on withdrawing US troops from Syria, Kinzinger and his colleagues effectively practiced congressional foreign policy advocacy that helped to stymie the president's plans and slow withdrawal from this strategic commitment. Lawmakers in the Syria Caucus found that their views aligned well with key actors inside and outside the government that supported engagement in Syria. A bipartisan group of lawmakers found like-minded supporters from organizations like the Center for Strategic and International Studies, the Atlantic Council, and the Heritage Foundation (Lantis 2021).

Finally, veterans' health care initiatives nicely illuminate the importance of advocacy coalition formation: Congresswoman Luria and her office maintained high levels of coordination with advocacy coalitions on issues related to veterans affairs and health care from the start. Her office identified the burn pits issue as an important area of focus, and she worked closely with other advocacy organizations to promote a strong government response. Throughout her work on the COVENANT Act in 2020–21, Luria supported much broader efforts to advance the legislation in both chambers. Her office worked especially closely with the legislative liaisons from the American Legion and the Iraq and Afghanistan Veterans of America (IAVA). In committee and subcommittee hearings in 2020, for example, Luria's staff drew together strong witness lists and letters of support for the case. Among the organizations represented at the hearing were the Disabled American Veterans, the American Legion, the Military Officers Association of America, the Wounded Warrior Project, and the Veterans Healthcare Policy Institute.

Changes in Defense Policy Directions or Outcomes

Many WoT military veterans in Congress appear attuned to adaptation and complexity and to making rapid corrections or changes in difficult strategic environments. Subjects interviewed for this project said that when they arrived at Capitol Hill, they quickly recognized the political lay of the land. With strong party leadership and centralized control, they did not expect to drive most legislative packages as junior members. On the contrary, they followed a path of identifying issues that concerned them personally (often reflecting their perspectives as military veterans with foreign deployments) and then "seizing" these issues or affiliating themselves strongly with them to advance them through the political process. Indeed, this pattern of championing issues and pursuing executive branch solutions is so profound that it represents one of the more significant insights from the larger study, challenging mixed results of prior roll-call voting analyses (Bianco and Markham 2001; Robinson et al. 2018).

Veterans in this project sought out more immediate solutions to challenges through action within, or increased congressional oversight of, executive branch policies. They were determined to change policies and they became leading advocates for reform (Mintrom and Luetjens 2017; Burden 2007). Consistent with Lupton's arguments (2017), this study sought to test the impact of military service where military expertise would be highly applicable. This study confirmed that WoT veteran lawmakers may be inclined to pursue traditional legislative processes to attempt to achieve objectives, but when faced with legislative roadblocks, they are equally likely to employ alternative strategies of activism that reflect their conviction and creativity in the policy process.

There are numerous examples of this dynamic at work. For example, when faced with the proposition that the Trump administration would actually withdraw US Special Operations troops from Syria and allow a vacuum of power, Adam Kinzinger took the issue as a personal and professional challenge. He began to speak out publicly against the action and try to press congressional action—but he was also keenly aware of their limited power and influence in these circumstances. He maneuvered to expand his advocacy coalition for policy influence and determine ways to try to effectively block an executive order. Similarly, Representatives Mike Waltz and Jason Crow sought creative ways to pursue changes in policies associated with the Afghanistan War and Special Immigrant Visas. When the White House made clear they would not reverse the decision to withdraw troops, even after chaos erupted in Kabul, these veterans determined that the most immediate pathway to achieve their objectives was to bolster informal advocacy networks that had contacts on the ground in Kabul and who could assist those in crisis.

Theoretical Implications

This study draws from modified theories of foreign policy entrepreneurship and advocacy to expand our understanding of some of the dynamics at work on Capitol Hill today. It shows the power of descriptive and substantive representation in the policy process and it demonstrates how even junior lawmakers who are WoT veterans can take on defense policy concerns. And when "frontal assaults" to promote policy changes might fail, this study suggests that WoT veterans might use "envelopment maneuvers" through the trenches of the policy process to try to achieve their objectives. They often employ multiple tools of influence to leverage the defense policy process.

This study also reinforces the value of studying congressional foreign policy advocacy as much, or perhaps more, than pure entrepreneurship (Lantis 2019). Insights help us bridge theories of congressional foreign policy entrepreneurship literature and advocacy coalition studies from public policy studies, offering a much more comprehensive picture of foreign policy activism today. A new generation of military veterans on Capitol Hill readily acknowledges their roles as advocates for policy correction and improvement. For example, senior congressional staff members described how Representative Ted Lieu saw the crisis in Yemen unfolding and was one of the first to address reports of human rights violations and see these as an issue of concern. He became an advocate for changing US relations with Saudi Arabia to achieve policy corrections. Lieu employed networking tactics and even used Twitter and other social media outlets to conduct a full-frontal assault on the executive branch decision-making process.

Advocacy often involves both direct and indirect strategies of engagement. For instance, one of the strongest, indirect tools for policy influence was WoT veteran coordination with nongovernmental organizations through advocacy coalitions. All members of Congress interviewed for this project expressed their appreciation for the work of nongovernmental organizations and said that their staffs had worked closely with these groups to multiply their interest. In this context, WoT veterans exhibited some of the same skills and inclinations to shape policy through the marketplace of ideas along with advocacy communities and humanitarian organizations. WoT veterans worked closely with well-established veteran organizations like Veterans of Foreign Wars and the American Legion, but they also coordinated policy ideas with specific groups and even ad hoc organizations created to respond to particular challenges.

This study also speaks to the civil-military relations literature, including debates about whether and how prior military experiences impact the decision-making of elected officials, and if so, how? As noted in chapter 1, many scholars agree on the general idea of these connections, but the civil-military relations literature remains divided on exactly how they are realized. For example, studies show that there are distinctive differences between the attitudes of civilians and military veterans (Feaver and Kohn 2001; Dempsey 2010) and their estimations of potential costs and benefits of policy choices (Brooks 2020; Stadelmann, Portmann, and Eichenberger 2015, 143; Grossman, Manekin, and Miodownik 2015). Related research examines learning processes and their impact on political activism (Dudley and Gitelson 2002) as well as how experiences, motivations, and preferences help shape lawmakers' perspectives toward domestic and foreign policies (Burden 2007; DiCicco and Fordham 2018; Swers 2013; Kriner and Shen 2014).

However, other research counters that personal values, ideology, and party affiliation ultimately have the strongest impact on political behavior and that individuals who "self-select" to join the volunteer military may be driven primarily by their own belief structures and ideologies (Burden 2007; Horowitz, Stam, and Ellis 2015). Research suggests that select individuals may be attracted to military service and that the experience, in turn, amplifies hawkish personal views (Jost, Meshkin, and Schub 2018; Endicott 2020; Navajas et al. 2020). In

184 Staying in the Fight

other words, military socialization may not be the primary causal agent for changes in attitudes (Jennings and Markus 1977), and attitudinal differences between veterans and civilians might not be significant or lasting (Bachman et al. 2000; Bianco 2005; DiCicco and Fordham 2018).

This study suggests a connection between military experiences of veterans of Iraq and Afghanistan and their defense policy positions in Congress. Case evidence suggests that some WoT veterans in Congress were certainly concerned about the scope of executive authority on these questions. Advocates for policy change often drew connections between their military experiences, their understanding of constitutional restrictions, and the need for caution regarding the use of troops in conflict. Consistent with contemporary treatments of the question (e.g., Lupton 2022), this study also finds that the relationship between military experience and subsequent behavior of lawmakers in office is complex and multidimensional (Lupton 2017, 2022). While this project did not examine distinctive differences between the attitudes of civilians and military veterans and their implications (Feaver and Kohn 2001; Dempsey 2010; Grossman, Manekin, and Miodownik 2015; Hong and Kang 2017), it did focus on how experiences, motivations, and preferences help shape lawmakers' perspectives on defense policy. In reality, a mix of factors, including military socialization experiences, personal values, ideology, and party affiliation, appeared to influence their political behavior.

Looking Back, Looking Ahead: More Veterans in Congress?

The WoT generation of veterans in Congress today appears to share common understandings, such as beliefs about the use of military force, strong congressional oversight of executive branch policies related to the military and defense policy, and a sense of individual and moral responsibility to achieve critical goals. This study has demonstrated how the actions of WoT military veterans have helped shape Afghanistan policy, US aid to Saudi Arabia, Syria policy, Ukraine policy, and veterans' affairs and public health.

The American public continues to support the engagement of the military in society and politics. Recent surveys find that Americans have a "great deal" or "fair amount" of trust in the military. However, there is also a dynamic tension at work here: while citizens support the military as an institution, they do not tend to trust elected officials. For example, in a 2018 Pew Survey, 75 percent of respondents stated that they had "not too much" trust or no trust "at all" for these individuals. This figure had increased to 78 percent by 2021. These tensions were further magnified by events and circumstances in 2020, including the COVID-19 pandemic and the unrest across the United States in the wake of the killing of George Floyd. A survey conducted in February

Findings and Conclusion   185

2021 found declining levels of trust and confidence in the military along with greater concerns about domestic threats to democracy and public safety. Groups that demonstrated the most marked drop in public trust for the military included people under the age of thirty, Black voters, Democrats, and women (Losey 2021).

While many scholars are understandably pessimistic about governance in today's polarized politics (Jeong and Quirk 2019), this book shows how lawmakers with military experience in Congress can help overcome some practical challenges. Voters may distrust Congress as an institution, for example, but support their elected representatives with military experience. The results of the study also push back on the idea of a widespread collapse of collegiality and bipartisanship in Congress (Moreno et al. 2021). Military veterans may play an important role in responding to this dysfunction in their commitments to bipartisanship. A number of prominent veterans have joined the Problem Solvers Caucus, a collection of twenty-nine Democrats and twenty-nine Republicans who champion "normal business" on Capitol Hill, including a deliberative and open process that will produce legislation through committee hearings, markups, and floor amendments. In early 2021, the caucus challenged party leaders to correct a system in which ways that many bills have been fast-tracked to the House floor, bypassing committees, with limited information available to members. Moderates claimed that their role was magnified in a Congress with very narrow majorities in the House and Senate and the importance for bills to gain bipartisan support to pass both houses and ultimately be signed into law by the president. The best way to enact meaningful legislation, they argued, would be "by having a deliberative and open process that promotes transparency and allows members to help shape legislation through committee hearings, markups, and floor amendments." They concluded, "We should not be afraid to deliberate and debate" (Problem Solvers Caucus 2021).

That said, this study does illuminate concerns about a potential blurring of lines of the separation between civilian and military control of government. Some experts with whom I spoke for this study expressed concerns that the traditional norm of the professional military that it is apolitical appears to be eroding in the face of contemporary developments. This speaks directly to the civil-military relations literature on whether lawmakers with military experience bring valuable perspectives to political debates about foreign policy and whether their service influences their policy preferences. This situation becomes even more complicated when we recognize that higher rates of guard and reserve duty activation for operations in conflict zones since September 11, 2001, means the United States has effectively adopted an operational reserve. Members of Congress who serve have been called up for active duty, donning the uniform and serving in different theaters and then

186   *Staying in the Fight*

returning to their offices on Capitol Hill. For example, Adam Kinzinger's unit in the Wisconsin Air National Guard was deployed to the US-Mexico border in 2019 to support increased border security operations ordered by President Trump. Trent Kelly, a Republican House member from Mississippi, served in Congress at the same time that he rose to the rank of major general in the National Guard. Kelly is a combat veteran who has served multiple tours of duty in Iraq, and he was a member of the House Armed Services Committee. As a result, expert Jessica Blankshain (2019) argues that some veterans often "have more in common with their active duty counterparts than with average Americans." This raises interesting questions about the propriety of this arrangement, including whether reserve officers who also serve in Congress can or should criticize orders from their commander-in-chief (Golby, Feaver, and Dropp 2017).

Experts continue to disagree about whether the presence of more veterans in elected office would augment or undermine the democratic processes of foreign and defense policymaking. For example, retired US Army colonel and Georgetown professor Heidi Urben believes that military service experience during the WoT, especially combat deployments, promotes informed perspectives for this new generation of lawmakers. She identifies common patterns of activism across party lines and numerous public statements by veterans in Congress about how their service has shaped their political strategies and goals. At the same time, she reminds us that veterans' "common service doesn't mean their policy goals are always going to align," and partisanship remains important (author's interview, October 2, 2021). Another retired senior military officer interviewed for this book points out that while longtime service veterans could provide a "wealth of information" to shape foreign policymaking, "the problem comes when these individuals don't provide unbiased advice." Indeed, their input in the policy process can have the effect of "sidelining, understating, or actively destroying the other potential policy choices" (author's interview, September 9, 2021).

Finally, the events of January 6 remind us that WoT veterans play an important role as both stewards of and potential challengers to the stability of American democracy. Their activism on defense policies and in veterans' affairs have shaped the pathways of government commitments abroad and at home. Some WoT veterans moved almost directly from the battlefield to the halls of Congress, and they have risen up in the ranks of Congress and brought their considerable skills and perspectives to bear in decision-making. They have championed important causes and urged presidents to make prudent decisions about the use of force. Other WoT veterans have become caught up in the extreme partisanship and polarization of contemporary American politics, potentially limiting their impact. These dynamics will likely continue to unfold in fascinating ways.

Avenues for Future Research

This project has also identified some promising avenues for further research. First, this study finds links between military experience and *policy processes* and thus broadens the treatment of these dynamics for the civil-military relations and foreign policy analysis literatures by identifying the connections and thinking behind military socialization and lawmakers' approaches to issues of concern. This fills a needed gap in the civil-military relations literature that could be further developed in future research. Future mixed-method studies could more systematically analyze legislators' uses of traditional and nontraditional advocacy tools including bill cosponsorship, committee activities, legislative amendments, public letters, and coordination with advocacy groups. This suggests that the linkage could be further parsed or analyzed to capture the nuances of these connections and project patterns of strategies of engagement by veterans in the policy process.

Second, this study raises interesting questions about veterans' ideologies in relation to their policy activism. Further study is needed, for example, on the myriad factors that might influence veterans' high bipartisan index scores, including the district that they are representing in Washington. For example, a statistical analysis of a broader dataset of veterans in Congress could explore possible correlations between bipartisanship and mixed, or purple, districts as well as whether veterans are more likely to practice congressional oversight when they are in the majority or minority party in Congress. Are there patterns of connections between the ideology of the WoT veteran in Congress and strongly conservative or liberal electorates? How does socioeconomic status and racial and ethnic diversity in districts impact WoT veteran lawmakers' representation and willingness to engage in bipartisanship and congressional oversight of the executive?

Third, this study also sets the stage for further research on gender and WoT military veterans in Congress. It features two case studies among a much larger universe of examples of female veterans' activism in the policy process. Female WoT veterans represent the largest share of any female veteran cohort in Congress in US history, and they are making their voices heard on critical issues like defense policy and veterans affairs. Indeed, the number of female combat veterans in politics is also on the rise, providing a distinctive combination of experiences that we would expect to influence the policy process. However, with the notable exception of the recent book *Service above Self: Women Veterans and American Politics*, by Erika Smith (2022), there are not enough published works on these important, changing patterns of representation and the policymaking process.

Fourth, this study highlights a complex reality in the policy world: it shows how elected representatives and their staffs are in constant communication inside the political system with fellow lawmakers and executive branch bureaucracies and outside the system with their constituents and civil society actors. As I indicated in a prior study (2019, 312), the "push-and-pull dynamic illustrated [here] appears to be a more accurate reflection of the pressures on policymaking today. Indeed, it may capture a 'new normal' for players in Washington, DC." This new study has only scratched the surface of this complex reality, and the power of advocacy coalitions to shape the policy process is worthy of much greater scrutiny. But this also raises issues related to the true nature of the democratic process by illustrating a surprising level of coordination.

Finally, at a time of intense polarization and partisanship, there is a need for more granular and personal studies of dynamics in the policymaking process, including the role played by military veterans. In the American system of checks and balances, Congress has traditionally focused its efforts on challenging executive authority. The arrival of this new generation of veterans during a period of broader political volatility has set up a potential collision course, and this raises fascinating questions about whether the executive-legislative balance of power is changing in the contemporary era and whether the emergence of a new veteran cohort would be more or less likely to challenge executive authority to call up troops for domestic security operations. In sum, this study sets the stage for further research on timely questions about civilian and military influence in the policymaking process that lies at the heart of American democratic stability.

Acknowledgments

This study is the product of four years of research work, and I am indebted to many institutions and individuals for their support. The seeds of this project were planted during my fieldwork on a related study of freshmen lawmakers in Washington, DC, in 2017, where I learned about the power of different groups of new members of Congress and their distinctive perspectives. I launched this study two years later and conducted more than forty interviews with lawmakers, congressional staff members, and experts in Washington. Those open and frank discussions helped solidify my understanding of the power of congressional foreign policy advocacy and the distinct leanings of a new generation of military veterans on Capitol Hill. While many interviews were conducted confidentially, I am able to publicly thank the following individuals in DC for their helpful perspectives: Representative Jason Crow (D-CO), Representative Mike Waltz (R-FL), Representative Steve Stivers (R-OH), and Mary Kaszynski, VoteVets director of advocacy. I also benefited from many discussions and interviews with my colleagues and experts in the academy, including Danielle Lupton, Heidi Urben, Jessica Blankshain, Jeremy Teigen, Jeffrey Baker, Mark Jacobson, Charles Allen, Lindsay Cohn, and Risa Brooks.

The College of Wooster and the directors of the Henry Luce III Fund for Distinguished Scholarship provided me with the research leave and grant funding that supported my interviews and archival research in Washington, DC. I had research assistance on this project from excellent Wooster students including Lilia Eisenstein, Emily Hasecke, and Abby Thomson, whose curiosity and interest in the project helped propel this work forward. I am also grateful for the support and understanding of my family as I worked intensively on this project and spent time away from home.

Finally, I thank the editors and staff members at the University Press of Kentucky, including Natalie O'Neal, who have been supportive of the project throughout its development. I also received very helpful guidance and suggestions from anonymous reviewers, whose contributions were critical in refining the arguments of the book. Needless to say, any errors in the manuscript remain my own.

Notes

1. Introduction

1. The Persian Gulf War (1991) involved sustained air operations and one hundred hours of ground war against Iraqi forces. There were only four active-duty veterans of this war still serving in Congress by 2021: Representatives Steven Palazzo (R-MS) and Trent Kelly (R-MS), along with Senators Gary Peters (D-MI) and Mark Kelly (R-AZ).

2. The author thanks an anonymous reviewer for spurring ideas for this summation.

3. To date, thirty-one of forty-six US presidents have served in the military.

4. That said, veterans are still somewhat overrepresented in Congress compared to the percentage of veterans in society today (about 7 percent).

5. This statistic refers to the number of living military veterans who were engaged in active duty or guard and reserve from September 11, 2001, to September 2021.

6. Many WoT veterans ran high-profile campaigns in 2020 that shook up the political status quo. Kentucky Democrat Amy McGrath, a Marine Corps pilot with combat experience, threatened the seat of incumbent senator Republican Majority Leader Mitch McConnell. In Arizona, Navy combat veteran Mark Kelly defeated incumbent Air Force combat veteran Senator Martha McSally, and Kelly's victory helped flip the Senate to Democratic Party control. Meanwhile, in the House, first-time Republican candidate August Pfluger campaigned heavily on his record as a pilot in combat missions against the Islamic State to win an open seat in the Texas Eleventh District. Several other newer veteran incumbents like Representative Elaine Luria (D-VA) and Jason Crow (D-CO) played up their military experience to hold on to seats in mixed "purple" districts.

7. For an excellent treatment of female veterans in American politics and the story of Tammy Duckworth, see Smith (2022).

8. The author thanks an anonymous reviewer for providing additional data and context for this discussion.

9. For the range of WoT veterans who served in Congress from 2007 to 2023, see table 1.1.

10. Fontana and Rosenheck (2008, 513) found some interesting comparisons between WoT veterans and previous generations of soldiers. On average, data show that WoT veterans are more likely to be younger, female, and working. They are less likely to be either married or separated/divorced, to ever have been incarcerated, or to report exposure to atrocities in the military. WoT veterans also reflect a higher percentage of Latino veterans compared to other cohorts.

11. The WoT veteran cohort is also more pessimistic about the value of their military operations. The Pew survey found that 64 percent of veterans said the Iraq War was

191

192 Notes to Pages 16–25

not worth fighting, and 58 percent of veterans said the same about Afghanistan (author's interview, December 6, 2021).

12. This system was a compromise between direct popular vote of the president and selection by Congress, implemented to help offset framers' concerns about the dominant will of uneducated voters and the marginalization of small states or particular groups (Edwards 2019).

13. It is important to stress that these plans contravened standard practice, including respect for the legitimacy of state electoral processes and certifications, as well as the "safe harbor" deadlines established for states to settle any outstanding contests or questions before ascertainment (Arceneaux and Truex 2022; Hill 2023).

14. These figures were concerning to experts since they constituted an overrepresentation of veterans in the insurrection versus the overall population (Steinhauer 2021).

15. Several patterns emerge from a close examination of these data: all WoT veterans who voted to decertify were Republicans and outspoken supporters of Donald Trump; many had tied their fate closely to that of the president; some had actually worked for him; and several veterans who voted to challenge the election results had been sworn into office only three days earlier.

2. Military Veterans and Policy Advocacy

1. This approach complements studies of descriptive and substantive representation, which argue that individual backgrounds, life experiences, and interests of lawmakers clearly influence the types of issues on which they focus (Dahlerup 1988; Childs and Krook 2006).

2. Critics of this interpretation might counter that WoT veterans are primarily junior legislators who are driven to "make their mark" on Capitol Hill by championing an issue in defense policy that will bolster their standing with voters. David Mayhew's (1974) claim that lawmakers are single-minded seekers of reelection and that in order to secure reelection, they advertise, credit claim, and take positions on issues could capture some dimensions of lawmaker motivations. But studies of distinctive groups of junior lawmakers in Congress and their impact on the policy process (Swers 2002; Lantis 2019) also demonstrate that identity and experience shapes distinctive policy agendas. In many cases, junior lawmakers—be they WoT veterans or not—take positions on foreign and defense policy issues that go well beyond the particular interests or purview of their districts and constituents.

3. WoT veterans have also learned from the campaign trail that narratives can be incredibly powerful (Meisel and Karlawish 2011; Nisbett and Ross 1980). Nevbahar Ertas (2015, 429) argues, "Narrative stories are vehicles that present individuals with vivid and emotion-laden information" (see also Shanahan, McBeth, and Hathaway 2011).

4. Steven Teles and Robert Saldin (2019, 4) argue the "space for cross-party coalition-building has shrunk," potentially limiting the ability of the government to unify in response to even serious foreign and domestic challenges (Rogowski and Sutherland 2016; Webster and Abramowitz 2017; Goldgeier and Saunders 2018; McKeon and Tess 2019).

5. For example, a number of prominent veterans have joined the Problem Solvers Caucus, a group of twenty-nine Democrats and twenty-nine Republicans who champion "normal business" on Capitol Hill, including a deliberative and open process that will produce legislation through committee hearings, markups, and floor amendments. The caucus has challenged party leaders to correct a system in which many bills have been fast-tracked to the House floor, bypassing committees, with limited information available to members. Another group, With Honor, is dedicated to the election and policy activism of military veterans in Congress. This group advocates for the election of more veterans to public service and contends that their presence will promote bipartisan solutions to enduring policy problems (Barcott and Wood 2017).

6. In addition, Robinson et al. (2018) and others remind us that there may be differences between correlations and causation when it comes to tendencies to cosponsor bills across the political aisle. Different factors can influence veterans' high bipartisan index scores, of course, including constituency pressures in competitive districts and strategies to overcome intense polarization.

7. Jonathan Pierce et al. (2017, 6) argue that coalitions are relatively stable, as a function of socialization and ideological background, and beliefs represent the "glue that binds" the coalition together. These vested players share policy core beliefs and views regarding problems and solutions related to power, authority structures, and delivery and implementation of policy goals. However, given the challenge of measuring complex belief structures, Paul Sabatier and Christopher Weible (2007) suggest that finding two or three core policy beliefs among actors may be sufficient to identify advocacy coalitions.

8. This approach stands in contrast to the study of roll-call vote outcomes, which Barry Burden (2007, 8) asserts, often misses "much of congressional reality" and tell only part of the story.

9. As James Lindsay (1992–93, 613) argues, legislative scorecards are not enough to measure success because "in any stable institutional arrangement people will act strategically" through alternative means, including the creation of new institutions and procedures.

10. Both Tulsi Gabbard and Scott Perry have remained in the news since they advocated for restraint in Syria. Gabbard chose not to run for reelection in Congress in 2020, and in October 2022, she resigned from the Democratic Party. Since that time, Gabbard has been an outspoken critic of the Biden administration in public forums. Perry was a Trump loyalist who remains in Congress, but he is reportedly under investigation by the Department of Justice for his efforts to interfere in the outcome of the 2020 election.

11. This example also recognizes the complexity in the policy process. While the advocacy of WoT veterans was critical to expedite the evacuation and protection of Afghans who had applied for special visas during the tumultuous summer and fall of 2021, the policy struggle continues regarding expediting the application processing and permanent settlement for Afghan refugees.

12. As Seawright and Gerring (2008, 294) observe, the "primordial task" of case selection "also sets out an agenda for studying those cases. This means that case selection and case analysis are intertwined."

13. For example, roll-call voting data patterns are typically reflective of patterns seen across the veteran cohort as well as broader levels of interest and engagement.

194 Notes to Pages 36–59

3. To the Rescue?

1. Gabbard's engagement on the issue showed her commitment to averting war with Syria but also reflected broader ideological inconsistencies that seemed to foreshadow her 2022 resignation from the Democratic Party and embrace of conservative positions. Gabbard went on to become a regular contributor on Fox News, where she strongly opposed US involvement in the Ukraine War, and she made a series of controversial political statements in 2023.

2. Kinzinger was one of only two Republicans named in 2021 to serve on the Select Committee to Investigate the January 6 attack on the US Capitol.

3. For example, citizen Donald Trump made clear as early as 2013 that he opposed intervention in Syria, tweeting, "We should stay the hell out of Syria, the 'rebels' are just as bad as the current regime. WHAT WILL WE GET FOR OUR LIVES AND $BILLIONS? ZERO" (original emphasis, quoted in Fandos 2017).

4. President Biden quietly approved the mission when he took office in January 2021, and at this writing (in January 2023), these troops have continued to help successfully counterbalance the interests of Turkey, Iran, and Russia in Syria interventions (author's interview, September 28, 2021).

5. Tammy Duckworth was the other female combat veteran from the Iraq War elected to represent the Eighth District of Illinois that year.

6. At the same time, Gabbard favored sensible gun control legislation, including bans on assault weapons. In 2020, Gabbard had a 0 percent rating from the National Rifle Association for her views.

7. Mike Gabbard eventually changed his party affiliation to Democrat, and he mounted an unsuccessful campaign to represent Hawaii in the US Congress in 2004 (Bolante 2004; Calamur 2017).

8. Only Democrats have represented Hawaii's Second District since its creation, and the general election was effectively no contest: her Republican opponent, David "Kawika" Crowley, was a self-described "homeless handyman" who ran an unconventional campaign. Crowley lost more support when he ridiculed Gabbard's religion, Hinduism, as inconsistent "with the constitutional foundation of the U.S. government" (Basu 2015).

9. Gabbard demonstrated an ideological inconsistency in her policy positions throughout her political career. For example, her position on gay and trans rights were somewhat unclear throughout her campaigns and during her service in Congress (Kessler 2016). Gabbard publicly endorsed same-sex marriage, though her ambiguity on other issues continued to draw ire from liberal groups throughout her time in Congress.

10. Notably, this challenge to President Obama also came from a legislator from his own home state.

11. These actions certainly seemed to foreshadow Gabbard's move to the political right and willingness to engage with different ideological perspectives.

12. There were many reasons for these criticisms. For example, Gabbard failed to inform the House leadership in advance of the trip, so Minority Leader Pelosi was not aware of the circumstances or nature of the trip when questioned by the media. The trip had also been funded by an activist group with ties to Syria, the Cleveland-based AAC-CESS group, which critics charged amounted to an illegal campaign donation. Others

denounced Gabbard's actions as a violation of the federal Logan Act, which prohibits unauthorized individuals from contacting foreign governments that are in dispute with the United States (BBC News 2017).

4. Strained Ties

1. Saudi Arabia is the birthplace of Osama bin Laden, the founder of the al-Qaeda terrorist network who issued fatwas against the United States for its "occupation" of the holy land in the 1990s. Salafist jihadism found fertile soil in some extremist schools and mosques in Saudi Arabia. Fifteen of the nineteen hijackers who carried out the September 11, 2001, terror attacks on the United States were Saudi nationals.

2. The timing of the operations was also significant: The United States and other great powers had just completed a landmark nuclear agreement with Iran that offered the opportunity for expanded relations. The Saudis raised these concerns and sought reassurance of US backing.

3. Lieu's district, which runs along the coast near Malibu, California, is among the wealthiest in the country (Green 2014a).

4. In another interview, Lieu said, "I taught the law of war when I was on active duty. You can't kill children, newlyweds, doctors and patients—those are exempt targets under the law of war, and the coalition has been repeatedly striking civilians. It is even worse that the US is aiding this coalition" (quoted in Prupis 2016; Ahmed and Ferguson 2016).

5. This organization, originally called Iraq Veterans Against the War, was composed of WoT military veterans who opposed American involvement in "endless wars."

6. Young also developed a strong relationship with Senator Chris Coons (D-DE) on foreign policy matters and this would later prove influential during the Biden presidency (2021–present).

5. Veterans and Afghanistan

1. This also speaks to the literature on why veterans run for office (Teigen 2018) and on the potential for bipartisan efforts to try to check the executive branch (Marshall and Haney 2022).

2. The concept of the SIV was codified in immigration law in the 1960s and provided special status for immigrants in certain circumstances who would not be subject to quotas (Bruno 2015).

3. In 2021, Metis was acquired by a larger private defense contractor, for which Waltz received $26 million for his share of the company.

4. Crow's district is quite diverse, with thirty thousand Ethiopian immigrants in the Denver metro area alone.

6. War on Terror Veterans and Public Health

1. The public health and safety of *active-duty* soldiers who are deployed abroad and in the United States fall under the direct purview of the Department of Defense (DoD). Soldiers who enlist for two years or longer become eligible for VA medical care for up to five years following their last activation.

196   Notes to Pages 120–145

2. Congress had created a new program called the War Risk Insurance Act before the war in 1914 (and later amended in 1917 and 1918) that was actually designed to limit federal spending by changing policies from lifelong pensions for soldiers in favor of life insurance and limited medical benefits for veterans.

3. While the Bonus Army march did not yield immediate results, it contributed to pressure by veterans for further expansion of benefits programs. The federal government also increased its budget for veterans affairs, and this expansion was only slowed by measures in the Roosevelt administration in the 1930s to respond to the Great Depression (Dickson and Allen 2020).

4. The author thanks student research assistant Emily Hasecke for her excellent work in gathering some of this information.

5. In its legal finding, the court said that while the law dictated dismissal of the case, the ruling did not "mean that the Court is unsympathetic to the claims of the Plaintiffs" and concluded that the best remedy would be "through the military and the legislative processes, not through the judiciary" (quoted in Das and Kellay 2017, 317).

6. Notably, Luria had another ally in this fight: President Biden himself viewed the burn pits issue as personal because he believed that his son, Major Beau Biden, suffered from a rare form of brain cancer that was likely linked back to toxic burn pit exposure. Biden championed the issue publicly, saying during the campaign: "We're going to make sure that no veteran is locked out of treatment for conditions related to toxic exposures from burn pits or elsewhere, or traumatic brain injuries they experienced in the line of duty." However, as the issue slowly ground through Congress in 2020 and 2021, the president drew on latent support from congressional advocates to advance administrative policy changes, including the creation of direct pathways of presumption of illness causation and treatment.

7. At this writing, Stivers is both the president and chief executive officer for the Ohio Chamber of Commerce and an assistant adjutant general for the Ohio Joint Force Headquarters, based in Columbus, Ohio.

8. Both Sherill and Stivers were tireless in their efforts to garner as much bipartisan support for the bill as they could. In November 2020, Sherrill hosted a screening at the US Capitol of *To Be of Service*, a documentary that highlighted the relationship between veterans and their service dogs, and both lawmakers personally appealed to their colleagues to support the bill. During Trump's State of the Union address in February 2019, Stivers hosted Vietnam veteran Walter Parker and service dog to help promote the value of the legislation.

9. Concerns about these issues multiplied during the COVID-19 pandemic, when about twenty veterans per day became victims of suicide.

10. Notably, the legislation would not require the VA to pay the costs for service dog adoption and training. Nonprofit organizations would continue to provide the animals, even as the VA administered and organized the pilot program (O'Neill 2021).

7. The Ukraine War and the Fight for Democracy

1. UN Charter Article 2(4) prohibits member states from using or threatening to use force against one another.

Notes to Pages 146–161   197

2. Cooperation with European allies was also at question on this issue, as many were reluctant to block imports of Russian oil and gas at the time. Nearly half of all Russian oil exports annually go to Europe, and so countries like Germany were extremely reluctant to take such a measure.

3. Gallego also gained public attention for leading a recall effort against Maricopa County sheriff Joe Arpaio, who had cracked down harshly on immigration and illegally used taxpayer money to investigate whether Barack Obama was really born in the United States.

4. Meijer remained in the reserves and eventually went on to attend graduate school, earning a master's in business administration degree from New York University in 2017. He then returned to Michigan, where he worked as a business analyst for a real estate company based in Detroit

5. Amash later announced that he would not run for reelection.

6. The trip reportedly "infuriated the House leadership and some officials at the Pentagon and the State Department" who believed that it diverted needed personnel and resources from the larger mission (Cole et al. 2021). House Speaker Pelosi was reportedly so incensed that she issued a public warning to all other members of the House to not engage in similar activities.

References

Abramson, Jeff. 2021. "US Arms Sales under Review." *Arms Control Today* 51 (2): 25–26.

Ackerman, Spencer. 2013. "U.S. Military Intervention in Syria Would Create 'Unintended Consequences.'" *The Guardian*, July 22, 2013. https://www.theguardian.com/world/2013/jul/22/us-military-intervention-syria.

Adkins, Robinson E. 1967. *Medical Care of Veterans*. Report Prepared for the House Committee on Veterans' Affairs, 90th Congress, 1st session.

Adler, Jessica L. 2017. *Burdens of War: Creating the United States Veterans Health System*. Baltimore: Johns Hopkins University Press.

Aggarwal, Neil Krishan. 2015. *Mental Health in the War on Terror*. New York: Columbia University Press.

Aghamohammadi, Zahra, and Ali Omidi. 2018. "The Prospect of the United States and Saudi Arabia Relations in Light of Khashoggi Murder." *World Sociopolitical Studies* 2 (4): 605–32.

Ahmed, Akbar Shahid, and Amber Ferguson. 2016. "This Congressman Doesn't Buy Obama's Excuses for Supporting Saudi Arabia in Yemen." HuffPost, April 28, 2016. https://www.huffpost.com/entry/ted-lieu-barack-obama-saudi-arabia-yemen_n_571e8a26e4b01a5ebde305a5.

Akin, Gib, and Ian Palmer. 2000. "Putting Metaphors to Work for Change in Organization." *Organizational Dynamics* 28 (3): 67–79.

Allen, Charlotte. 2017. "Congressman Lieu Urges Climate, Environmental Policy Action." *The Hoya*, September 8, 2017. https://thehoya.com/congressman-lieu-urges-climate-environmental-policy-action/.

Al-Salhy, Suadad, and Tim Arango. 2014. "Sunni Militants Drive Iraqi Army Out of Mosul." *New York Times*, June 10, 2014. https://www.nytimes.com/2014/06/11/world/middleeast/militants-in-mosul.html.

"Ambassador Julianne Smith: 'Even if We Debate the Pros and Cons' with Poland over MiGs, 'This Alliance Is Rock Solid.'" 2022. Andrea Mitchell Reports, March 9, 2022. https://www.msnbc.com/andrea-mitchell-reports/watch/amb-julianne-smith-even-if-we-debate-the-pros-cons-with-poland-over-migs-this-alliance-is-rock-solid-134967877696.

American Legion. 2022. "In Support of Veterans Exposed to Burn Pits." March 3, 2022. https://www.legion.org/veteransbenefits/255094/support-veterans-exposed-burn-pits.

Anderson, Kevin B. 2022. "The January 6 Insurrection: Historical and Global Contexts." *Critical Sociology* 48 (6): 901–7.

"Another Way to Serve: After 20 Years in Navy, Elaine Luria Running for Congress." 2018. *Southern Jewish Life Magazine*, March 7, 2018.

200　References

Arceneaux, Kevin, and Rory Truex. 2022. "Donald Trump and the Lie." *Perspectives on Politics* 36 (1): 1–17.

Arizona PBS. 2022. "Congressman Ruben Gallego Speaks on the War in Ukraine." February 28, 2022. https://azpbs.org/horizon/2022/03/congressman-ruben-gallego-speaks-on-the-war-in-ukraine/.

Associated Press. 2022. "House to Vote on Bill to Help Veterans Exposed to Burn Pits." Associated Press, March 3, 2022. https://www.npr.org/2022/03/03/1084114117/house-to-vote-on-bill-to-help-veterans-exposed-to-burn-pits.

Bacevich, Andrew. 2011. "Whose Army?" *Daedalus* 140 (3): 122–34.

Bachman, Jerald, Peter Freedman-Doan, David Segal, and Patrick O'Malley. 2000. "Distinctive Military Attitudes among U.S. Enlistees, 1976–1997: Self-Selection Versus Socialization." *Armed Forces & Society* 26 (4): 561–85.

Baker, M. S. 2014. "Casualties of the Global War on Terror and Their Future Impact on Health Care and Society: A Looming Public Health Crisis." *Military Medicine* 179 (4): 348–55.

Baker, Peter, Mujib Mashal, and Michael Crowley. 2019. "How Trump's Plan to Secretly Meet with the Taliban Came Together and Fell Apart." *New York Times*, September 8, 2019. https://www.nytimes.com/2019/09/08/world/asia/afghanistan-trump-camp-david-taliban.html.

Baran, Jonathan, Alex Horton, and Elizabeth Dwoskin. 2021. "An Army of Veterans and Volunteers Organizes Online to Evacuate Afghans, from Thousands of Miles Away." *Washington Post*, August 26, 2021, A1.

Barcott, Rye, and James Wood. 2017. "Why More Veterans Should Run for Office." *Time*, November 9, 2017. http://time.com/5014163/veterans-run-for-office/.

Barnes, Julian E., and Thomas Gibbons-Neff. 2021. "U.S. Should Slow Withdrawal from Afghanistan, Bipartisan Panel Urges." *New York Times*, February 3, 2021. https://www.nytimes.com/2021/02/03/us/politics/afghanistan-biden-trump-troops-withdrawal.html.

Bartel, Bill. 2018. "Mermaid Factory Owner, Retired Navy Officer to Take on Rep. Scott Taylor in Election | Local Politics." *Virginia Pilot* (online), January 8, 2018.

Bartels, Larry, and Simon Jackman. 2014. "A Generational Model of Political Learning." *Electoral Studies* 33:7–18.

Basu, Tanya. 2015. "Hindus Are Thriving in America, but There's Only One in Congress." *The Atlantic*, March 5, 2015. https://www.theatlantic.com/politics/archive/2015/03/hindus-in-american-politics/386941/.

BBC News. 2017. "Tulsi Gabbard's Syria Meeting with Assad Sparks Outcry." January 27, 2017. https://www.bbc.com/news/world-us-canada-38774701.

Beach, Derek, and Rasmus Brun Pedersen. 2018. "Selecting Appropriate Cases When Tracing Causal Mechanisms." *Sociological Methods and Research* 47 (4): 837–71.

Beals, Monique Beals. 2022. "The 11 Senate Republicans Who Opposed Advancing Aid for Ukraine." Yahoo News, May 16, 2022. https://news.yahoo.com/11-senate-republicans-opposed-advancing-020925673.html.

Bergman, Solveig. 2004. "Collective Organizing and Claim Making on Child Care in Norden: Blurring the Boundaries between the Inside and the Outside." *Social Politics: International Studies in Gender, State & Society* 11 (2): 217–46.

Best, Rebecca, and Greg Vonnahme. 2019. "Military Service and Legislative Agendas: A Study of Legislators in Four States." *Armed Forces & Society* 47 (2): 367–85.

Bianco, William. 2005. "Last Post for 'The Greatest Generation': The Policy Implications of the Decline of Military Experience in the U.S. Congress." *Legislative Studies Quarterly* 30 (1): 85–102.

Bianco, William, and Jamie Markham. 2001. "Vanishing Veterans: The Decline of Military Experience in the U.S. Congress." In *Soldiers and Civilians: The Civil-Military Gap and American National Security*, edited by Peter Feaver and Richard H. Kohn, 275–87. Cambridge, MA: MIT Press.

Bin Khaled Al-Saud, Abdullah. 2017. "Deciphering IS's Narrative and Activities in the Kingdom of Saudi Arabia." *Terrorism and Political Violence* 32 (3): 469–88.

Binder, Sarah. 2003. *Stalemate: Causes and Consequences of Legislative Gridlock*. Washington, DC: Brookings Institution Press.

Blanchard, Christopher M., and Alfred B. Prados. 2007. "Saudi Arabia: Terrorist Financing Issues." Congressional Research Service. Washington, DC: Library of Congress.

Blankshain, Jessica. 2019. "Should Elected Officials Be Allowed to Serve in the Military? It's Complicated." Military, March 8, 2019. https://www.military.com/daily-news/2019/03/08/should-elected-officials-be-allowed-serve-military-its-complicated.html.

———. 2020. "A Primer on U.S. Civil-Military Relations for National Security Professionals." Air University Press: Wild Blue Yonder Online Journal, April 29, 2020. https://www.airuniversity.af.edu/Wild-Blue-Yonder/Article-Display/Article/2255807/a-primer-on-us-civilmilitary-relations-for-national-security-practitioners/.

Blankshain, Jessica Deighan. 2014. "Essays on Interservice Rivalry and American Civil-Military Relations." PhD diss., Harvard University.

Bleich, Erik, and Robert Pekkanen. 2013. "How to Report Interview Data." In *Interview Research in Political Science*, edited by Layna Mosley, 84–105. Ithaca, NY: Cornell University Press.

Bock, Sara W. 2021. "From the Corps to Capitol Hill: Marine Veterans of the 117th Congress Continue Service to the Country." *Leatherneck Magazine*, July 2021. https://mca-marines.org/wp-content/uploads/From-the-Corps-to-Capitol-Hill.pdf.

Boghani, Priyanka. 2016. "A Staggering New Death Toll for Syria's War." PBS Frontline, February 11, 2016. http://www.pbs.org/wgbh/frontline/article/a-staggering-new-death-toll-for-syrias-war-470000/.

Bolante, Rona. 2004. "Who Is Mike Gabbard?" *Honolulu Magazine*, August 1, 2004. http://wwwhonolulumagazine.com/Honolulu-Magazine/August-2004/Who-is-Mike-Gabbard/.

Bond, Jon R. 2019. "Contemporary Presidency: Which Presidents Are Uncommonly Successful in Congress? A Trump Update." *Presidential Studies Quarterly* 49 (4): 898–908.

Brooks, Risa. 2019. "Integrating the Civil-Military Relations Subfield." *Annual Review of Political Science* 22 (1): 379–98.

———. 2020. "Paradoxes of Professionalism: Rethinking Civil-Military Relations in the United States." *International Security* 44 (4): 7–44.

———. 2021. "Are US Civil-Military Relations in Crisis?" *US Army War College Quarterly: Parameters* 51 (1): 7.

Brooks, Risa, Jim Golby, and Heidi Urben. 2021. "Crisis of Command: America's Broken Civil-Military Relationship Imperils National Security." *Foreign Affairs* 100:64–68.

References

Browne, Ryan, and Barbara Starr. 2018. "Trump Says U.S. Will Withdraw from Syria 'Very Soon.'" CNN, March 29, 2018. https://www.cnn.com/2018/03/29/politics /trump-withdraw-syria-pentagon/index.html.

Bruno, Andorra. 2015. "Iraqi and Afghan Special Immigrant Visa Programs." Congressional Research Service Report #R43725, January 20, 2015. https://afghanwarnews .info/pubs/SIVCRS20Jan15.pdf.

Burden, Barry. 2007. *Personal Roots of Representation*. Princeton, NJ: Princeton University Press.

Burtin, Oliver. 2020. "The History of Veterans' Policy in the United States: A Comparative Overview." *Historical Social Research/Historische Sozialforschung* 45 (2): 239–60.

Cahn, Emily. 2015. "Todd Young Announces Indiana Senate Bid." Roll Call, July 12, 2015. https://www.rollcall.com/2015/07/12/todd-young-announces-indiana-senate-bid/.

Calamur, Krishnadev. 2017. "The GOP's Favorite Democrat Goes to Syria." *The Atlantic*, January 18, 2017. https://www.theatlantic.com/politics/archive/2017/01/tulsi-gabbard -syria/508367/.

Cam, Deniz. 2021. "Meet the Michigan Congressman—and Billionaire's Son—Who Voted to Impeach Trump." *Forbes*, January 16, 2021. https://www.forbes.com/sites /denizcam/2021/01/16/peter-meijer-michigan-congressman-and-billionaires-son -who-voted-to-impeach-trump/?sh=37b8bc953a07.

Carney, Jay. 2021. "Afghanistan, Biden, and the Taliban: Here's What We Know." *New York Times*, August 25, 2021. https://www.nytimes.com/live/2021/08/25/world /afghanistan-taliban-kabul-biden-news.

Carney, Jordain, and Olivia Beavers. 2022. "Bipartisan Band of Brothers: The West Point Grads Coming to Congress." Politico, November 26, 2022. https://www.politico .com/news/2022/11/26/west-point-grads-congress-midterm-results-00070710.

Carpenter, Ted Galen. 2013. "Tangled Web: The Syrian Civil War and Its Implications." *Mediterranean Quarterly* 24 (1): 1–11.

Carter, Ralph G., and James M. Scott. 2009. *Choosing to Lead: Understanding Congressional Foreign Policy Entrepreneurs*. London: Duke University Press.

Catalina, Camia. 2013. "Iraq Vet: Syria Strike Is a 'Mistake.'" *USA Today*, September 9, 2013. https://www.usatoday.com/story/onpolitics/2013/09/09/tulsi-gabbard-syria -obama-congress/2785323/.

Childs, Sarah, and Mona Krook. 2006. "Gender and Politics: The State of the Art." *Politics* 26 (1): 18–28.

Clark, Bryan. 2021. "Transcript: The Future of the U.S. Navy: A Conversation with Representative Elaine Luria." The Hudson Institute, March 17, 2021. https://www .hudson.org/research/16761-transcript-the-future-of-the-u-s-navy-a-conversation -with-representative-elaine-luria.

Clark, Wesley. 2018. "Want a Politician You Can Trust? Elect a Veteran in November." *Baltimore Sun*, April 16, 2018. https://www.baltimoresun.com/opinion/op-ed/bs -ed-op-0427-veteran-politicians-20180425-story.html.

CNN. 2021. "Tulsi Gabbard Fast Facts." January 5, 2021. https://abc17news.com /politics/national-politics/2021/01/05/tulsi-gabbard-fast-facts/.

Cohen, Marshall, and Hannah Rabinowitz. 2021. "These Veterans Swore to Defend the Constitution; Now They're Facing Jail Time for the U.S. Capitol Riot." CNN,

November 9, 2021. https://www.cnn.com/2021/11/09/politics/january-6-veterans-military/index.html.

Cole, Devan, Ryan Nobels, Zachary Cohen, and Oren Liebermann. 2021. "Two Congressmen Traveled to Afghanistan amid Frantic Evacuation Efforts." CNN Politics, August 24, 2021. https://www.cnn.com/2021/08/24/politics/seth-moulton-peter-meijer-afghanistan-trip/index.html.

Congressional Research Service. 2022. "Legal Sidebar: The Law of War and the Russian Invasion of Ukraine." Report #LSB10710. March 16, 2022. https://sgp.fas.org/crs/row/LSB10710.pdf.

Congressional Veterans Caucus. 2021. "Representative Steve Stivers: Army." http://caucus.militarytimes.com/speaker/steve-stivers/#.YZ6XqC_MzBI.

"Congressman Lieu Promoted to Rank of Air Force Colonel." 2016. *Beverly Press*, June 23, 2016. https://beverlypress.com/2016/06/congressman-lieu-promoted-rank-air-force-colonel/.

Cordell, Kasey. 2020. "Inside Congressman Jason Crow's Intense First Year." *5280 Magazine*, January 2020. https://www.5280.com/2019/12/inside-congressman-jason-crows-intense-first-year/.

Cormack, Lindsey. 2018. *Congress and U.S. Veterans: From the GI Bill to the VA Crisis*. Santa Barbara, CA: Praeger.

Coughlin, S. S., and A. Szema. 2019. "Burn Pits Exposure and Chronic Respiratory Illnesses among Iraq and Afghanistan Veterans." *Journal of Environment and Health Sciences* 5 (1): 13–24.

Crow, Jason. 2019. "Congressman Crow on Trump's Plan to Divert Military Funding for Border Wall." September 4, 2019. Press Release. https://crow.house.gov/media/press-releases/congressman-crow-trumps-plan-divert-military-funding-border-wall.

———. 2020. "Representatives Crow and Cheney Introduce Bipartisan Afghanistan Oversight Bill." June 5, 2020. Press Release. https://crow.house.gov/media/press-releases/representatives-crow-and-cheney-introduce-bipartisan-afghanistan-oversight.

Cummings, William, Deirdre Shesgreen, and David Jackson. 2019. "A Stain on America's Honor: Lindsey Graham Says Trump's Syria Pullout Abandons Kurds, Helps ISIS." *USA Today*, October 7, 2019. https://www.usatoday.com/story/news/world/2019/10/07/trump-defends-syria-withdrawal/3896039002/.

Curry, James. 2015. *Legislating in the Dark: Information and Power in the House of Representatives*. Chicago: University of Chicago Press.

Dahlerup, Drude. 1988. "From a Small to a Large Minority: Women in Scandinavian Politics." *Scandinavian Political Studies* 11 (4): 275–98.

Das, Onita, and Anika Kellay. 2017. "Private Security Companies and Other Private Service Providers and Environmental Protection in Jus Post Bellum: Policy and Regulatory Challenges." In *Environmental Protection and Transitions from Conflict to Peace*, edited by Carsten Stahn, Jens Iverson, and Jennifer S. Easterday. Oxford: Oxford University Press.

Date, S. V. 2021. "Anti-Immigrant Trump Aide Stephen Miller Laid Groundwork for Disastrous Afghan Evacuation." HuffPost, August 25, 2021. https://www.huffpost.com/entry/afghan-allies-stephen-miller_n_6126b40ee4b06e5d80c95654.

204 References

De Luce, Dan. 2017. "Trump Nominee Concedes Saudi Blockade of Yemen Could Be Violating U.S. Law." Foreign Policy, December 19, 2017. https://foreign policy.com/2017/12/19/trump-nominee-concedes-saudi-siege-of-yemen-could-be -violating-u-s-law/.

De Luce, Dan, and Ken Dilanian. 2022. "Can the U.S. and NATO Provide Ukraine with Enough Weapons?" NBC News, March 31, 2022. https://www.nbcnews.com/politics /national-security/can-us-nato-provide-ukraine-enough-weapons-rcna22066.

De Luce, Dan, and Robbie Gramer. 2017. "GOP Senator Presses Trump Administration over Deadly Saudi Blockade in Yemen." Foreign Policy, December 4, 2017. https://foreignpolicy.com/2017/12/04/gop-senator-presses-trump-administration -over-deadly-saudi-blockade-in-yemen-state-department-nomination-newstead -international-law-diplomacy-congress-senate/.

De Luce, Dan, and Mushtaq Yusufzai. 2019. "Proposed U.S. Deal with Taliban Uses Name of Insurgency's Former 'Emirate.'" August 28, 2019. https://www.nbcnews.com/news /world/proposed-u-s-deal-taliban-uses-name-insurgency-s-former-n1047091.

de Yoanna, Michael. 2021. "Tens of Thousands of Afghan Allies Could Be Left behind or Saved, Rep. Crow and Others Say." KUNC, August 16, 2021.

Demirjian, Karoun. 2016. "Saudi Arabia Is Facing Unprecedented Scrutiny from Congress." Washington Post, September 21, 2016. https://www.washingtonpost .com/news/powerpost/wp/2016/09/21/saudi-arabia-is-facing-unprecedented-scrutiny -from-congress/.

Dempsey, Jason. 2010. Our Army: Soldiers, Politics, and American Civil-Military Relations. Princeton, NJ: Princeton University Press.

Denham, Ryan. 2019. "Kinzinger's Rising Star Burns a Bit Brighter in Trump Era." WGLT, July 12, 2019. https://www.wglt.org/post/kinzingers-rising-star-burns-a-bit -brighter-trump-era#stream/0.

Desiderio, Andrew. 2019. "Senate Rebuffs Trump with Vote Cutting off U.S. Support in Yemen." Politico, March 13, 2019. https://politi.co/2TLiMPv.

———. 2021. "Meet the Republican Building a McCain Model on Foreign Policy." Politico, March 13, 2021. https://www.politico.com/news/2021/03/13/todd -young-foreign-policy-475314.

DeYoung, Karen. 2019. "Collapse of Afghanistan Peace Talks Spotlights Internal Trump Administration Divisions." Washington Post, September 8, 2019. https://www .washingtonpost.com/national-security/collapse-of-afghanistan-peace-talks-spotlights -internal-trump-administration-divisions/2019/09/08/c7d57412-d24b-11e9-86ac -0f250cc91758_story.html.

DiCicco, Jonathan, and Benjamin Fordham. 2018. "The Things They Carried: Generational Effects of the Vietnam War on Elite Opinion." International Studies Quarterly 62 (1): 131–44.

Dickson, Paul, and Thomas B. Allen. 2020. The Bonus Army: An American Epic. New York: Courier Dover.

Doblansky, Christine. 2016. "Ted Lieu Promotion to Lt. Colonel." Asian American Press, June 15, 2016. https://aapress.com/government/u-s-rep-ted-lieu-promoted -to-colonel-in-usar/.

Dudley, Robert, and Alan Gitelson. 2002. "Political Literacy, Civic Education, and Civic Engagement: A Return to Political Socialization?" Applied Developmental Science 6 (4): 175–82.

"Durbin, Kinzinger Support Trump's Missile Strike in Syria." 2017. CBS News 2, Chicago, April 7, 2017. https://chicago.cbslocal.com/2017/04/07/syria-missile-strike-donald-trump-chemical-weapons-dick-durbin-adam-kinzinger/.

Eaton, Sabrina. 2021. "House Adopts Veterans' Service Dog Measure from Retiring Rep. Steve Stivers." Cleveland, May 12, 2021. https://www.cleveland.com/open/2021/05/house-adopts-veterans-service-dog-measure-from-retiring-rep-steve-stivers-of-ohio.html.

Edmondson, Catie. 2022. "Why the Once-Hawkish Heritage Foundation Opposed Aid to Ukraine." *New York Times*, May 27, 2022. https://www.nytimes.com/2022/05/27/us/politics/ukraine-aid-heritage-foundation.html.

Edwards, George C., III. 2019. *Why the Electoral College Is Bad for America*. New Haven, CT: Yale University Press.

Elder, G. H., Jr., C. Gimbel, and R. Ivie. 1991. "Turning Points in Life: The Case of Military Service and War." *Military Psychology* 3 (3): 215–31.

Endicott, Travis W. 2020. "Combat Experience and the Foreign Policy Positions of Veterans." *Social Science Quarterly* 101 (4): 1413–29.

Entman, Robert. 1993. "Framing: Toward Clarification of a Fractured Paradigm." *Journal of Communication* 43 (4): 51–58.

Ertas, Nevbahar. 2015. "Policy Narratives and Public Opinion Concerning Charter Schools." *Politics & Policy* 43 (3): 426–51.

Fandos, Nicholas. 2017. "Trump's View of Syria; How it Evolved in 19 Tweets." *New York Times*, April 7, 2017. https://www.nytimes.com/2017/04/07/us/politics/donald-trump-syria-twitter.html.

Feaver, Peter, and Richard Kohn. 2001. "The Gap and What It Means for American National Security." In *Soldiers and Civilians: The Civil-Military Gap and American National Security*, edited by Peter Feaver and Richard Kohn, 459–74. Cambridge, MA: MIT Press.

Feerick, John D. 2021. "The Electoral College: Time for a Change?" *Fordham Law Review* 90:395.

Feldman, Martha, Kaj Sköldberg, Ruth Brown, and Debra Horner. 2004. "Making Sense of Stories: A Rhetorical Approach to Narrative Analysis." *Journal of Public Administration Research and Theory* 14 (2): 147–70.

Feltman, Jeffrey, and Hrair Balian. 2021. "The United States Needs a New Syria Policy." Brookings Institution, January 29, 2021. https://www.brookings.edu/blog/order-from-chaos/2021/01/29/the-united-states-needs-a-new-syria-policy/.

Filkins, Dexter. 2019. "John Bolton on the War Path." *New Yorker*, May 6, 2019. https://www.newyorker.com/magazine/2019/05/06/john-bolton-on-the-warpath.

Fleisher, Richard, and Jon Bond. 1983. "Beyond Committee Control: Committee and Party Leader Influence on Floor Amendments in Congress." *American Politics Research* 11 (2): 131–61.

Flynn, Meagan. 2021. "Who Said It?—Rep. Elaine Luria (D), or a Republican?" *Washington Post*, July 24, 2021. https://www.washingtonpost.com/local/virginia-politics/elaine-luria-military-spending-democrats/2021/07/23/19e981e2-eb06-11eb-ba5d-55d3b5ffcaf1_story.html.

Fontana, Alan, and Robert Rosenheck. 2008. "Treatment-Seeking Veterans of Iraq and Afghanistan Comparison with Veterans of Previous Wars." *Journal of Nervous and Mental Disease* 196 (7): 513–21.

206   References

Ford School Policy Talks. 2021. "Elissa Slotkin and Peter Meijer: Voices across the Aisle in a Challenging Time." February 16, 2021. https://fordschool.umich.edu/video/2021/elissa-slotkin-and-peter-meijer-voices-across-aisle-challenging-time.

Fordham, Benjamin. 2001. "Military Interests and Civilian Politics: The Influence of the Civil-Military 'Gap' on Peacetime Military Policy." In *Soldiers and Civilians: The Civil-Military Gap and American National Security*, edited by Peter Feaver and Richard Kohn, 327–60. Cambridge, MA: MIT Press.

Fowler, Linda L. 2017. *Watchdogs on the Hill: The Decline of Congressional Oversight of U.S. Foreign Relations*. Princeton, NJ: Princeton University Press.

Franke, Volker. 2001. "Generation X and the Military: A Comparison of Attitudes and Values between West Point Cadets and College Students." *Journal of Political and Military Sociology* 29 (1): 92–119.

Freking, Kevin. 2021. "GOP Rep. Steve Stivers Resigns to Run Ohio Commerce Chamber." WIVB, Channel 4, April 19, 2021. https://www.wivb.com/news/political-news-news/gop-rep-steve-stivers-resigns-to-run-ohio-commerce-chamber/.

Fuhrmann, Matthew, and Michael Horowitz. 2015. "When Leaders Matter: Rebel Experience and Nuclear Proliferation." *Journal of Politics* 77 (1): 72–87.

"Full Biography for Ted Lieu." April 11, 2014. http://www.smartvoter.org/2014/11/04/ca/state/vote/lieu_t/bio.html.

Gallego, Ruben. 2022a. "Gallego Votes for the Ukraine Democracy Defense Lend-Lease Act." Office of Congressman Ruben Gallego, April 28, 2022. https://rubengallego.house.gov/media-center/press-releases/gallego-votes-ukraine-democracy-defense-lend-lease-act.

———. 2022b. "Rep. Gallego Leads Bipartisan Congressional Delegation to Ukraine." Press Release, December 12, 2022. https://rubengallego.house.gov/media-center/press-releases/rep-gallego-leads-bipartisan-congressional-delegation-ukraine.

Gallego, Ruben, with Jim DeFelice. 2021. *They Called Us "Lucky": The Life and Afterlife of the Iraq War's Hardest Hit Unit*. New York: Custom House.

Gamboa, Suzanne. 2021. "Rep. Ruben Gallego Writes an Ode to His Fellow Marines, Veterans in New Book." NBC News, November 9, 2021. https://www.nbcnews.com/news/latino/rep-ruben-gallego-writes-ode-fellow-marines-vets-new-book-rcna4972.

Gambone, Michael D. 2021. *The New Praetorians: American Veterans, Society, and Service from Vietnam to the Forever War*. Boston: University of Massachusetts Press.

Gamson, William. 1995. "Constructing Social Protest." In *Social Movements and Culture*, edited by H. Johnston and B. Klandermans, 85–106. Minneapolis: University of Minnesota Press.

Garand, James, and Kelly Burke. 2006. "Legislative Activity and the 1994 Republican Takeover: Exploring Changing Patterns of Sponsorship and Cosponsorship in the U.S. House." *American Politics Research* 34 (2): 159–88.

Gause, F. Gregory, III. 2018a. "Fresh Prince: The Schemes and Dreams of Saudi Arabia's Next King." *Foreign Affairs*, May/June 2018.

———. 2018b. "From 'Over the Horizon' to 'Into the Backyard': The US-Saudi Relationship in the Gulf." In *The Middle East and the United States*, edited by David W. Lesch and Mark L. Haas, 326–40. London: Routledge.

———. 2018c. "Why the U.S. Should Stay Out of Saudi Politics." *Foreign Affairs*, December 18, 2018.

Gearan, Anne, and Carol Morello. 2018. "Trump: U.S. Expenditures in Middle East Have Been a Mistake." *Washington Post*, February 12, 2018. https://www.washington post.com/politics/trump-us-expenditures-in-middle-east-have-been-a-mistake/20 18/02/12/684e7592-1010-11e8-9065-e55346f6de81_story.html.

Geis, A., and Schlag, G. 2017. "'The Facts Cannot Be Denied': Legitimacy, War and the Use of Chemical Weapons in Syria." *Global Discourse* 7 (2): 285–303.

Gelpi, Christopher, and Peter Feaver. 2002. "Speak Softly and Carry a Big Stick? Veterans in the Political Elite and the American Use of Force." *American Political Science Review* 96 (4): 779–93.

George, Alexander L. 1979. "Case Studies and Theory Development." In *New Approaches in Theory, History, and Policy*, 42–68. New York: Free Press.

George, Alexander L., and Andrew Bennett. 2005. *Case Studies and Theory Development in the Social Sciences*. Cambridge, MA: MIT Press.

Gerring, John, and Lee Cojocaru. 2015. "Selecting Cases for Intensive Analysis: A Diversity of Goals and Methods." *Sociological Methods & Research* 45 (3): 392–423. https://doi.org/10.1177/0049124116631692.

Gittelson, Ben. 2022. "Tough Decision for Biden: Russia Oil Ban Would Trigger Higher Gas Prices." ABC News, March 7, 2022. https://abcnews.go.com/Politics /tough-decision-biden-russia-oil-ban-trigger-higher/story?id=83296953.

Glasser, R. J. 2011. *Broken Bodies, Shattered Minds: A Medical Odyssey from Vietnam to Afghanistan*. Palisades, NY: History Publishing Company.

Goffman, Erving. 1974. *Frame Analysis: An Essay on the Organization of Experience*. Cambridge, MA: Harvard University Press.

Golby, James, Peter Feaver, and Kyle Dropp. 2017. "Elite Military Cues and Public Opinion about the Use of Military Force." *Armed Forces & Society* 44 (1): 44–71.

Goldberg, Jeffrey. 2019. "A Nation Coming Apart." *The Atlantic*, December 2019. https://www.theatlantic.com/magazine/archive/2019/12/a-nation-coming-apart/ 600730/.

Goldberg, Jonah. 2019. *Suicide of the West: How the Rebirth of Tribalism, Populism, Nationalism, and Identity Politics Is Destroying American Democracy*. New York: Crown.

Goldberg, J. J. 2020. "American Jews and the Domestic Arena: Focus on the 2018 Midterm Elections." In *American Jewish Year Book 2019*, edited by Arnold Dashefsky and Ira M. Sheskin, 91–96. London: Springer.

Goldberg, M. S. 2010. "Death and Injury Rates of U.S. Military Personnel in Iraq." *Military Medicine* 175 (4): 220–26.

Goldgeier, James, and Elizabeth Saunders. 2018. "The Unconstrained Presidency: Checks and Balances Eroded Long before Trump." *Foreign Affairs* 97 (5): 144–56.

Gordon, Suzanne. 2018. *Wounds of War: How the VA Delivers Health, Healing, and Hope to the Nation's Veterans*. Ithaca, NY: Cornell University Press.

Green, Matthew. 2019. *Legislative Hardball: The House Freedom Caucus and the Power of Threat-Making in Congress*. Cambridge: Cambridge University Press.

Green, Nick. 2014a. "Election 2014: Sen. Ted Lieu Claims Victory in Bid to Replace Henry Waxman in Congress." *Daily Breeze*, November 5, 2014. https://www.daily breeze.com/2014/11/05/election-2014-sen-ted-lieu-claims-victory-in-bid-to-replace -henry-waxman-in-congress/.

208 References

———. 2014b. "Torrance's Ted Lieu Assumes Leadership Role among Freshman Democrats in Congress." *Torrance Daily Breeze*, November 18, 2014. https://www.dailybreeze.com/2014/11/18/torrances-ted-lieu-assumes-leadership-role-among-freshman-democrats-in-congress/.

Griffith, James. 2020. "Community Service and Voting among Veterans and Nonveterans Using a National Sample of College Undergraduates." *Armed Forces & Society* 46 (2): 323–41.

Groppe, Maureen. 2016. "Todd Young Relies on Marine Experience in Surprise Battle for Senate Seat." *IndyStar*, October 30, 2016. https://www.indystar.com/story/news/politics/2016/10/30/young-battles-indianas-biggest-democratic-name-help-republicans-keep-senate/92828712/.

Grossman, Guy, Devorah Manekin, and Dan Miodownik. 2015. "The Political Legacies of Combat: Attitudes toward War and Peace among Israeli Ex-Combatants." *International Organization* 69 (4): 981–1009.

Grube, Nick. 2020. "Tulsi Gabbard Is Refocusing Her Military Career in California." Honolulu Civil Beat, October 20, 2020. https://www.civilbeat.org/2020/10/tulsi-gabbard-is-refocusing-her-military-career-in-california/.

Gstalter, Morgan. 2018. "GOP Lawmaker: Trump's Video on Syria Troop Withdrawal 'Really Kind of Tacky.'" *The Hill*, December 20, 2018. https://thehill.com/homenews/house/422335-gop-lawmaker-trumps-video-on-syrian-troop-withdrawal-really-kind-of-tacky.

Guerrero, Mayra, and Leonard A. Jason. 2020. "Social Network Cohesion among Veterans Living in Recovery Homes." *Military Behavioral Health* 9 (1): 55–68.

Haaretz. 2018. "Trump: USA Shouldn't Be the Policeman of the Middle East—We Get 'Nothing.'" Haaretz and Reuters, December 20, 2018. https://www.haaretz.com/us-news/trump-tweets-syria-withdrawal-should-be-no-surprise-1.6765143.

Hall, Andrew, and Kenneth Shepsle. 2014. "The Changing Value of Seniority in the U.S. House: Conditional Party Government Revised." *Journal of Politics* 76 (1): 98–113.

Hammond, Susan. 1991. "Congressional Caucuses and Party Leaders in the House of Representatives." *Political Science Quarterly* 106 (2): 277–94.

Hanna, Michael Wahid, and Peter Salisbury. 2021. "The Shattering of Yemen: Why Ending the War Is More Difficult than Ever." *Foreign Affairs*, August 19, 2021. https://www.foreignaffairs.com/articles/united-states/2021-08-19/shattering-yemen.

Hansen, Ronald J. 2022. "After Zelenskyy Speech, Arizona Delegation Calls for More Aid to Ukraine without Combat." *Arizona Central*. https://www.azcentral.com/story/news/politics/arizona/2022/03/16/arizona-delegation-calls-more-aid-ukraine-after-zelensky-speech/7060294001/.

Harbridge, Laurel. 2015. *Is Bipartisanship Dead?* Cambridge: Cambridge University Press.

Harrell, Harlan. 2021. "The 'Beautiful Struggle' of Student Veterans in the Canopy of the Community College: A Phenomenological Study." Drexel University.

Harris, Peter. 2019. "Is Tulsi Gabbard Right about Syria? She's Not Wrong." *National Interest*, August 14, 2019. https://nationalinterest.org/feature/tulsi-gabbard-right-about-syria-she's-not-wrong-73526.

Heffernan, Shayne. 2017. "Rep. Tulsi Gabbard the Only Democrat Fighting ISIS." Live Trading News, March 2, 2017. https://www.livetradingnews.com/rep-tulsi-gabbard-democrat-fighting-isis-32468.html.

Hersman, Rebecca. 2000. *Friends and Foes How Congress and the President Really Make Foreign Policy*. Washington, DC: Brookings Institution Press.

Hickey, Patrick T. 2022. "Virginia's 7th Congressional District: Birth of a Bellwether." In *The Roads to Congress 2020*, edited by Sean D. Foreman, Marcia L. Godwin, and Walter Clark Wilson, 185–206. Cham: Palgrave Macmillan.

Hill, Ginny. 2017. *Yemen Endures: Civil War, Saudi Adventurism and the Future of Arabia*. Oxford: Oxford University Press.

Hill, Walter W. 2023. "The Electoral College." In *The United States Presidential Election of 2020: Evidence-Based and Nonpartisan Perspectives*, edited by Abdul Karim Bangura, 95–104. Lanham, MD: Lexington Books.

Hiltermann, Joost. 2017. "The Kurds Are Right Back Where They Started." *The Atlantic*. October 31, 2017. https://www.theatlantic.com/international/archive/2017/10/history-of-the-kurds/544316/.

———. 2018. "The Kurds: Betrayed again by Washington." *The Atlantic*, December 22, 2018. https://www.theatlantic.com/international/archive/2018/12/chaos-washington-kurds-stranded/578941/.

Holsti, Ole. 2001. "Of Chasms and Convergences: Attitudes and Beliefs of Civilians and Military Elites at the Start of a New Millennium." In *Soldiers and Civilians: The Civil-Military Gap and American National Security*, edited by Peter Feaver and Richard Kohn, 85–100. Cambridge, MA: MIT Press.

Hong, Ji Yeon, and Woo Chang Kang. 2017. "Trauma and Stigma: The Long-Term Effects of Wartime Violence on Political Attitudes." *Conflict Management and Peace Science* 34 (3): 264–86.

Horowitz, Michael, and Allan Stam. 2014. "How Prior Military Experience Influences the Future Militarized Behavior of Leaders." *International Organization* 68 (3): 527–59.

Horowitz, Michael, Allan Stam, and Cali Ellis. 2015. *Why Leaders Fight*. Cambridge: Cambridge University Press.

"House Committee on Veterans' Affairs Hearing Report #116-698." December 28, 2020. Washington, DC: US Government Publishing Office.

"House Member Rips GOP as 'Party of No' for Vote against Ukraine Aid." 2022. MSNBC, May 12, 2022. https://www.msn.com/en-us/news/politics/house-member-rips-gop-as-party-of-no-for-vote-against-ukraine-aid/vi-AAXceUY?ocid=Bing NewsSearch.

Howard, Michael. 2017. "Tulsi Gabbard, True Maverick." *Paste Magazine*, February 1, 2017. https://www.pastemagazine.com/politics/tulsi-gabbard/tulsi-gabbard-true-maverick/.

Huntington, Samuel. 1957. *The Soldier and the State: The Theory and Politics of Civil-Military Relations*. Cambridge, MA: Belknap Press of Harvard University Press.

Inbody, Donald. 2016. *The Soldier Vote: War, Politics, and the Ballot in America*. London: Palgrave Macmillan.

"Indiana 9th District Congressional Debate." 2010. C-SPAN, October 18, 2010. https://www.c-span.org/video/?296074-1/indiana-9th-congressional-district-debate.

Institute of Medicine (US) Committee on the Initial Assessment of Readjustment Needs of Military Personnel, Veterans, and Their Families. 2010. *Returning Home from Iraq and Afghanistan: Preliminary Assessment of Readjustment Needs of Veterans, Service Members, and Their Families*. Washington, DC: National Academies Press. https://www.ncbi.nlm.nih.gov/books/NBK220071/.

Jackson, Jon. 2022. "Adam Kinzinger Slams GOP Criticism of Biden: 'Feeds into Putin's Narrative.'" *Newsweek*, February 23, 2022. https://www.newsweek.com/adam-kinzinger-slams-gop-criticism-biden-feeds-putins-narrative-1681809.

Jackson, Joshua, Felix Thoemmes, Kathrin Jonkmann, Oliver Lüdtke, and Ulrich Trautwein. 2012. "Military Training and Personality Trait Development: Does the Military Make the Man, or Does the Man Make the Military?" *Psychological Science* 23 (3): 270–77.

Jakupcak, Matthew, Jessica Cook, Zac Imel, Alan Fontana, Robert Rosenheck, and Miles McFall. 2009. "Post-Traumatic Stress Disorder as a Risk Factor for Suicidal Ideation in Iraq and Afghanistan War Veterans." *Journal of Traumatic Stress* 22 (4): 303–6.

Janowitz, Morris. 1960. *The Professional Soldier*. New York: Free Press.

Jenkins-Smith, Hank. 1990. *Democratic Politics and Policy Analysis*. Pacific Grove, CA: Brooks/Cole.

Jenkins-Smith, Hank, and Paul Sabatier. 1994. "Evaluating the Advocacy Coalition Framework." *Journal of Public Policy* 14 (2): 175–203.

Jenkins-Smith, Hank, Carol Silva, Kuhika Gupta, and Joseph Ripberger. 2014. "Belief System Continuity and Change in Policy Advocacy Coalitions: Using Cultural Theory to Specify Belief Systems, Coalitions, and Sources of Change." *Policy Studies Journal* 42 (4): 484–508.

Jennings, M. Kent, and Gregory Markus. 1977. "The Effect of Military Service on Political Attitudes: A Panel Study." *American Political Science Review* 71 (1): 131–47. https://doi.org/10.2307/1956958.

Jeong, Gyung-Ho, and Paul Quirk. 2019. "Division at the Water's Edge: The Polarization of Foreign Policy." *American Politics Research* 47 (1): 58–87.

Johnsen, Gregory D. 2021. "The End of Yemen." Brookings Institution, March 25, 2021. https://www.brookings.edu/blog/order-from-chaos/2021/03/25/the-end-of-yemen/.

Johnson, Tim, and Christopher Dawes. 2016. "Do Parents' Life Experiences Affect the Political and Civic Participation of Their Children? The Case of Draft-Induced Military Service." *Political Behavior* 38:793–816. https://doi.org/10.1007/s11109-016-9334-z.

Jones, Brian Adam. 2014. "The Dramatically Diminishing Number of Veterans in Congress." Task and Purpose, October 7, 2014. https://taskandpurpose.com/news/dramatically-diminishing-number-veterans-congress/.

Jones, Seth. 2018. "The U.S. Strategy in Afghanistan: The Perils of Withdrawal." CSIS, October 26, 2018. https://www.csis.org/analysis/us-strategy-afghanistan-perils-withdrawal.

Jordan, Chuck. 2019. "Sen. Young: Progress in Yemen Requires American Leadership." *The Hill*, January 8, 2019. https://thehill.com/blogs/congress-blog/foreign-policy/424266-sen-young-progress-in-yemen-requires-american-leadership.

Jost, Tyler, Kaine Meshkin, and Robert Schub. 2018. "Socialized Hawks? How Selection Explains Military Attitudes on the Use of Force." Unpublished working paper. https://www.tylerjost. com/uploads/1/1/0/4/110425699/socializedhawks_full.pdf.

Kaarbo, Juliet, and Ryan Beasley. 1999. "A Practical Guide to the Comparative Case Study Method in Political Psychology." *Political Psychology* 20 (2): 369–91.

Kabaservice, Geoffrey. 2012. *Rule and Ruin: The Downfall of Moderation and the Destruction of the Republican Party.* Oxford: Oxford University Press.

Kertzer, Joshua, Deborah Brooks, and Stephen Brooks. 2021. "Do Partisan Types Stop at the Water's Edge?" *Journal of Politics,* 2021. https://www.people.fas.harvard.edu/~jkertzer/Research_files/Against_Type_Web.pdf.

Kessler, Daniel, and Keith Krehbiel. 1996. "Dynamics of Cosponsorship." *American Political Science Review* 90 (3): 555–66.

Kessler, Glenn. 2016. "Bernie Sanders' Claim That Glass Steagal Banned Commercial Bank Loans to 'Shadow' Banks." *Washington Post,* January 11, 2016. https://www.washingtonpost.com/news/fact-checker/wp/2016/01/11/bernie-sanderss-claim-that-glass-steagall-banned-commercial-bank-loans-to-shadow-banks/.

Khaled, Fatima. 2022. "Vindman Calls Gabbard 'Agent of Russian Disinformation' after Fox Segment." *Newsweek,* August 13, 2022. https://www.newsweek.com/vindman-calls-gabbard-agent-russian-disinformation-after-fox-segment-1733443.

Kinder, John M. 2015. *Paying with Their Bodies: American War and the Problem of the Disabled Veteran.* Chicago: University of Chicago Press.

Kinzinger, Adam. 2021. "Representative Adam Kinzinger." Congress, June 19, 2021. https://www.congress.gov/member/adam-kinzinger/K000378.

Kinzinger, Adam, and Brendan Boyle. 2017. "Kinzinger and Boyle Announce Congressional Caucus for Syria." June 26, 2017. https://kinzinger.house.gov/news/documentsingle.aspx?DocumentID=399547.

Klingler, Jonathan, and Tyson Chatagnier. 2016. "Would You Like to Know More? Selection, Socialization, and the Political Attitudes of Military Veterans." http://dx.doi.org/10.2139/ssrn.2876839.

Knickmeyer, Ellen. 2021. "Biden Ending U.S. Support for Saudi-led Offensive in Yemen." Associated Press, February 4, 2021. https://apnews.com/article/biden-end-support-saudi-offenseive-yemen-b68f58493dbfc530b9fcfdb80a13098f.

Koger, Gregory. 2003. "Position Taking and Cosponsorship in the U.S. House." *Legislative Studies Quarterly* 28 (2): 225–46.

Kostiner, Joseph. 2009. "Saudi Arabia and the Arab–Israeli Peace Process: The Fluctuations of Regional Coordination." *British Journal of Middle Eastern Studies* 36 (3): 417–29.

Krehbiel, Keith. 1995. "Cosponsors and Wafflers from A to Z." *American Journal of Political Science* 39 (4): 906–23. https://doi.org/10.2307/2111662.

Krieg, Andreas. 2016. "Externalizing the Burden of War: The Obama Doctrine and US Foreign Policy in the Middle East." *International Affairs* 92 (1): 97–113.

Kriner, Douglas. 2010. *After the Rubicon: Congress, Presidents, and the Politics of Waging War.* Chicago: University of Chicago Press.

Kriner, Douglas, and Francis Shen. 2014. "Responding to War on Capitol Hill: Battlefield Casualties, Congressional Response, and Public Support for the War in Iraq." *American Journal of Political Science* 58 (1): 157–74.

212 References

Kube, Courtney. 2021. "Biden Administration to Increase Support for Veterans Exposed to Toxic Burn Pits While Serving Overseas." NBC News, November 11, 2021. https://www.nbcnews.com/news/military/biden-administration-increase-support -veterans-exposed-toxic-burn-pits-while-n1283689.

Kube, Courtney, and Carol E. Lee. 2019. "Trump Wants to Pull All U.S. Troops Out of Afghanistan by 2020 Election, Officials Say." NBC News, August 2, 2019. https:// www.nbcnews.com/news/military/trump-wants-pull-all-troops-out-afghanistan -2020-election-n1038651.

LaForgia, Michael, and Edward Wong. 2020. "War Crime Risk Grows for U.S. over Saudi Strikes in Yemen." *New York Times*, September 14, 2020. https://www.nytimes .com/2020/09/14/us/politics/us-war-crimes-yemen-saudi-arabia.html.

Lahut, Jake. 2020. "Gabbard Pitches Pro-Peace, Bipartisan Agenda." Keene Sentinel, January 22, 2020. https://www.sentinelsource.com/news/local/gabbard-pitches -pro-peace-bipartisan-agenda-to-sentinel-editorial-board/article_7ad42636-8503 -50c0-8e62-5a779a051d72.html.

Landay, Jonathan, and Steve Holland. 2019. "In Trump's Team, Misgivings Emerge over Any Deal with Taliban in Afghanistan: U.S. Officials." Reuters, August 30, 2019.

Landler, Mark, and Peter Baker. 2019. "Trump Vetoes Measure to Force End to U.S. Involvement in Yemen War." *New York Times*, April 6, 2019. https://www.nytimes .com/2019/04/16/us/politics/trump-veto-yemen.html.

Lantis, Jeffrey. 2019. *Foreign Policy Advocacy and Entrepreneurship*. Ann Arbor: University of Michigan Press.

———. 2021. "Military Veterans of the War on Terror: A New Generation of Congressional Foreign-Policy Advocacy." *Journal of Political & Military Sociology* 48 (1): 1–36.

Laporta, James. 2019. "Exclusive: Official Who Heard Call Says Trump Got 'Rolled' By Turkey and 'Has No Spine.'" *Newsweek*, October 7, 2019. https://www.newsweek .com/exclusive-official-who-heard-call-says-trump-got-rolled-turkey-has-no -spine-1463623.

Lasker, Judith. 1980. "Veterans' Medical Care: The Politics of an American Government Health Service." *Journal of Sociology & Social Welfare* 7 (3): 374–91.

Lawrence, George, and Thomas Kane. 1995. "Military Service and Racial Attitudes of White Veterans." In *The Military-State-Society Symbiosis*, edited by Peter Karsten, 235–55. London: Routledge.

Lazaroff, Tovah. 2018. "McGurck, Mattis Resign in Wake of U.S. Syria Pullout Declaration." *Jerusalem Post*, December 22, 2018. https://www.jpost.com/american-politics /mcgurk-mattis-resign-in-wake-of-us-syria-pullout-declaration-575132.

Leal, David L., and Jeremy M. Teigen. 2015. "Recent Veterans Are More Republican than Older Ones. Why?" *Washington Post*, November 11, 2015. https://www .washingtonpost.com/news/monkey-cage/wp/2015/11/11/recent-veterans-are-more -republican-than-older-ones-why/.

———. 2018. "Military Service and Political Participation in the United States: Institutional Experiences and the Vote." *Electoral Studies* 53 (1): 99–110.

LeBlanc, Paul. 2011. "Veterans Exposed to Burn Pits Will Get Expanded Health Care Support, White House Says." CNN, November 1, 2011. https://www.cnn

.com/2021/11/11/politics/military-exposure-burn-pits-biden-administration /index.html.

———. "Republican Reps Cite 9/11 Anniversary in Criticizing Trump's Decision to Invite Taliban to U.S. for Peace Talks." CNN, September 9, 2019. https://edition .cnn.com/2019/09/08/politics/michael-waltz-taliban-9-11-pompeo-cnntv/index .html.

Levine, Marianne. 2019. "Senate Rebukes Trump with Vote to Block Arms Sales to Saudi Arabia, UAE." Politico, June 20, 2019. https://politi.co/2IPL8AA.

Levinson, Nan. 2020. "More Veterans in Congress Could Mean Fewer Wars." *The Nation*, July 14, 2020. https://www.thenation.com/article/politics/congress-veterans-2020.

Lieu, Ted. 2015a. "Congressman Lieu Statement on White House Call for Investigation into Civilian Deaths in Yemen Airstrikes." Office of Congressman Ted Lieu, October 3, 2015. https://lieu.house.gov/media-center/press-releases/congressman-lieu-statement -white-house-call-investigation-civilian.

———. 2015b. "Public Statement on Rights Violations in Yemen." September 29, 2015. https://www.lieu.house.gov.

———. 2016. "Congressman Lieu Introduces Bipartisan Bill to Establish New Guidelines for Weapons Sales to Saudi Arabia." Office of Congressman Ted Lieu, April 22, 2016. https://lieu.house.gov/media-center/press-releases/congressman-lieu -introduces-bi-partisan-bill-establish-new-guidelines.

———. 2017. "Rep. Lieu Statement on House Passage of Lieu Amendment on Yemen." Office of Congressman Ted Lieu, July 14, 2017. https://lieu.house.gov/media-center /press-releases/rep-lieu-statement-house-passage-lieu-amendment-yemen.

———. 2021. "Public Statement on Military Support for Saudi Arabia." February 4, 2021. https://www.lieu.house.gov.

Lindsay, James. 1992–93. "Congress and Foreign Policy: Why the Hill Matters." *Political Science Quarterly* 107 (4): 607–28. https://doi.org/10.2307/2152287.

———. 1994. *Congress and the Politics of US Foreign Policy*. Baltimore: Johns Hopkins University Press.

Linskey, Annie, Tyler Pager, John Hudson, and Sean Sullivan. 2021. "Two Congress Members Make Unauthorized Trip to Kabul amid Evacuation Efforts." *Washington Post*, August 24, 2021. https://www.washingtonpost.com/politics/congress -kabul-trip-evacuation/2021/08/24/77f7673a-0501-11ec-a266-7c7fe02fa374 _story.html.

Londono, Ernesto, and Greg Miller. 2013. "CIA Begins Weapons Delivery to Syrian Rebels." *Washington Post*, September 11, 2013. https://www.washingtonpost.com /world/national-security/cia-begins-weapons-delivery-to-syrian-rebels/2013/09/11 /9fcf2ed8-1b0c-11e3-a628-7e6dde8f889d_story.html?utm_term=.b76acac65be9.

Long, David E. 2019. *The United States and Saudi Arabia: Ambivalent Allies*. London: Routledge.

Losey, Stephen. 2021. "The Military Is Resuming the Diversity Training that Trump Banned." Military, March 10, 2021. https://www.military.com/daily-news/2021/03 /08/military-resuming-diversity-training-trump-banned.html.

Lowande, Kenneth, Melinda Ritchie, and Erinn Lauterbach. 2019. "Descriptive and Substantive Representation in Congress: Evidence from 80,000 Congressional

Inquiries." *American Journal of Political Science* 63 (3): 644–59. https://doi.org/10.1111/ajps.12443.

Lugar, Richard, and Thomas Daschle. 2019. "Veterans Can Restore Trust in Congress." *Washington Post*, March 19, 2019. https://www.washingtonpost.com/opinions/veterans-can-restore-trust-in-congress-thats-why-we-created-a-new-caucus/2019/03/19/f5b88cd4-4a5b-11e9-b79a-961983b7e0cd_story.html.

Lupton, Danielle L. 2017. "Out of the Service: Into the House: Military Experience and Congressional War Oversight." *Political Research Quarterly* 70 (2): 327–39. https://doi.org/10.1177/1065912917691359.

———. 2018. "Military Experience and Congressional Decision-Making: The Impact of the Vietnam Draft Lottery and Cohort Effects." Paper presented to the Annual Meeting of the International Studies Association, 2018. Author's copy.

———. 2022. "Military Experience and Elite Decision-Making: Self-Selection, Socialization, and the Vietnam Draft Lottery." *International Studies Quarterly* 66 (1): sqab052.

Luria, Elaine. 2019. "From the Navy to Congress: Progressing from Physics to Policy Making." In *APS Division of Nuclear Physics Meeting Abstracts*. GA-003. Crystal City, VA: APS Division.

———. 2020a. "Press Release: Congresswoman Elaine Luria Participates in Hearing on Modernizing Veteran Eligibility for Care." Office of Congresswoman Elaine Luria, December 7, 2020. https://luria.house.gov/media/press-releases/congresswoman-elaine-luria-participates-hearing-modernizing-veteran-eligibility.

———. 2020b. "Public Statement on Veterans' Service." Elaine Luria for Congress, May 4, 2020. https://elaineforcongress.com/issues/.

———. 2021. "Press Release: Rep. Luria Urges House to Pass the COVENANT Act." 2021. Office of Congresswoman Elaine Luria, April 14, 2021. https://luria.house.gov/media/press-releases/rep-luria-urges-house-pass-covenant-act.

Lutz, Catherine, and Andrea Mazzarino, eds. 2019. *War and Health: The Medical Consequences of the Wars in Iraq and Afghanistan*. Vol. 4. New York: NYU Press.

Lyall, Sarah. 2021. "For Some, Afghanistan Outcome Affirms a Warning: Beware the Blob." *New York Times*, September 16, 2021. https://www.nytimes.com/2021/09/16/us/politics/blob-afghanistan-withdrawal-biden.html.

Lynch, Julia. 2013. "Aligning Sampling Strategies with Analytical Goals." In *Interview Research in Political Science*, edited by Layna Mosley, 31–44. Ithaca, NY: Cornell University Press.

Lynch, Michael, and Anthony Madonna. 2017. "Broken Record: Causes and Consequences of the Changing Roll Call Voting Record in the U.S. Congress." https://static1.squarespace.com/static/590b42623a04112426074d15/t/59a041e2c534a5ecfb429de6/1503674852306/LynchMadonna2017.pdf.

Malkasian, Carter. 2021. *The American War in Afghanistan: A History*. Oxford: Oxford University Press.

Malley, R., and S. Pomper. 2021. "Accomplice to Carnage: How American Enables War in Yemen." *Foreign Affairs* 100:73–79.

Mannheim, Karl. (1936) 1955. *Ideology and Utopia: An Introduction to the Sociology of Knowledge*. London: Harcourt.

Marshall, Bryan W., and Patrick J. Haney. 2022. "The Impact of Party Conflict on Executive Ascendancy and Congressional Abdication in US Foreign Policy." *International Politics* 59 (4): 661–86.

Martinez, Shandra. 2012. "Meijer Heir Puts His Military Experience to Use Helping Hurricane Sandy Victims." Michigan Live, November 19, 2012. https://www.mlive .com/business/west-michigan/2012/11/meijer_heir_puts_his_military.html.

Mason, Kara. 2019. "'It Was Surreal for Me': Congressman Crow Sees Afghanistan Again as a Lawmaker, Not a Soldier." The Colorado Sentinel, October 24, 2019. https:// sentinelcolorado.com/news/metro/it-was-surreal-for-me-congressman-crow-sees -afghanistan-again-as-a-lawmaker-not-a-soldier/.

Mattiace, Gaia. 2017. "Panelists Call for Bipartisan Solution in Syria." *The Hoya*, February 17, 2017. https://thehoya.com/panelists-call-for-bipartisan-solution-in-syria/.

Mayhew, David. 1974. "Congressional Elections: The Case of the Vanishing Marginals." *Polity* 6 (3): 295–317. https://www.journals.uchicago.edu/doi/abs/10.2307/3233931.

Mazzetti, Mark, and Eric Schmidt. 2016. "Quiet Support for Saudis Entangles U.S. in Yemen." *New York Times*, March 13, 2016. https://www.nytimes.com/2016/03/14 /world/middleeast/yemen-saudi-us.html.

McBeth, Mark, Michael Jones, and Elizabeth Shanahan. 2014. "The Narrative Policy Framework." In *Theories of the Policy Process*, edited by Paul A. Sabatier and Christopher M. Weible, 225–66. Boulder, CO: Westview Press.

McCarthy, Niall. 2019. "The Annual Cost of the War in Afghanistan since 2001 [Infographic]." *Forbes*, September 12, 2019. https://www.forbes.com/sites/niallmccarthy /2019/09/12/the-annual-cost-of-the-war-in-afghanistan-since-2001-infographic/#11 59e0391971.

McCormick, D. 2018. "Vote 'Veteran' to Get the Job Done." *Washington Post*, May 23, 2018. https://www.washingtonpost.com/opinions/vote-veteran-to-get-the-jobdone /2018/05/23/3ae4c9fc-5ea9-11e8-b2b8-08a538d9dbd6_story.html?noredirect¼on & utm_term¼.3a737dc2e589.

McDermott, Monika L., and Costas Panagopoulos. 2015. "Be All That You Can Be: The Electoral Impact of Military Service as an Information Cue." *Political Research Quarterly* 68 (2): 293–305.

McDonald, Ryan. 2017. "The Rise of Ted Lieu." Easy Reader & Peninsula, June 8, 2017. https://easyreadernews.com/rise-ted-lieu-south-bay-congressman-emerges -national-leader-trump-opposition/.

McDonough, Denis. 2021. "Transcript: Meet the Press Interview with Courtney Kube." November 11, 2021. https://twitter.com/ckubeNBC/status/1458887499867168770.

McKeon, Brian, and Caroline Tess. 2019. "How Congress Can Take Back Foreign Policy." *Foreign Affairs*, January 2019. https://www.foreignaffairs.com/articles /united-states/2018-11-07/how-congress-can-take-back-foreign-policy.

McVicar, Brian. 2019. "'West Michigan Needs a New Voice in Congress', Says Amash Challenger Peter Meijer." Michigan Live, July 3, 2019. https://www.mlive.com /news/grand-rapids/2019/07/west-michigan-needs-a-new-voice-in-congress-says -amash-challenger-peter-meijer.html.

Meisel, Zachary, and Jason Karlawish. 2011. "Narrative vs Evidence-Based Medicine-And, Not Or." *Journal of the American Medical Association* 306 (18): 2022–23.

216 References

Memmott, Mark. 2013. "Kerry Says Assad, A 'Thug and Murderer,' Was Behind Attack." National Public Radio, August 30, 2013. https://www.npr.org/sections/thetwo-way /2013/08/30/217211589/coming-up-kerry-statement-about-the-crisis-in-syria.

Mendoza, Jim. 2013. "The Gabbards: Raising Hawaii's Next Political Star (Part 1)." Hawaii News Now, February 1, 2013.

Micinski, Nicholas R. 2018. "Refugee Policy as Foreign Policy: Iraqi and Afghan Refugee Resettlements to the United States." *Refugee Survey Quarterly* 37 (3): 253–78.

Miller, Aaron David. 2017. *Search for Security: Saudi Arabian Oil and American Foreign Policy*. Chapel Hill: UNC Press Books.

Miller, Joshua. 2010. "Into the Wild Blue Yonder: Adam Kinzinger's Flight from Air Force Pilot to Congressman." ABC News, November 11, 2010. https://abcnews.go.com /Politics/adam-kinzinger-beats-illinois-incumbent-deborah-halvorson-congressman /story?id=12118583.

Mintrom, Michael. 2019. "So You Want to Be a Policy Entrepreneur?" *Policy Design and Practice* 2 (4): 307–23.

Mintrom, Michael, and Joannah Luetjens. 2017. "Policy Entrepreneurs and Foreign Policy Decision Making." *Oxford Research Encyclopedia of Politics*. https://doi .org/10.1093/acrefore/9780190228637.013.463.

Moreno, Dario, Eduardo Gamarra, Patrick Murphy, and David Jolly. 2021. *A Divided Union: Structural Challenges to Bipartisanship in America*. New York: Routledge.

Mullen, Mike, and Elliot Ackerman. 2018. "Can Veterans Rescue Congress from Its Partisan Paralysis?" *USA Today*, July 2, 2018. https://www.usatoday.com/story /opinion/2018/02/07/veterans-can-rescue-congress-partisan-paralysis-mike-mullen -elliott-ackerman-column/309188002.

Naiman, Robert. 2017. "Back Murphy-Paul-Lieu-Yoho Limits on Weapons to Saudis." MoveOn, 2017. https://sign.moveon.org/petitions/back-murphy-paul-lieu.

Navajas, Joaquín, Barrera Lemarchand, Federico, Viktoriya Semeshenko, and Pablo Balenzuela. 2020. "Polarizing Crowds: Consensus and Bipolarization in a Persuasive Arguments Model." *Chaos: An Interdisciplinary Journal of Nonlinear Science* 30 (6): 063141.

Naylor, Brian. 2022. "President Biden Warns That the Threat of a Russian Invasion of Ukraine is 'Very High.'" NPR, February 17, 2022. https://www.npr.org /2022/02/17/1081428801/biden-russia-ukraine-invasion.

Nelson, Joshua. 2019. "Representative Michael Waltz Says U.S. Troop Pullout from Syria Sets Conditions for ISIS 2.0." Fox News Interview, October 14, 2019. https:// www.foxnews.com/media/rep-michael-waltz-says-u-s-troops-pullout-from-syria -sets-conditions-for-isis-2-0.

Nelson, Thomas. 2011. "Issue Framing." In *The Oxford Handbook of American Public Opinion and the Media*, edited by Robert Y. Shapiro and Lawrence R. Jacobs, 189–203. Oxford: Oxford University Press.

Nelson, Thomas, Zoe Oxley, and Rosalee Clawson. 1997. "Toward a Psychology of Framing Effects." *Political Behavior* 19:221–46.

Neukam, Stephen. 2023. "Group of Moderate Democrats Lobbying against Defense Spending Cuts." *The Hill*, January 11, 2023. https://thehill.com/policy/3808776 -group-of-moderate-democrats-lobbying-against-defense-spending-cuts/.

Nicas, Jack. 2022. "Ukraine War Threatens to Cause a Global Food Crisis." *New York Times*, March 20, 2022. https://www.nytimes.com/2022/03/20/world/americas/ukraine-war-global-food-crisis.html.

Nielson, Suzanne, and Don Snider. 2009. *American Civil-Military Relations: The Soldier and the State in a New Era.* Baltimore: Johns Hopkins University Press.

Nisbett, Richard, and Lee Ross. 1980. *Human Interference: Strategies and Shortcomings of Social Judgement.* Englewood Cliffs, NJ: Prentice Hall.

Nissenbaum, Dion, and Nancy Youssef. 2019. "U.S. Military Now Preparing to Leave as Many as 1,000 Troops in Syria." *Wall Street Journal*, March 17, 2019. https://www.wsj.com/articles/u-s-military-now-preparing-to-leave-as-many-as-1-000-troops-in-syria-11552853378.

Norton, Ben. 2016a. "A Congressman Campaigns to 'Stop the Madness' of U.S. Support for Saudi Bombings in Yemen." The Intercept, August 22 2016. https://theintercept.com/2016/08/22/a-congressman-campaigns-to-stop-the-madness-of-u-s-support-for-saudi-bombing-in-yemen/.

———. 2016b. "'Look Like War Crimes to Me': Congressman Raises Concerns over U.S. Support for Saudi War in Yemen." Salon, March 17, 2016. https://www.salon.com/2016/03/17look_like_war_crimes_to_me_congressman_raises_concerns_over_u_s_support_for_saudi_war_in_yemen/.

Norwegian Refugee Council. "Time for UN Security Council to Act on Yemen." February 1, 2018. https://www.nrc.no/news/2018/february/time-for-un-security-council-to-act-on-yemen/.

Nteta, Tatishe, and Melinda Tarsi. 2016. "Self-selection versus Socialization Revisited: Military Service, Racial Resentment, and Generational Membership." *Armed Forces & Society* 42 (2): 362–85.

Oakford, Samuel, and Peter Salisbury. 2016. "Yemen: The Graveyard of the Obama Doctrine." *The Atlantic*, September 23, 2016. https://www.theatlantic.com/international/archive/2016/09/yemen-saudi-arabia-obama-riyadh/501365/.

O'Dowd, Peter. 2019. "GOP Rep. Waltz Afghanistan War Veteran, Has Concerns about US Withdrawal." WBUR, February 1, 2019. https://www.wbur.org/hearandnow/2019/02/01/michael-waltz-afghanistan-troop-withdrawal.

O'Haire, M. 2010. "Companion Animals and Human Health: Benefits, Challenges, and the Road Ahead." *Journal of Veterinary Behavior* 5 (5): 226–34.

O'Hanlon, Michael. 2019. "5,000 Troops for 5 Years: A No Drama Approach for Afghanistan." Brookings Institution, August 16, 2019. https://www.brookings.edu/articles/5000-troops-for-5-years-a-no-drama-approach-to-afghanistan-for-the-next-us-president/.

Olenick, M., M. Flowers, and V. J. Diaz. 2015. "U.S. Veterans and Their Unique Issues: Enhancing Health Care Professional Awareness." *Advances in Medical Education and Practice* 6 (4): 635–39.

O'Neill, Stephanie. 2021. "More Veterans with PTSD Will Soon Get Help from Service Dogs Thanks to the PAWS Act." NPR News, November 26, 2021. https://www.npr.org/sections/health-shots/2021/11/26/1045708726/more-veterans-with-ptsd-will-soon-get-help-from-service-dogs-thank-the-paws-act.

Ortiz, Stephen R., ed. 2015. *Veterans' Policies, Veterans' Politics: New Perspectives on Veterans in the Modern United States.* Tallahassee: University Press of Florida.

218   References

Ottaway, David. 2009. "The King and Us: US-Saudi Relations in the Wake of 9/11." *Foreign Affairs* 88 (4): 121–26.

Parker, Ashley, and Jeremy Peters. 2015. "Veterans in Congress Bring Rare Perspective to Authorizing War." *New York Times*, February 17, 2015. https://www.nytimes.com/2015/02/18/us/bringing-a-rare-perspective-to-authorizing-war.html.

Parker, Kim, Ruth Igielnik, Amanda Barroso, and Anthony Cilluffo. 2019. "The American Veteran Experience and the Post-9/11 Generation." Pew Research, September 10, 2019. https://www.pewresearch.org/social-trends/2019/09/10/the-american-veteran-experience-and-the-post-9-11-generation/.

Parlapiano, Alicia, Anjali Singhvi, Jon Huang, and Thomas Kaplan. 2017. "Where Top Lawmakers Stand on Syria: Now and in 2013." *New York Times*, April 7, 2017. https://www.nytimes.com/interactive/2017/04/07/us/politics/congress-quotes-on-syria-airstrikes.html.

Payne, J. Sayre. 2018. "A Duty Owed: The Failure of the Special Immigrant Visa Program and Its Message to Allies and Enemies." *University of Dayton Law Review* 44:631.

PBS NewsHour. 2018. "Rep.-elect Waltz, a former Green Beret, Shares His Congressional Vision." November 14, 2018. https://www.pbs.org/newshour/show/rep-elect-waltz-a-former-green-beret-shares-his-congressional-vision.

Pergram, Chad. 2022. "New Fight in Congress over War Powers with U.S. Troops in Eastern Europe." Fox News, February 8, 2022. https://www.foxnews.com/politics/war-powers-congress-9-11-ukraine-tensions.

"Peter Meijer Pushes for Expanded Sanctions on Members of Russia's Parliament." 2022. Forbes Breaking News, May 7, 2022. https://www.bing.com/videos/search?q=peter+meijer+ukraine&&view=detail&mid=C2860CBA658C1E67438BC2860CBA658C1E67438B&rvsmid=26EED0533AB7004C641226EED0533AB7004C6412&FORM=VDRVRV.

Pfingsten, Patrick. 2021. "Willing to 'Put My Career on the Line' over Direction of GOP." *The Illinoize*, April 16, 2021. https://www.theillinoize.com/articles/kinzinger-willing-put-my-career.

Phillips, Amber. 2015. "Rep. Tulsi Gabbard: The Democrat That Republicans Love and the DNC Can't Control." *Washington Post*, October 15, 2015.

Pierce, Jonathan, Holly Peterson, Michael Jones, Samantha Garrard, and Theresa Vu. 2017. "There and Back Again: A Tale of the Advocacy Coalition Framework." *Policy Studies Journal* 45 (1): S13–S46.

Pion-Berlin, David, and Danijela Dudley. 2020. "Civil-Military Relations: What Is the State of the Field." In *Handbook of Military Sciences*, edited by A. Sookermany, 1–22. Cham: Springer.

Pizzaro, Sierra. 2022. "Two Americas: PAWS Act Is in Effect for Veterans with PTSD." KRIS 6 News, January 7, 2022. https://www.kristv.com/news/local-news/two-americas-paws-act-is-in-effect-for-veterans-with-ptsd.

Platt, Matthew, and V. Sinclair-Chapman. 2008. "Legislative Problem-Solving: Exploring Bill Sponsorship in Post-War America." https://scholar.google.com/scholar?hl=en&as_sdt=0%2C36&q=Platt+and+Sinclair-Chapman+2008&btnG=.

Poisson, Chelsey, Sheri Boucher, Domenique Selby, Sylvia P. Ross, Charulata Jindal, Jimmy T. Efird, and Pollie Bith-Melander. 2020. "A Pilot Study of Airborne Hazards and Other Toxic Exposures in Iraq War Veterans." *International Journal of Environmental Research and Public Health* 17 (9): 3299.

Portnoy, Jenna. 2019b. "The Story of a Virginia Swing District Town Hall: From Cheers to Jeers." *Washington Post*, October 4, 2019. https://www.washingtonpost.com/local/virginia-politics/the-story-of-a-virginia-swing-district-town-hall-from-cheers-to-jeers/2019/10/04/3d5441e6-e485-11e9-a331-2df12d56a80b_story.html.

Powers, Scott. 2019. "Michael Waltz Bill Would Tie Afghanistan Withdrawal to Taliban Concessions." Florida Politics, April 3, 2019. https://floridapolitics.com/archives/292623-michael-waltz-bill-would-tie-afghanistan-withdrawl-to-taliban-concessions/.

———. 2021. "Mike Waltz, Two Democrats Plead for Biden Administration to Help Ukraine Now." Florida Politics, December 14, 2021. https://floridapolitics.com/archives/480182-mike-waltz-two-democrats-plead-for-administration-to-help-ukraine-now/.

Problem Solvers Caucus. 2021. "Press Release." March 29, 2021. https://problemsolverscaucus.house.gov/media.

Prupis, Nadia. 2016. "Lawmakers, Peace Groups Team Up to Block 'Disturbing' U.S.-Saudi Arms Deal." Common Dreams, August 23, 2016. https://lieu.house.gov/media-center/in-the-news/lawmakers-peace-groups-team-block-disturbing-us-saudi-arms-deal.

Radford, Jynnah, and Jens Manuel Krogstad. 2017. "Afghans Who Worked for U.S. Government Make Up Growing Share of Special Immigrant Visa Recipients." Pew Research Center, December 11, 2017. https://media3.nooneleft.org/WF/_transactionServerFiles/886/2021/6/23/Pew-Research-Special-immigrant-visas-increasingly-go-to-Afghans-who-worked-for-US-government-_-Pew-Research-Cente-1.pdf.

Ragin, Charles. 2013. "New Directions in the Logic of Social Inquiry." *Political Research Quarterly* 66 (1): 171–74.

———. 2014. *The Comparative Method: Moving beyond Qualitative and Quantitative Strategies*. Berkeley: University of California Press.

Rainey, Michael. 2022. "Who's Keeping an Eye on $40 Billion in Ukraine Aid?" *Fiscal Times*, June 2, 2022. https://www.yahoo.com/now/keeping-eye-40-billion-ukraine-225408316.html.

Ramani, Samuel. 2019. "In the Demise of the Taliban Peace Talks, Russia is the Winner." Foreign Policy, September 11, 2019. https://foreignpolicy.com/2019/09/11/in-the-demise-of-the-taliban-peace-talks-russia-is-the-winner/.

Raskin, Jamie. 2022. "Trump Coup Will Be Focus of House Hearings." April 18, 2022. Press Conference Transcript. https://politicalwire.com/2022/04/18/trump-coup-attempt-will-be-focus-on-house-hearings/.

Recchia, Stefano. 2015. *Reassuring the Reluctant Warriors: U.S. Civil-Military Relations and Multilateral Intervention*. Ithaca, NY: Cornell University Press.

Remnick, David. 2014. "Going the Distance: On and Off the Road with Barack Obama." *New Yorker*, January 19. https://www.newyorker.com/magazine/2014/01/27/going-the-distance-david-remnick.

"Rep. Ruben Gallego: We Need to Be Fully Committed to Saving Ukraine." 2022. Andrea Mitchell Reports, February 24, 2022. https://www.msnbc.com/andrea-mitchell-reports/watch/rep-ruben-gallego-we-need-to-be-fully-committed-to-saving-ukraine-133951557936.

220 References

"Representative Tulsi Gabbard, Legislation Record." Congress. Accessed March 9, 2017. https://www.congress.gov/member/tulsi-gabbard/G000571.

"Republican Congressman and Veteran Shares His Thoughts on Troops Withdrawing from Syria." 2018. NPR, December 19, 2018. https://www.npr.org/2018/12/19 /678294382/republican-congressman-and-veteran-shares-his-thoughts-on-troops -withdrawing-fro.

Reuters News Service. 2016. "Congresswoman Quits Democratic National Committee, Endorses Bernie Sanders." February 28, 2016. https://www.reuters.com/article/us -usa-election-sanders-gabbard/congresswoman-quits-democratic-national -committee-endorses-bernie-sanders-idUSMTZSAPEC2S9JDNKG.

Rhidenour, Kayla B., Ashley K. Barrett, and Kate G. Blackburn. 2019. "Heroes or Health Victims? Exploring How the Elite Media Frames Veterans on Veterans Day." *Health Communication* 34 (4): 371–82.

Riley-Topping, Rory. 2019. "The Benefit of Electing Veterans: More Bipartisan Law-making." *The Hill*, June 26, 2019. https://thehill.com/opinion/campaign/450457-the -benefits-of-electing-veterans-is-more-bipartisan-lawmaking.

Ripon Advance News Service. 2020. "Stivers Introduces Bill to Strengthen Suicide Prevention Program for Veterans." August 27, 2020. https://riponadvance.com/ stories/stivers-introduces-bill-to-strengthen-suicide-prevention-program-for -veterans/.

Robinson, G. Lee, Joseph Amoroso, Isaiah (Ike) Wilson III, and Richard Yon. 2018. "Veterans and Bipartisanship." *Armed Forces & Society* 46 (1): 132–62.

———. 2020. "Veterans and Bipartisanship." *Armed Forces & Society* 46 (1): 132–62.

Roblin, Sebastien. 2018. "The Battle at Hudaydah: How Saudi Arabia Is Trying to Cut Off Houthi Rebels' Maritime Supply Lines." National Interest, June 27, 2018. https://nationalinterest.org/blog/the-buzz/battle-hudaydah-how-saudi-arabia -trying-cutoff-houthi-rebels-26380.

Rocca, Michael, and Gabriel Sanchez. 2008. "The Effect of Race and Ethnicity on Bill Sponsorship and Cosponsorship in Congress." *American Politics Research* 36 (1): 130–52. https://doi.org/10.1177/1532673X07306357.

Roche, Darragh. 2021. "Freshman Republicans Send Letter to Joe Biden: 'We Can Rise Above the Partisan Fray'". Newsweek, January 20. https://www.newsweek.com /freshman-republicans-letter-joe-biden-rise-above-partisan-fray-1563043.

Rodriguez, Kerri E., Nancy R. Gee, Aubrey H. Fine, and Janet P. Trammell. 2021. "Dogs Supporting Human Health and Well-Being: A Biopsychosocial Approach." *Frontiers in Veterinary Science* 8: 630–45.

Rodriguez, Sabrina. 2023. "Can Ruben Gallego's Senate Campaign Energize Latino Vot-ers in Arizona?" *Washington Post*, February 1, 2023. https://www.washingtonpost .com/politics/2023/02/01/ruben-gallego-senate-arizona/.

Rogin, Josh. 2019. "Tulsi Gabbard's Syria Record Shows Why She Can't Be President." *Washington Post*, August 1 2019. https://www.washingtonpost.com/opinions/global -opinions/tulsi-gabbards-syria-record-shows-why-she-cant-be-president/2019/08 /01/f804c790-b497-11e9-8949-5f36ff92706e_story.html.

Rogowski, Jon, and Joseph Sutherland. 2016. "How Ideology Fuels Affective Polariza-tion." *Political Behavior* 38:485–508. https://doi.org/10.1007/s11109-015-9323-7.

Rojas, Warren, and Brent D. Griffiths. 2022. "Democratic Rep. Ruben Gallego, an Iraq War Vet, Said He Was Prepared to 'Kill Somebody' on Jan. 6th." Business Insider, April 22, 2022. https://sports.yahoo.com/democratic-rep-ruben-gallego-iraq-1447 49615.html.

Roman, P., and D. Tarr. 2001. "Military Professionalism and Policymaking: Is There a Civil-Military Gap at the Top? If So, Does It Matter?" In *Soldiers and Civilians: The Civil-Military Gap and American National Security*, edited by Peter Feaver and Richard Kohn, 403–28. Cambridge, MA: MIT Press.

Rossomando, John. 2023. "Tulsi Gabbard Sounds Like a Republican Now." MSN, April 23, 2023. https://www.msn.com/en-us/news/politics/tulsi-gabbard-sounds -like-a-republican-now/ar-AA190svB.

Roth, Claire. 2021. "Representative Steve Stivers to Resign from Congress." WKSU, April 21, 2021. https://www.wksu.org/government-politics/2021-04-19/rep-steve -stivers-to-resign-from-congress.

Rudalevige, Andrew. 2006. *The New Imperial Presidency: Renewing Presidential Power after Watergate*. Ann Arbor: University of Michigan Press.

Ryan, Missy. 2023. "Arab Embrace of Assad Underscores Divergence with U.S. over Syria." *Washington Post*, May 19, 2023. https://www.washingtonpost.com/national -security/2023/05/19/syria-assad-arab-league-sanctions/.

Ryan, Missy, and Josh Dawsey. 2018. "U.S. Troops to Be Pulled Out of Syria Quickly, White House Says." *Washington Post*, December 19, 2018. https://www.washington post.com/world/national-security/trump-administration-plans-to-pull-us-troops -from-syria-immediately-defense-official-says/2018/12/19/4fcf188e-0397-11e9-b5df -5d3874f1ac36_story.html.

Sabatier, Paul A. 1986. "Top-Down and Bottom-Up Approaches to Implementation Research: A Critical Analysis and Suggested Synthesis." *Journal of Public Policy* 6 (1): 21–48.

———. 1988. "An Advocacy Coalition Framework of Policy Change and the Role of Policy-Oriented Learning Therein." *Policy Sciences* 21 (2): 129–68.

Sabatier, Paul A., and Christopher Weible. 2007. "The Advocacy Coalition Framework: Innovations and Clarifications." In *Theories of the Policy Process*, edited by Paul A. Sabatier and Christopher M. Weible, 189–220. Boulder, CO: West Press.

Saenz, Arlette. 2022. "Biden Administration Adds Nine Rare Respiratory Cancers with Ties to Burn Pits to List of Service-Connected Disabilities." CNN Politics, April 25, 2022. https://www.cnn.com/2022/04/25/politics/burn-pits-cancer-veterans/index .html.

Sanneh, Kelefa. 2017. "What Does Tulsi Gabbard Believe?" *New Yorker*, November 6. https://www.newyorker.com/magazine/2017/11/06/what-does-tulsi-gabbard-believe.

Schaffner, Brian, and Patrick Sellers. 2010. *Winning with Words: The Origins and Impact of Political Framing*. New York: Routledge.

Schulhofer-Wohl, Jonah. 2021. "The Obama Administration and Civil War in Syria, 2011–2016: US Presidential Foreign Policy-Making as Political Risk Management." *Journal of Transatlantic Studies* 19 (4): 517–47.

Schultz, Kenneth. 2017. "Perils of Polarization for U.S. Foreign Policy." *Washington Quarterly* 40 (4): 7–28. https://doi.org/10.1080/0163660X.2017.1406705.

Schumacher, Tobias, Dimitris Bouris, and Maja Olszewska. 2016. "Of Policy Entrepreneurship, Bandwagoning, and Free-Riding: EU Member States and the Multilateral Cooperation Frameworks for Europe's Southern Neighborhood." *Global Affairs* 2 (3): 259–72.

Scott, Steven, Heather Belanger, Rodney Vanderploeg, and Jill Paul Massengale. 2006. "Mechanism-of-Injury Approach to Evaluating Patients with Blast-Related Polytrauma." *Journal of the American Osteopathic Association* 106 (5): 265–70.

Scoville, Ryan. 2017. "A Legal Analysis of Rep. Tulsi Gabbard's Trip to Syria." Lawfare (Blog), February 14, 2017. https://www.lawfareblog.com/legal-analysis-rep-tulsi -gabbards-trip-syria.

Seal, Karen H., Thomas J. Metzler, Kristian S. Gima, Daniel Bertenthal, Shira Maguen, and Charles R. Marmar. 2009. "Trends and Risk Factors for Mental Health Diagnoses among Iraq and Afghanistan Veterans Using Department of Veterans Affairs Health Care, 2002–2008." *American Journal of Public Health* 99 (9): 1651–58.

Sears, D. O., and S. Levy. 2003. "Childhood and Adult Political Development." In *Oxford Handbook of Political Psychology*, edited by D. O. Sears, L. Huddy, and R. Jervis, 60–109. Oxford: Oxford University Press.

Seawright, Jason, and John Gerring. 2008. "Case Selection Techniques in Case Study Research: A Menu of Qualitative and Quantitative Options." *Political Research Quarterly* 61 (2): 294–308.

Sechser, Todd. 2004. "Are Soldiers Less War-Prone than Statesmen?" *Journal of Conflict Resolution* 48 (5): 746–74. https://doi.org/10.1177/0022002704268025.

Seligman, Lara. 2021. "Speed Equals Safety: Inside the Pentagon's Controversial Decision to Leave Bagram Early." Politico, September 28, 2021. https://www.politico .com/news/2021/09/28/pentagon-decision-leave-bagram-514456.

Senate Resolution SJ 54. 2018. "S.J.Res.54—A Joint Resolution to Direct the Removal of United States Armed Forces from Hostilities in the Republic of Yemen That Have Not Been Authorized by Congress." Congress, December 19, 2018. https://www .congress.gov/bill/115th-congress/senate-joint-resolution/54.

Serhan, Yasmeen. 2017. "The Organization That Sent Tulsi Gabbard to Syria." *The Atlantic*, January 30, 2017. https://www.theatlantic.com/news/archive/2017/01/the -organization-that-sent-tulsi-gabbard-to-syria/514763/.

Settersten, R. A., Jr. 2006. "When Nations Call: How Wartime Military Service Matters for the Life Course and Aging." *Research on Aging* 28:12–36.

Shanahan, Elizabeth A., Michael Jones, and Mark McBeth. 2011. "Policy Narratives and Policy Processes." *Policy Studies Journal* 39 (3): 535–61.

Shanahan, Elizabeth A., Michael Jones, Mark McBeth, and Claudio Radaelli. 2018. "The Narrative Policy Framework." In *Theories of the Policy Process*, edited by Christopher M. Weible, 173–213. New York: Routledge.

Shanahan, Elizabeth A., Mark K. McBeth, and Paul L. Hathaway. 2011. "Narrative Policy Framework: The Influence of Media Policy Narratives on Public Opinion." *Politics & Policy* 39 (3): 373–400.

Sharkey, D. Harkins, T. Schickedanz, and C. Baird. 2014. "Department of Defense Participation in the Department of Veterans Affairs Airborne Hazards and Open Burn Pit Registry: Process, Guidance to Providers, and Communication." *US Army Medical Department Journal* 2014:44–50.

Shear, Michael D., David E. Sanger, Helene Cooper, Eric Schmitt, Julian E. Barnes, and Lara Jakes. 2021. "Miscue after Miscue, U.S. Exit Plan Unravels." *New York Times*, August 21, 2021, A1.

Sherrill, Mikie. 2020. "Rep. Sherrill Delivers Unanimous Passage of Bipartisan Bill to Pair Veterans with Service Dogs." Insider NJ, February 5, 2020. https://www.insidernj.com /press-release/rep-sherrill-delivers-unanimous-passage-bipartisan-bill-pair-veterans -service-dogs/.

Shesgreen, Debra. 2018. "'Stop Starving People as Instrument of War,' One Republican's Blunt Message to Saudis—and Trump." *USA Today*, October 30, 2018. https:// www.usatoday.com/story/news/world/2018/10/30/why-sen-todd-young-became -leading-critic-saudi-led-war-yemen/1738004002/.

Shinkman, Paul D. 2019. "Trump's Consideration of Afghanistan Withdrawal Spurs Criticism." U.S. News and World Report, August 16, 2019. https://www.usnews .com/news/world-report/articles/2019-08-16/trumps-consideration-of-afghanistan -withdrawal-spurs-criticism.

Shpeer, M., and W. T. Howe. 2020. "Socialization, Face Negotiation, Identity, and the United States Military." *International Journal of Communication* 14 (3): 726–44.

Simon, Caroline. 2021. "House Passes Bill to Authorize 8,000 More Visas for Afghan Allies." Roll Call, July 22, 2021. https://www.rollcall.com/2021/07/22/house-passes -bill-to-authorize-8000-more-visas-for-afghan-allies/.

Sinha, Shreeya. 2015. "Obama's Evolution on ISIS." *New Yorker*, June 9, 2015. https:// www.nytimes.com/interactive/2015/06/09/world/middleeast/obama-isis-strategy .html.

Sjursen, Danny. 2017. "The Last Great Debate: Congressional Veterans and the First Persian Gulf War." *World Affairs* 180 (1): 8–41.

Slatore, Christopher G., Michael J. Falvo, Shannon Nugent, and Kathleen Carlson. 2018. "Afghanistan and Iraq War Veterans: Mental Health Diagnoses Are Associated with Respiratory Disease Diagnoses." *Military Medicine* 183 (5–6): e249–e257.

Smith, Erika Cornelius. 2022. *Service above Self: Women Veterans in American Politics.* Lawrence: University of Kansas Press.

Smith, Steven. 2007. *Party Influence in Congress.* Cambridge: Cambridge University Press.

Sobel, Richard. 2001. *The Impact of Public Opinion on U.S. Foreign Policy since Vietnam.* New York: Oxford University Press.

Sonmez, Felicia. 2019. "Trump Faces Bipartisan Criticism for Syria Withdrawal." *Washington Post*, October 13, 2019. https://www.washingtonpost.com/politics /trump-faces-bipartisan-criticism-for-syria-withdrawal/2019/10/13/35da3026 -edde-11e9-8693-f487e46784 aa_story.html.

Sparrow, James T. 2011. *Warfare State: World War II Americans and the Age of Big Government.* Oxford: Oxford University Press.

Special to Richland Source. 2019. "Balderson Partners with Democrat to Join Civility & Respect Caucus." Richland Source, June 21, 2019. https://www.richlandsource .com/news/balderson-partners-with-democrat-to-join-civility-and-respect-caucus /article_e87d7860-93ba-11e9-adca-3fc22cd85f6b.html.

Stadelmann, David, Marco Portmann, and Reiner Eichenberger. 2015. "Military Careers of Politicians Matter for National Security Policy." *Journal of Economic Behavior & Organization* 116:142–56. https://doi.org/10.1016/j.jebo.2015.04.001.

Steinhauer, Jennifer. 2021. "In the Battle for the Capitol, Veterans Fought on Opposite Sides." *New York Times*, February 8, 2021. https://www.nytimes.com/2021/02/08/us/politics/capitol-riot-trump-veterans-cops.html.

Stevens, Rosemary. 1991. "Can the Government Govern? Lessons from the Formation of the Veterans Administration." *Journal of Health Politics, Policy, and Law* 16 (2): 281–315.

Stewart, Phil, and Warren Strobel. 2016. "U.S. to Halt Some Arms Sales to Saudi, Citing Civilian Deaths in Yemen Campaign." Yahoo Finance, December 13, 2016. https://finance.yahoo.com/news/us-halt-arms-sales-saudi-203516070.html.

Stivers, Steve. 2021. "No Party Has a Monopoly on Good Ideas: Listen To Those You Disagree With." *Columbus Dispatch*, May 17, 2021. https://www.dispatch.com/story/opinion/columns/guest/2021/05/17/steve-stivers-americans-must-listen-to-not-vilify-those-they-disagree/5126316001/.

Stroupe, Kevin T., Rachael Martinez, Timothy P. Hogan, Elisa J. Gordon, Beverly Gonzalez, Ibuola Kale, Chad Osteen, et al. 2019. "Experiences with the Veterans' Choice Program." *Journal of General Internal Medicine* 34 (10): 2141–49.

Sulkin, Tracy. 2011. *The Legislative Legacy of Congressional Campaigns*. Cambridge: Cambridge University Press.

Swarens, Tim. 2018. "How Todd Young Took on Donald Trump's Team—and Won." *IndyStar*, December 19, 2018. https://www.indystar.com/story/opinion/columnists/tim-swarens/2018/12/19/swarens-how-sen-todd-young-took-donald-trumps-team-and-won/2350678002/.

Swers, Michele. 2002. *The Difference Women Make: The Policy Impact of Women in Congress*. Chicago: University of Chicago Press.

———. 2013. *Women in the Club: Gender and Policy Making in the Senate*. Chicago: University of Chicago Press.

Szema, Anthony, Niely Mirsaidi, Bhumika Patel, Laura Viens, Edward Forsyth, Jonathan Li, Sophia Dang, et al. 2017. "Proposed Iraq/Afghanistan War-Lung Injury (IAW-LI) Clinical Practice Recommendations: National Academy of Sciences' Institute of Medicine Burn Pits Workshop." *American Journal of Men's Health* 11 (6): 1653–63.

Tam, Kenric, and Jivianne T. Lee. 2021. "Increased Prevalence of Upper and Lower Respiratory Disease in Operation Enduring Freedom and Operation Iraqi Freedom US Veterans." *Journal of Occupational and Environmental Medicine* 63 (3): 262–64.

Tama, Jordan. 2020. "Forcing the President's Hand: How the US Congress Shapes Foreign Policy through Sanctions Legislation." *Foreign Policy Analysis* 16 (3): 397–416.

Tarrow, Sidney. 1998. "'The Very Excess of Democracy': State Building and Contentious Politics in America." In *Social Movements and American Political Institutions*, edited by Anne N. Costain and Andrew S. McFarland, 20–38. Boulder, CO: Rowman & Littlefield.

———. 2005. *The New Transnational Activism*. New York: Cambridge University Press.

Tasolides, Justin. 2022. "Senate Unanimously Passes Bill to Expand Health Care for Veterans Exposed to Burn Pits." New York 1, February 16, 2022. https://www.ny1.com/all-boroughs/news/2022/02/16/senate-burn-pit-veterans-congress.

Taylor, G., V. Rush, and A. Deck. 2008. *Screening Health Risk Assessment Burn Pit Exposures, Balad Air Base, Iraq and Addendum Report (IOH-RS-BR-TR-2008-0001/*

USACHPPM 47-MA-08PV-08). Brooks City-Base, TX: Air Force Institute for Operational Health and U.S. Army Center for Health Promotion and Preventative Medicine.

Teigen, Jeremy. 2007. "Debt of a Nation: Understanding the Treatment of Military Veterans in the United States." *Armed Forces & Society* 33 (3): 438–44.

———. 2015. "Conventional and Distinctive Policy Preferences of Early-Twenty-First Century Veterans." In *Veterans' Policies, Veterans' Politics: New Perspectives on Veterans in the Modern United States*, edited by Stephen R. Ortiz, 263–80. Tallahassee: University Press of Florida.

———. 2018. *Why Veterans Run: Military Service in American Presidential Elections, 1789–2016*. Philadelphia: Temple University Press.

Teles, Steven, and Robert Saldin. 2019. "The Future Is Faction." Niskanen Center, November 25, 2019. https://www.niskanencenter.org/the-future-is-faction/.

Telhami, Shibley, and Connor Kopchick. 2020. "A Recent Poll Shows How Americans Think about the War in Afghanistan." Brookings Institution, January 9, 2020. https://www.brookings.edu/blog/order-from-chaos/2020/01/09/a-recent-poll -shows-how-americans-think-about-the-war-in-afghanistan/.

Theriault, Sean. 2008. *Party Polarization in Congress*. New York: Cambridge University Press.

Thiessen, Marc. 2022. "Ukraine War: What Happened Today." NPR, March 17, 2022. https://www.npr.org/2022/03/17/1087186668/russia-ukraine-war-what-happened -today-march-17.

Thomas, L. Eugene. 1971. "Political Attitude Congruence between Politically Active Parents and College-Age Children: An Inquiry into Family Political Socialization." *Journal of Marriage and the Family* 33:375–86.

Thompson, Alex. 2019. "Seth Moulton Discloses PTSD, Unveils Military Mental Health Proposal." Politico, May 28, 2019. https://www.politico.com/story/2019/05/28 /seth-moulton-ptsd-mental-health-1345848.

Thurber, James, and Antoine Yoshinaka. 2015. *American Gridlock: The Sources, Character, and Impact of Political Polarization*. Cambridge: Cambridge University Press.

Tilly, Charles, and Sidney Tarrow. 2006. *Contentious Politics*. Boulder, CO: Paradigm.

Tisdall, Simon. 2015. "U.S. Changes Its Tune on Syrian Regime Change as ISIS Threat Takes Top Priority." *The Guardian*, January 25, 2015. https://www.theguardian.com /us-news/2015/jan/25/us-syrian-regime-change-isis-priority.

Transcript of Hearing. House Committee on Veterans' Affairs, December 2, 2020. https://docs.house.gov/meetings/VR/VR00/20201202/111107/HHRG-116-VR00 -Wstate-CzarneckiT-20201202.pdf.

Tyson, A. S. 2018. "Taking the Hill: Why More Veterans Are Running for Congress." *Christian Science Monitor*, May 25, 2018.

US Chamber of Commerce. 2021. "Back to Business with Representative Peter Meijer." February 26, 2021. https://www.uschamber.com/improving-government/back -business-rep-peter-meijer.

US Senate Foreign Relations Committee. 2017. "Flashing Red: The State of Global Humanitarian Affairs." United States Senate Committee on Foreign Relations, March 22, 2017. https://www.foreign.senate.gov/hearings/flashing-red-the-state-of -global-humanitarian-affairs-032217.

Vespa, Jonathan E. 2020. "Those Who Served: America's Veterans from World War II to the War on Terror." ACS-43, *American Community Survey Reports*, U.S. Government Census Report, June 2020. https://www.census.gov/content/dam/Census /library/publications/2020/demo/acs-43.pdf.

Vest, B. M., J. Kulak, V. M. Hall, and G. G. Homish. 2018. "Addressing Patients' Veteran Status: Primary Care Providers' Knowledge, Comfort, and Educational Needs." *Family Medicine* 50 (6): 455–61.

Waltz, Michael. 2014. *Warrior Diplomat: A Green Beret's Battles from Washington to Afghanistan*. Washington, DC: Potomac Books.

———. 2021. "Waltz Introduces Resolution Condemning Biden's Failure in Afghanistan." Office of Congressman Michael Waltz. December 30, 2021. https://waltz .house.gov/news/documentsingle.aspx?DocumentID=534.

Wasburn, P. C., and T. J. A. Covert. 2017. *Making Citizens: Political Socialization Research and Beyond*. Berlin: Springer.

Watson Institute. 2020. "Costs of War Project. U.S. and Allied Injuries." https://watson .brown.edu/costsofwar/costs/human/military/wounded.

Wawro, Gregory. 2010. *Legislative Entrepreneurship in the US House of Representatives*. Ann Arbor: University of Michigan Press.

Weber, Gustavus A., and Laurence F. Schmeckebier. 1934. *The Veterans' Administration: Its History, Activities, and Organization*. Washington, DC: Brookings Institution.

Webster, Steven, and Alan Abramowitz. 2017. "The Ideological Foundations of Affective Polarization in the U.S. Electorate." *American Politics Research* 45 (4): 621–47.

Weed, Matthew C. 2017. "A New Authorization for the Use of Military Force against the Islamic State: Issues and Current Proposals." Congressional Research Service Report 7-5700, February 21, 2017. https://apps.dtic.mil/dtic/tr/fulltext/u2/1028524.pdf.

Wehrman, Jessica. 2017. "Lawmakers Pushing for Columbus to Get National Veterans Museum." *Dayton Daily News*, September 14, 2017. https://www.daytondailynews .com/news/state--regional-govt--politics/lawmakers-pushing-for-columbus-get -national-veterans-museum/2RohxHkbk5VDCfpGaBBIHJ/.

Weible, Christopher M., Paul A. Sabatier, and Kelly McQueen. 2009. "Themes and Variations: Taking Stock of the Advocacy Coalition Framework." *Policy Studies Journal* 37 (1): 121–40.

Weisman, Jonathan. 2022. "Ukraine War Shifts the Agenda in Congress, Empowering the Center." *New York Times*, March 15, 2022.

Weissert, Will. 2021. "Elaine Luria's Pro-Navy, Centrist Identity May Get Test over Jan. 6 Committee." *Virginia-Pilot*, July 24, 2021. https://www.pilotonline.com /government/nation/vp-nw-luria-jan-6-20210724-v2mewmgki5apnkeizxmrqs cixy-story.html.

Widener, Laura. 2019. "Sen. Lindsey Graham Slams Trump's Syria Withdrawal as 'Stain on America's Honor' and 'Big Win for ISIS.'" American Military News, October 7, 2019. https://americanmilitarynews.com/2019/10/sen-lindsey-graham-slams -trumps-syria-withdrawal-as-stain-on-americas-honor-and-big-win-for-isis/.

Williams, Jordan. 2021. "Gallego Leads Congressional Delegation to Ukraine." *The Hill*, December 13, 2021. https://thehill.com/homenews/house/585568-gallego -leads-congressional-delegation-to-ukraine/.

Wilson, Rick, and Cheryl Young. 1997. "Cosponsorship in the U.S. Congress." *Legislative Studies Quarterly* 22 (1): 25–43.

Windrem, Robert, and Ben Popkin. 2019. "Russian Propaganda Machine Discovers 2020 Democratic Candidate Tulsi Gabbard." NBC News, February 2, 2019. https://www.nbcnews.com/politics/2020-election/russia-s-propaganda-machine-discovers-2020-democratic-candidate-tulsi-gabbard-n964261.

Wire, Sarah D. "A Bronze Star Recipient Watches the Fall of Afghanistan from Congress—And Wants Answers." *Los Angeles Times*, August 24, 2021. https://www.stripes.com/theaters/us/2021-08-24/bronze-star-recipient-jimmy-panetta-afghanistan-wants-answers-2655633.html.

Wolfgang, Ben. 2018. "It's Time to Act in Syria, Rep. Adam Kinzinger Says in Blistering Assault on U.S. Strategy." *Washington Times*, September 14, 2018.

Yahoo News. 2021. "Gallego Leads Congressional Delegation to Ukraine." Yahoo News, December 13, 2021. https://news.yahoo.com/gallego-leads-congressional-delegation-ukraine-180734181.html.

Yam, Kimmy. 2020. "How Ted Lieu's Asian American Upbringing Led to His Role as Twitter's Political Clapback King." NBC News, July 22, 2020. https://www.nbcnews.com/news/asian-america/how-ted-lieu-s-asian-american-upbringing-led-his-role-n1234615.

Yanow, Dvora. 2000. *Conducting Interpretive Policy Analysis*. Thousand Oaks, CA: Sage.

Zillman, Donald. 2006. "Where Have All the Soldiers Gone II: Military Veterans in Congress and the State of Civil-Military Relations." *Maine Law Review* 58 (1): 135–57.

Author's Interviews with Confidential Sources

Author's interview, March 20, 2017.
Author's interview, August 9, 2021.
Author's interview, August 16, 2021.
Author's interview, September 9, 2021.
Author's interview, September 10, 2021.
Author's interview, September 16, 2021.
Author's interview, September 21, 2021.
Author's interview, September 28, 2021.
Author's interview, September 29, 2021.
Author's interview, September 30, 2021.
Author's interview, October 2, 2021.
Author's interview, October 4, 2021.
Author's interview, October 6, 2021.
Author's interview, October 12, 2021.
Author's interview, October 13, 2021.
Author's interview, October 14, 2021.
Author's interview, October 15, 2021.
Author's interview, October 16, 2021.

Author's interview, October 18, 2021.
Author's interview, October 19, 2021.
Author's interview, October 20, 2021.
Author's interview, October 26, 2021.
Author's interview, November 5, 2021.
Author's interview, November 8, 2021.
Author's interview, November 9, 2021.
Author's interview, November 16, 2021.
Author's interview, December 6, 2021.
Author's interview, June 14, 2022.
Author's interview, June 21, 2022.
Author's interview, June 22, 2022.
Author's interview, July 1, 2022.
Author's interview, October 15, 2022.

Index

advocacy coalitions, as strategy for policy influence, 27–28, 30, 46, 57, 73, 83, 98, 113, 115, 130, 141, 156, 169–70, 178, 180–83, 188

Afghanistan War, 1–2, 5, 11–14, 17, 18, 19–20, 24–27, 29–30, 33, 37–38, 40, 43, 53, 69, 80, 88–93, 97–118, 121, 123, 126, 132–33, 141–42, 150, 160–61, 167, 174, 176–77, 179–82, 184

Air Force, 6–10, 32, 38, 64–67, 80, 146, 173

al-Qaeda terrorist organization, 53–54, 58–59, 78, 82, 87, 91–92, 98, 100, 102

American Legion, 115, 120–21, 131–32, 141–42, 156, 181, 183

Army Rangers, 11, 30, 109

Army Reserve, 6–10, 32, 159

Assad, Bashar al-, 36–37, 39–42, 44–45, 49, 51–54, 57–59, 146, 179

Austin, Lloyd, 145

authorization for the use of military force, 52, 57–58, 175

Bacon, Don, 8, 41, 93, 152

Biden, Joe, administration of, 1–2, 11, 16, 18–19, 24, 31, 49, 59–60, 62, 64, 75, 85–86, 88, 94, 97–99, 101, 105–7, 114–17, 132–33, 144–47, 149, 151–52, 156–59, 161, 163, 167, 170, 175

bin Laden, Osama, 87

bipartisanship, 1, 11, 18–21, 25, 27–29, 30, 32, 36, 41–42, 45, 53–54, 58, 60, 68, 72–73, 76, 79–80, 93, 104, 107, 112–14, 116, 123–24, 126, 130, 132, 134–35, 137, 141, 146–47, 150, 152,

156, 158–59, 161, 163–64, 168–70, 175, 177–79, 181, 185, 187

Blinken, Antony, 145

Blue Water Navy Vietnam Veterans Act of 2019, 44, 71, 110, 125, 137, 140, 154–55

Bronze Star, 102, 134

Brookings Institution, 84, 99

burn pits, 13, 19, 55, 71, 110–11, 118, 121–26, 130–33, 142, 153, 155, 166, 168, 176, 180–81

Bush, George W., administration of, 3–4, 45, 86–88, 91

Camp David, 24, 88, 99–100

Capitol Hill, 1–3, 11–12, 14, 19, 23, 25–26, 28–29, 51, 59, 66, 90, 93, 106–7, 116–17, 120, 125, 131–32, 145, 158, 163, 169, 172–73, 177–78, 181–83, 185–86

CARES Act, 71, 90, 96, 110, 128, 130, 137

Center for Strategic and International Studies, 46, 98–99, 181

chemical weapons, 35–36, 39, 42, 48, 52, 59

Cheney, Liz, 48, 89, 100, 113

China, People's Republic of, 43, 58, 69–70

Clinton, Hillary, 53

Conceding our Veterans' Exposure Now and Necessitating Training (COVENANT) Act, 126–27, 129, 139, 181

Congressional Hispanic Caucus, 157

Council on Foreign Relations, 98

230 Index

counterterrorism, 24, 27, 46, 54, 62, 77–78, 83, 89, 91–93, 99, 114, 179
COVID-19, 43, 96, 110, 130, 137, 184
Crow, Jason, 8, 11, 17–18, 29–30, 32–33, 62, 101–17, 173–75, 178, 180, 182

Democrat Party, 157
Dempsey, Martin, 51
Department of Defense (DOD), 48, 63, 69, 108, 114, 122
Department of Veterans Affairs (VA), 13
DeSantis, Ron, 6, 11
disability, 13, 119, 120, 121, 124–25, 130–33, 138–39
Disabled American Veterans, 131, 181
Duckworth, Tammy, 5, 7, 58

Electoral College, 16
Ernst, Joni, 1, 7, 19, 146

Floyd, George, 184
For Country Caucus, 11, 19, 93, 97, 104, 107, 159

Gabbard, Tulsi, 7, 19, 29, 32–33, 35–36, 45, 48–60, 173–75, 178–79, 181
Gallagher, Mike, 8, 164
Gallego, Ruben, 11, 17, 19, 32–33, 66, 68, 122, 144, 147–58, 173–75, 178
GI Bill, 119–20
Golden, Jared, 8, 20
Gonzalez, Tony, 20
Graham, Lindsey, 6, 45–46, 48, 93
Green Berets, 11, 89, 174

Hamid Karzai International Airport, 89, 102, 117
Hezbollah, 41, 57
Honoring our PACT Act, 69, 132–33, 153
Houlahan, Chrissy, 8, 93
House Armed Services Committee (HASC), 50, 76, 86, 90, 103, 113, 156, 175, 186
House Foreign Affairs Committee (HFAC), 37, 38, 41, 52, 65, 113, 162–63

human rights, 28, 35, 42, 66–67, 69–71, 74, 77, 84, 109, 111–12, 115, 167, 170, 174, 183
Human Rights Watch, 84

immigration policy, 15, 101, 104, 113–15, 160
International Security Assistance Force (ISAF), 87
Iran, 37, 39–43, 45, 47–48, 54–57, 59, 62–63, 69, 71, 75, 80, 94–96, 110, 154, 165, 179; Iran Threat Reduction and Syria Human Rights Act, 42
Iraq and Afghanistan Veterans of America (IAVA), 131, 142, 181
Iraq War, 1, 26, 51, 57, 106, 122, 148, 151, 158
Islamic State (ISIS), 37–40, 45, 47, 54, 57–59, 82
issue framing, as strategy for advocacy, 18, 21, 23–25, 30, 39, 65, 77, 91, 104, 125, 135, 150, 161, 177–78

January 6, 2021, insurrection, 14–18, 48, 150, 160, 163, 168, 171

Kabul, Afghanistan, 87, 89, 92, 98, 101, 105–6, 112, 116–18, 161, 176, 182
Kaine, Tim, 45, 80
Kaszynski, Mary, 12, 126
Kelly, Mark, 8
Kelly, Trent, 7, 15, 186
Khalilzad, Zalmay, 91, 100
Khashoggi, Jamal, killing of, 63, 72, 79
Kinzinger, Adam, 1, 6, 15, 19, 32–34, 36–48, 59, 114, 146, 163, 173, 175, 178–79, 181–82, 186
Kurds, 40, 45, 47, 65

Lee, Barbara, 169, 175
Lieu, Ted, 7, 18, 32–33, 60–61, 64–75, 77, 173–74, 178–79, 183
Lugar, Richard, 27, 32, 76
Luria, Elaine, 8, 19, 32–33, 119, 123–33, 136, 142, 173, 176, 178–81

Index 231

Marines, 6–10, 17, 20, 32, 75–77, 99, 122, 124, 147–48, 150–51, 158, 174
Mattis, James, 42, 46, 47
McCain, John, 46
Meijer, Peter, 9, 32, 33, 107, 114, 144–45, 158–71, 173, 175–76, 178
Middle East, 11, 18, 27, 29, 37, 39–42, 46–47, 50, 53, 58, 62, 64, 66, 68, 75, 80, 86–87, 89–90, 92, 99, 101, 104, 121, 124, 126, 129–30, 138, 173
MiG-29 fighter jets, 146, 150, 158
Milley, Mark, 125
Moulton, Seth, 7, 11, 41, 66, 106, 122, 152, 161, 164, 176, 178
Murphy, Chris, 5–6, 48, 68, 73, 79

National Defense Authorization (NDAA) Act, 72, 74, 88, 152
National Guard, 1–2, 5–11, 15–16, 32, 48–50, 60, 66, 90, 102, 108, 110–11, 130, 133–36, 167, 173, 186
Naval Academy, 76, 77, 123, 138, 173
Navy, 5, 6–10, 20, 32, 44, 71, 76, 110, 123, 126, 137–38, 140, 154–55, 173
New Democrat Coalition, 124, 126
no-fly zone, 145–47, 152, 157–58, 162–63

Obama, Barack, administration of, 19, 29, 31, 35–37, 39, 45, 50, 52–54, 61, 63–64, 66–68, 73
Operation Enduring Freedom, 38
Operation Iraqi Freedom, 38, 133–34

Pakistan, 87, 89, 91–92, 102
Panetta, Jimmy, 1, 3, 8, 68, 93
Paul, Rand, 54, 68, 72–73, 165
PAWS (Puppies Assisting Wounded Servicemembers) Act, 44, 70, 94, 96, 108, 110, 133–34, 137, 141–43, 154, 167
Pelosi, Nancy, 50, 59, 66
Perry, Scott, 7, 29
policy entrepreneur, 18, 25, 28–29, 31, 182
post-traumatic stress disorder (PTSD), 2, 13, 19, 44, 119, 122, 133, 135, 137–38, 140–41, 151, 172

Problem Solvers Caucus, 124, 126, 147, 163, 169, 185
Putin, Vladimir, 11, 69, 94, 145–46, 150, 152, 157, 161, 164, 166

Qatar, 91, 134

refugees, in Afghanistan, 18–19, 24, 70, 75, 86, 89, 101, 104–6, 109, 114, 116–18, 152, 159, 161, 164, 174, 176
Republican Party, 37, 46, 68, 103, 134
Reserve Officers' Training Corps (ROTC), 96, 102, 173
Russia, 1, 11, 19–20, 24, 37, 39, 49, 54, 58, 60, 69, 94, 108, 144–47, 149–52, 155–58, 162, 170, 179

Saudi Arabia, kingdom of, 18, 33, 37, 59, 61–64, 66–75, 77–80, 82–85, 174, 178–79, 183–84; and blockade of ports, 63, 75, 78
Senate Foreign Relations Committee (SFRC), 46, 60, 83
Sherrill, Mikie, 5, 8, 68, 138
Socialization: military experiences, 20–23; versus "self-selection" thesis, 23
Special Immigrant Visa program, for select Afghanistan citizens, 1, 18, 33, 86, 88, 101, 114, 116, 179, 182
Stivers, Steve, 6, 19, 23, 32, 33, 119, 133–42, 173, 176–78, 180
Syrian Civil War, 18, 21, 29; case study of US policy responses to, 35–60

Taiwan, 20, 64, 95
Taliban, 1, 24, 43, 82, 86–95, 97–102, 104–6, 109, 112, 114, 115–17, 167
Tillerson, Rex, 46, 78
Trump, Donald, administration of, 1, 15–19, 24, 29, 31, 35–39, 46–49, 59, 61, 64–65, 68, 71–75, 78–80, 84–93, 97–101, 103–5, 107, 112, 114, 117, 123, 141, 160, 163, 168, 170–71, 179, 181–82, 186
Turkey, 40, 42, 45, 48, 55

232   *Index*

Ukraine War, 1–2, 19, 21, 24, 33, 49,
    60, 69, 94, 108, 144–59, 161–71,
    178, 184
US Chamber of Commerce, 134,
    169–70

veterans, and health care, 19
Veterans of Foreign Wars (VFW), 120,
    131, 156
Vietnam War, 3, 14, 16, 44, 71, 110, 120,
    125, 130, 133, 137, 140, 154–55
VoteVets, 10, 12, 73, 99, 126, 170

Waltz, Michael, 8, 11, 18, 26, 29–30,
    32–33, 41, 86, 89–101
West Point, 79, 159
Wounded Warrior Project, 131, 181

Yemen, 18, 33, 61–68, 73–75, 77–80,
    82–85
Young, Todd, 6, 18, 32–33, 61–62, 64, 73,
    75–84, 73, 178–79

Zelenskyy, Volodymyr, 2, 146, 150,
    158, 163

About the Author

Jeffrey Lantis is professor of political science at the College of Wooster. His research specializations include foreign policy analysis, international norm theory, emerging technologies and international security, and strategic culture. A former Fulbright Senior Scholar in Australia, he is the author of more than a dozen books, including *Congress and the Battle for U.S. Foreign Policy*, with Patrick Homan (Palgrave Macmillan, 2020); *Foreign Policy Advocacy and Entrepreneurship* (University of Michigan Press, 2019); *Arms and Influence: U.S. Technology Innovations and the Evolution of International Security Norms* (Stanford University Press, 2016); and *The Life and Death of International Treaties* (Oxford University Press, 2008). He is the editor of *Teaching International Relations*, with James Scott, Ralph Carter, and Brandy Jolliff Scott (Elgar, 2021); *Foreign Policy in Comparative Perspective: Domestic and International Influences on State Behavior*, 2nd ed. (Sage/CQ Press, 2013); and other volumes. In addition, Lantis has published more than seventy-five journal articles and book chapters on US foreign policy, Congress, strategic culture, and technology and international security. He has served as a visiting scholar at the Institute for Security and Conflict Studies at the Elliott School of International Affairs at George Washington University, the School of Politics and International Relations at the Australian National University, the Norman Paterson School of International Affairs at Carleton University, and the German Council on Foreign Relations.

Lantis is also an award-winning teacher of foreign policy analysis and international security. He was named the International Studies Association's 2020 Distinguished Teacher-Scholar by the Active Learning in International Affairs Section (ALIAS) of the International Studies Association (ISA), and he was a recipient of the ISA Deborah Gerner Innovative Teaching in International Studies Award (with Kent Kille and Matthew Krain). Lantis is the past director of the ISA's Innovative Pedagogy Conference Initiative, organizing conferences for ISA in association with other professional meetings, and he is the coeditor of the ISA flagship journal *International Studies Perspectives*. He has led advanced seminars and workshops at the Ruprecht-Karls-Universität in

234 About the Author

Heidelberg, Germany; the Moscow State Institute of International Relations, Russia (MGIMO-University); the Universidad del Rosario in Colombia; the University of South Australia; and the Institute for International Relations at the University of Brasilia. Lantis received his doctorate in political science from Ohio State University.